The History and Politics of Free Movement within the European Union

Europe's Legacy in the Modern World

Series Editors: *Martti Koskenniemi and Bo Stråth (University of Helsinki, Finland)*

The 19th century is often described as Europe's century. This series aims to explore the truth of this claim. It views Europe as a global actor and offers insights into its role in ordering the world, creating community and providing welfare in the 19th century and beyond. Volumes in the series investigate tensions between the national and the global, welfare and warfare, property and poverty. They look at how notions like democracy, populism and totalitarianism came to be intertwined and how this legacy persists in the present day world.

The series emphasizes the entanglements between the legal, the political and the economic and employs techniques and methodologies from the history of legal, political and economic thought, the history of events, and structural history. The result is a collection of works that shed new light on the role that Europe's intellectual history has played in the development of the modern world.

Published

Historical Teleologies in the Modern World, Henning Trüper, Dipesh Chakrabarty and Sanjay Subrahmanyam

Europe's Utopias of Peace, Bo Stråth

Political Reform in the Ottoman and Russian Empires, Adrian Brisku

European Modernity: A Global Approach, Bo Stråth and Peter Wagner

The Contested History of Autonomy, Gerard Rosich

Caesarism in the Post-Revolutionary Age: Crisis, Populace and Leadership, Markus J. Prutsch

Orientalism, Philology, and the Illegibility of the Modern World, Henning Trueper

The History and Politics of Free Movement within the European Union: European Borders of Justice, Saila Heinikoski

Forthcoming

Social Difference in Nineteenth-Century Spanish America: An Intellectual History, Francisco A. Ortega

The History and Politics of Free Movement within the European Union

European Borders of Justice

Saila Heinikoski

BLOOMSBURY ACADEMIC
LONDON • NEW YORK • OXFORD • NEW DELHI • SYDNEY

BLOOMSBURY ACADEMIC
Bloomsbury Publishing Plc
50 Bedford Square, London, WC1B 3DP, UK
1385 Broadway, New York, NY 10018, USA
29 Earlsfort Terrace, Dublin 2, Ireland

BLOOMSBURY, BLOOMSBURY ACADEMIC and the Diana logo are
trademarks of Bloomsbury Publishing Plc

First published in Great Britain 2021
This paperback edition published in 2022

Copyright © Saila Heinikoski, 2021

Saila Heinikoski has asserted her right under the Copyright, Designs and Patents Act, 1988,
to be identified as Author of this work.

Cover image: © (Busà Photography / Getty Images)

All rights reserved. No part of this publication may be reproduced or
transmitted in any form or by any means, electronic or mechanical, including
photocopying, recording, or any information storage or retrieval system,
without prior permission in writing from the publishers.

Bloomsbury Publishing Plc does not have any control over, or responsibility for, any
third-party websites referred to or in this book. All internet addresses given in this
book were correct at the time of going to press. The author and publisher regret any
inconvenience caused if addresses have changed or sites have ceased to exist,
but can accept no responsibility for any such changes.

Every effort has been made to trace copyright holders and to obtain their permissions
for the use of copyright material. The publisher apologizes for any errors or omissions and
would be grateful if notified of any corrections that should be incorporated in future reprints
or editions of this book.

A catalogue record for this book is available from the British Library.

A catalog record for this book is available from the Library of Congress.

ISBN: HB: 978-1-3501-5054-6
PB: 978-1-3502-3306-5
ePDF: 978-1-3501-5055-3
eBook: 978-1-3501-5056-0

Series: Europe's Legacy in the Modern World

Typeset by Newgen KnowledgeWorks Pvt. Ltd., Chennai, India

To find out more about our authors and books visit www.bloomsbury.com
and sign up for our newsletters.

Contents

List of Figures		viii
List of Tables		ix
Acknowledgements		x

1 Introduction 1
   1.1 Free movement: An endangered principle? 1
   1.2 Filling a gap in mobility studies 3
   1.3 Normative social science from a new perspective 7
   1.4 Research questions and the structure of the book 9

2 The context: The history of free movement in Europe 13
   2.1 Historical overview of the regulation of people's movement 13
   2.2 Free movement: From an economic principle towards a fundamental right 17
   2.3 Security and immigration intertwined in the Schengen Area 19

3 Conceptual framework and methodology 25
   3.1 A conceptual framework of practical reasoning 25
   3.2 The empirical material 27
   3.3 Methodological underpinnings inspired by critical discourse analysis 30

4 Agreement dimension: Emphasis on common duties 35
   4.1 Agreement-based reasoning as a theoretical ideal: Equal moral worth 35
   4.2 Duty to comply with rules: Free movement of the Roma 38
   4.3 Duty of balancing between rules and security 45
   4.4 Duty of better implementation 51
   4.5 Rights-based Europe: Mobility justified by common rules 58

5 Community dimension: Reproducing the community of the European Union 61
   5.1 Community-based reasoning as a theoretical ideal: Focus on 'our duty' 61
   5.2 Duty stemming from 'a fundamental piece of European community' 63

	5.3	Duty stemming from responsibility towards future generations	67
	5.4	Duty stemming from deep diversity: The nation as primary responsibility	68
	5.5	Europe as identification: 'Our' mobility justified with values	73
6	Utility dimension: Optimizing concrete benefits		77
	6.1	Utility-based reasoning as a theoretical ideal: Strain or gain?	77
	6.2	Goal of maximizing functionality	79
	6.3	Goal of maximizing benefits	83
	6.4	Goal of minimizing costs	89
	6.5	'A Europe that delivers': Mobility justified with material benefits	94
7	Solidarity dimension: Solidarity as the ultimate aim		97
	7.1	Solidarity-based reasoning as a theoretical ideal: Wider sense of 'us'	97
	7.2	Goal of deeper Europeanness	100
	7.3	Goal of burden-sharing in immigration	105
	7.4	Goal to prevent negative transactionalism	108
	7.5	Europe of solidarity: Mobility justified as enhancing solidarity	110
8	Setting the scene: Migration policy histories of the analysed countries		113
	8.1	The history of migration policies in Germany: From Gastarbeiter to immigrants	113
	8.2	The history of French immigration policies: Republican assimilation	115
	8.3	Migration policy history in Italy: A late country of immigration	116
	8.4	Migration policy in the UK: Restrictions to mobility towards the country	118
	8.5	History of Spanish migration policy: Emigration and regularizations	120
	8.6	History of Romanian migration policy: Curtailing emigration	122
9	Free movement discourses by country		125
	9.1	German emphasis on free movement as a commonly agreed beneficial principle	125
	9.2	French focus on free movement rules	127
	9.3	Italian discussion on the free movement of specific groups	130
	9.4	The UK concerned about the control of free movement	131
	9.5	Spain connects free movement to European integration	133
	9.6	Romania focuses on the need to receive equal rights	135

	9.7 European Commission emphasizes EU Treaties	137
	9.8 Concluding remarks on the country-specific patterns of discourse	139
10	Free movement discourses as practical reasoning	143
	10.1 Who should stay and who should go?	143
	10.2 European political discourses: A few weak signals	147
	10.3 Practical reasoning: Contradictions in the free movement discourses	149
	10.4 'L'Europa è mobile', or the existence of 'European' discourses	151

Appendix Material selection and speaker-specific tables	153
Germany	153
France	154
Italy	155
The UK	156
Spain	157
Romania	158
European Commission	159
Notes	161
Bibliography	187
Index	223

Figures

1.1	Studies on EU mobility	4
1.2	Normative research fields related to this study	7
9.1	Matrix on the discursive emphases	141

Tables

3.1	Practical reasoning types	26
3.2	Theoretical framework of practical reasoning and examples	26
3.3	Empirical material of the study	29
4.1	Agreement-related discourses on free movement	59
5.1	Community utterances on free movement	74
6.1	Utilitarian discourses observed in the analysis	95
7.1	Solidary utterances regarding free movement	111
9.1	Free movement utterances by country	126
9.2	Different groups of utterances on free movement	140
10.1	Most encouraged and discouraged free movers	144
A.1	German free movement utterances, N=59	153
A.2	French free movement utterances, N=59	154
A.3	Italian free movement utterances, N=42	155
A.4	British free movement utterances, N=54	156
A.5	Spanish free movement utterances, N=40	158
A.6	Romanian free movement utterances, N=53	159
A.7	Commissioners' free movement utterance, N=72	160

Acknowledgements

This book is based on research originally started in 2013, when I had no idea how politicized the issue of free movement within the European Union was about to become, because of the Brexit referendum promised by the British Conservatives and the so-called migration crisis in autumn 2015. While employing my privilege to free movement as a visiting scholar during the writing process, both phenomena became very tangible.

In autumn 2015, I happened to be on a research visit in Catania, the Italian seaport in Sicily, where people rescued from the Mediterranean Sea are brought. I could witness the migratory situation with my own eyes. During my morning runs, I could see asylum-seekers lining up at the bus station of Catania. On TV, the only programme that did not address migration was Detto Fatto, an afternoon programme for housewives. It became obvious that free movement is not the same for everyone on the European soil.

The Brexit referendum showed that not even the movement of EU citizens was accepted everywhere. On Friday, 24 June 2016, I woke up at 5 am in Trento, Northern Italy. I had signed up for a breakfast run event, which I deemed a great way to start celebrating the Midsummer Eve. When I had gone to bed, it seemed that Bremain would defeat the Brexit camp. In the early morning, I checked the news and read that the majority of Brits had voted in favour of leaving the EU. As I went outside, I saw people wearing the same blue t-shirt as me, preparing for the run. I was wondering: don't you know what has happened? I could not understand what the heck was going on.

Couple of days later, on Monday, 27 June, I was watching football in a street pizzeria. The match was England vs. Iceland and there was a Brit sitting next to me. Eventually, tiny Iceland won, against all odds, and knocked England out of the tournament. The Englishman, who had lived in Italy for ten years and spoke fluent Italian, left cursing: 'I've been kicked out of Europe twice this week', he said.

In addition to these and other memorable experiences around Europe, the writing of this book has benefited from exchanges with numerous people before and after the defence of my doctoral dissertation, on which a bulk of the text is based.

I am grateful to the editors of the series, Professor Martti Koskenniemi and Professor emeritus Bo Stråth, for accepting this book in the series and for their valuable and insightful comments. I also remain indebted to two anonymous reviewers. Without their comments, this book would have looked very different. I wish to express my gratitude for all the editorial help I received from Bloomsbury during the process, especially to Laura Reeves and Rhodri Mogford.

This research would not have been possible without funding. I would like to thank Kone Foundation for funding my PhD project and the project 'Demilitarisation in an increasingly militarised world'. Sincere thanks are also in order for Wihuri

Foundation, University of Turku Research Grant Fund, the Department of Philosophy, Contemporary History and Political Science at the University of Turku, the Academy of Finland-funded Centre of Excellence in Law, Identity and the European Narratives (funding decision number 312154) and the Finnish Institute of International Affairs. I am grateful for COST Action RECAST (Reappraising Intellectual Debates on Civic Rights and Democracy in Europe) for funding my Short-Term Scientific Mission in Bologna and my participation in workshops with great colleagues in inspiring environments. I would like to thank all the institutions where I have worked during these years and all my amazing co-workers, especially Director Sia Spiliopoulou Åkermark from the Åland Islands Peace Institute, with whom me and Pirjo Kleemola-Juntunen also co-authored our first international monograph, *Demilitarisation and International Law in Context: The Åland Islands* (2018).

The most sincere thanks are in order for all people who contributed to this book. First and foremost, I would like to thank Professor Henri Vogt for being my PhD supervisor and for providing me tremendous help along the way. My deepest gratitude goes to Professor Peo Hansen, who gave me invaluable comments both in the four-hour defence and in our discussions afterwards. I would also like to thank everyone who commented on my texts before the defence, including my pre-examiners and colleagues as well as all my fellow seminar and conference participants all over Europe. I regret my word limit does not allow me to list each name, but I wish to specifically express my gratitude for all participants to the Political Science research seminar at the University of Turku. Thanks for still keeping me on the list!

Many of the most important and greatest moments in writing this book, and in my life too, have taken place in Italy. I would like to thank Fulvio Attinà, Marco Brunazzo and Sonia Lucarelli, respectively, for providing me the possibility to fill my scholarly and physical appetite *presso le Università di Catania, Trento e Bologna*.

Most importantly, I wish to thank my family and friends. *Kiitos* Tatu. *Mi raccomando, eh!*

As always, any remaining errors are my own.

On Brexit day, 31 January 2020, Helsinki
Saila Heinikoski

1

Introduction

La donna è mobile
Qual piuma al vento,
muta d'accento
e di pensiero
(Giuseppe Verdi, Rigoletto 1851)

1.1 Free movement: An endangered principle?

This study examines political discourses on free movement within the European Union from 2004 through mid-2016. While European politicians from across the continent hold a wide range of views with respect to the idea of free movement, the types of practical reasoning that they subscribe to seem to nonetheless follow a number of recognizable patterns. Through the analysis of free movement discourses in six major European countries – UK, Germany, France, Italy, Spain and Romania – and in the European Commission,[1] this book seeks to make sense of these patterns. To do this, it will develop a conceptual framework of practical reasoning, theoretically applicable in many a field of politics and policy; practical reasoning refers to argumentation with which people seek to justify human practices, theirs and others' (Kratochwil 1989: 37, cf. Searle 2001: 124). The primary aim of the book is thus to provide a broad, systematized overview of free movement perceptions in Europe from the perspective of high-level politics. The actual use of the conceptual framework and the comparison between the inherent differences of the analysed countries compose the two significant sub-aims of the analysis. Along the way, the study will say a great deal about the ways in which people across the continent understand 'Europeanness' and the process of European integration.

When I began working on this study in 2013, the utterances of British politicians on Eastern European migrants were what had originally awoken my interest. The inflow of large numbers of citizens from new member states under post-2004 conditions – the UK was one of the only countries, together with Ireland and Sweden, that granted free access for Central and Eastern European workers – seemed to be highly problematic for the country's political leaders to justify. The unquestionable economic benefits of labour mobility failed to generate public support for the policy of free movement and assuage fears of 'welfare tourism', resulting in the British decision to leave the European Union.

When the right to free movement assumed a pivotal role in the British EU membership considerations overall, I became increasingly aware of the centrality of mobility for the entire process of European integration as well as of its moral and legal complexities. In addition to being a fundamental right (Roberts and Sakslin 2009), labour mobility is also an integral part of the single market (Rumford 2007); it relates to the Schengen Agreement and border control (Carrera et al. 2011); it involves concerns related to irregular migrants and the regularization amnesties of such migrants in member states (Finotelli and Arango 2011);[2] and it reflects approaches towards European cooperation in general (Kuhn 2015). This also meant that my original intention to limit my approach to mobility among EU citizens proved too narrow. Free movement closely relates to who is allowed to move freely in the European Union and who is not, and which political actors can ultimately make decisions in this respect. Indeed, free movement is a fundamental question of justice on several different levels.

In light of recent (2015–19) political developments, particularly terrorist attacks and the so-called migration crisis, the complexity and internal tensions of the question of free movement have become increasingly evident – and this certainly does not decrease the relevance of this study. The deaths from terrorism have made political leaders and scholars across the continent question whether open democracies can be protected when the idea and practice of free movement prevail (Council of the European Union 2016, Tammikko 2017). Nationalistic populist parties throughout Europe have exploited this new alleged security risk, apparently emanating from unchecked free movement. Even more importantly, migration from outside Europe has proved to be *the* issue that most severely challenges free movement and the rationale of European integration. Not only are the EU member states unable to implement common policies vis-à-vis migrants, but politicians across the continent face increasing difficulties in justifying why the citizens of 'arbitrary' European countries can live and work anywhere they want in Europe while others, 'outsiders', cannot. The reintroduction of border controls at certain internal borders highlights the lack of trust and worry about not knowing who crosses the borders. Although officially intended to maintain public order, such measures easily contribute to the alienation and presentation of people who are fleeing from war and conflict zones as potential threats. Another example of contradictions is the (unsuccessful) state-specific quotas for 'sharing the burden' of asylum seekers established by the European Council in autumn 2015, which require that the asylum seekers *stay* in the country designated to them[3] – an idea that clearly undermines the free movement ideal (cf. Kmak 2015).

The migration context links the discussion on free movement in the European Union to the global framework of mobility. With conflicts persisting in the Middle East and North Africa, and population numbers increasing in the Global South, migration pressure on the Union seems unlikely to weaken. The question why Western 'global insiders' may move around pretty much as they wish, while the stateless 'global outsiders' tend to carry the label of illegal and 'dangerous' people, will remain pertinent.

It is morally impossible to justify the proposition that people who are the worst-off need to carry the main burden of global structural failures and crises (see also Guild 2005: 14, Cetti 2012: 19). In many respects, this book provides an introduction to, and framework for, understanding this current state of affairs.

An important conceptual distinction should also be made here at the outset. In the EU discourse, 'free movement' in the European Union is consistently separated from 'migration', a term referring to migration from outside the European Union. However, since the mid-2000s, certain national politicians in Europe have started to refer to EU mobility with the term '(im)migration', which has a more negative connotation than 'freedom' (see, e.g. Hansen 2008). This and other discursive implications in the political debates will be further elaborated in the present study.

This book began with a quotation from Giuseppe Verdi's opera Rigoletto. In the Duke of Mantua's famous *canzone* entitled *La donna è mobile*, 'mobile' refers to fickle or flighty: the voice and thoughts of a woman are constantly and confusingly changing. In the Europe of today, 'mobility' is mainly discussed with regard to the EU's free movement policies, but as this book will show, these policies also encompass the sense of mobility intended by Verdi: political attitudes are complex and contradictory, and no unified European voice can be found.

1.2 Filling a gap in mobility studies

To my knowledge, attitudes towards free movement in Europe have not been systematically studied through analysis of contemporary high-level political discourses. It is also difficult to find single-authored, comparative and Europe-wide studies on free movement discourses. The existing works often address free movement through various kinds of case studies or generally from the historical–legal viewpoint (e.g. Giubboni 2007, Johns 2013, Maas 2013, Recchi 2013, Tonkiss 2013a, Chatty 2015, McMahon 2015). My aim is to offer a diversified, multidimensional picture of the phenomenon without subscribing to a single theoretical orientation. The book illustrates, inter alia, that free movement in the EU involves more than just concerns of national security or the migrants' rights, which are often the focus of mobility research (Sasse 2005, cf. Chatty 2015). In fact, the entire study could be seen as an effort to define or illustrate what free movement *actually* means in today's Europe.

This book could be characterized as an analysis of mobility discourses at the high political level. In order to analyse practical reasoning through political discourses, it introduces a new conceptual framework and illustrates its usability in the European context. There is an underlying element of normativity in the analysis, which is why the study can also be classified under the umbrella of normative social science (see Section 1.3). However, my objective is not to evaluate what is morally the best approach for realizing the right to free movement but to show how free movement has been justified or criticized. Figure 1.1 illustrates some adjacent fields of study concerning mobility in the European Union; it should be noted, however, that there is considerable overlap between what I have categorized as different fields of study. In addition to being inspired by the debates, I wish to contribute to the debates with this book.

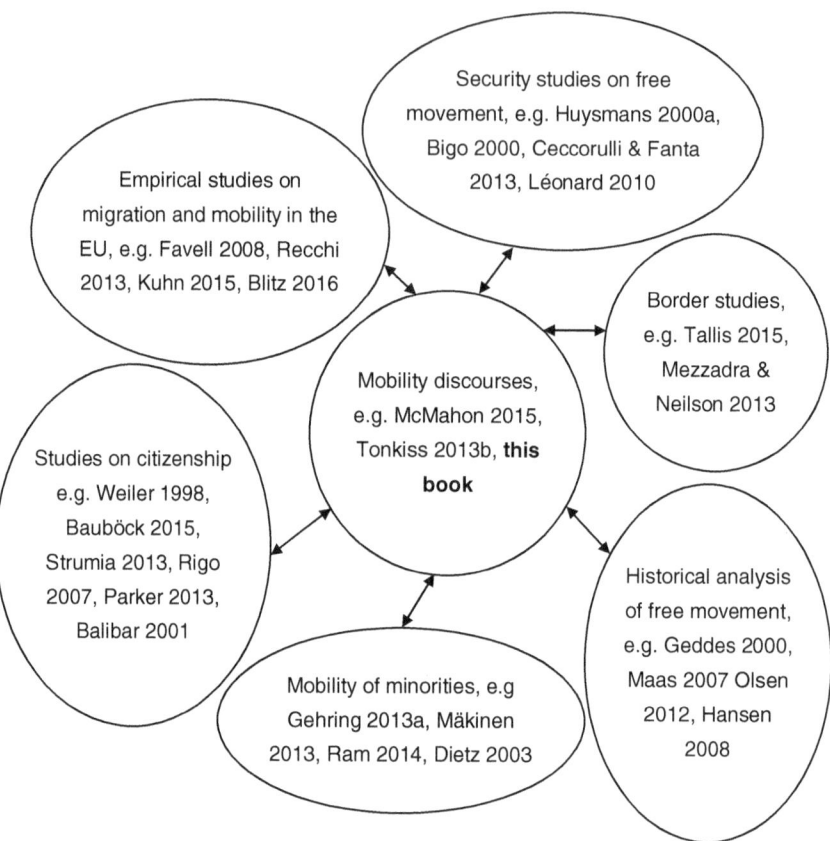

Figure 1.1 Studies on EU mobility (categorization by the author).

Many of the works that relate to free movement in the EU are thoroughly *empirical studies*; they have a sociologically inspired orientation, usually approaching the issue of free movement and European identity from the movers' perspective. Ettore Recchi argues that although mobility plays a crucial role in the construction of Europe, it should be complemented with a true sense of solidarity and identity in order to create a unified Europe (Recchi 2013: 213, 2015). Theresa Kuhn develops several policy suggestions for developing such an identity: for example, less educated people should be provided with more opportunities for transnational activities, while highly educated people tend to be pro-European anyway (Kuhn 2015: 154–5). Adrian Favell focuses on the highly educated pioneers of European integration that he terms 'Eurostars' and concludes that they have been successful as pioneers, but mobility loses its distinctive value when it becomes more common (Favell 2008: 229–30). Brad K. Blitz has analysed immigration and free movement policies in case studies concerning different professional groups in five EU countries, noting that there are still barriers preventing EU nationals from utilizing their right to free movement. For example, national labour markets may discriminate against other EU nationals or make it more difficult for nationals to return to their home country (Blitz 2016: 14). This study also has an empirical orientation in the sense that the body of the work consists of a vast amount of empirical material. I also refer to the host of existing empirical studies while discussing the inferences I make.

A number of studies focusing on *mobility discourses* observe the host society's political and public stances. These studies argue, for example, that free movement may increase nationalist rhetoric and tendencies, creating a situation that Katherine Tonkiss – focusing on the British approaches – calls a 'post-national dilemma' (Tonkiss 2013a: 98–100). Another focus of research has been the observation of how a certain group of movers is discussed in different host countries: for example, Simon McMahon argues that Romanian migrants have been positively received in Spain while they have been greeted with hostility in Italy (McMahon 2015). While Tonkiss and McMahon focus on analysing a single host society or a single group of movers, respectively, the aim of the book is to provide a more comprehensive and diversified picture. This book can be included in this category of mobility discourse studies; the multidimensional perspective of this study complements and contradicts the views provided by Tonkiss and McMahon from the host country perspective. As I will outline in the book, the approaches in the UK or towards the Roma present a small but significant part of the overall picture of free movement discourses in Europe.

There are a number of studies that primarily seek to create a long-term historical overview of free movement policies. Willem Maas claims that EU citizenship has evolved through efforts to create a community instead of a free market area (Maas 2007: 7), while Espen D. H. Olsen holds a contrary view of the same development, maintaining that economic integration has been the key feature (Olsen 2012: 26). Andrew Geddes, for his part, has analysed immigration policies towards third-country nationals from the perspective of European integration as contributing to the development of a 'Fortress Europe' (Geddes 2000). Peo Hansen arrives at similar conclusions, arguing that free movement policies have served to alienate third-country nationals (Hansen 2008).

Yet another strand of contributions concentrates on the *citizenship* issues, in particular with respect to third-country nationals (Shaw 2007, Strumia 2013). Many of the earlier mentioned works are primarily interested in EU citizenship rather than free movement as such (Bellamy, Castiglione and Shaw 2006a). However, EU citizenship does revolve around the right to free movement, as also noted by Enrica Rigo, who argues that the objective of European citizenship is a way of guaranteeing and controlling mobility (Rigo 2007). Moreover, legal scholars have written on the multidimensional nature of European Union citizenship centred around the right to free movement (Weiler 1998). Several political theory studies also demonstrate the exclusive nature of EU citizenship related to the question of mobility (Balibar 2001, Parker 2013). Rainer Bauböck focuses on the normative issues of citizenship, arguing that free movement should be complemented with more wide-ranging political rights (Bauböck 2015).

Physical *borders* are also of interest in mobility studies: the permeable external borders of the EU in Eastern Europe (Tallis 2015) or border issues from a theoretical point of view (Mezzadra and Neilson 2013), whereby it is argued that the European border regimes result in the 'selective and differential inclusion of migrants' (Mezzadra 2006: 39). Physical borders mainly relate to the Schengen Area, and this study illustrates how border-free physical movement and the legal right to free movement are also intertwined in European political discourses.

Security plays a special role in European discourses on free movement (Bigo 2000: 171–204, Huysmans 2000a, 2006, Léonard 2010, Ceccorulli and Fanta 2013). The security implications related to the position of immigrants, European border politics and European identity have been increasingly discussed after the establishment of the 'Area of Freedom, Security and Justice' in 1999 (Bigo 2000, Huysmans 2000b, Balibar 2001). The public demands for the exclusion of third-country nationals have also become more vocal in correlation with the rising numbers of migrants during the twenty-first century. The more exclusionary that the policies become, the more attention that scholarly debates pay to the 'securitization' of migration (Mitsilegas, Monar and Rees 2003, Huysmans 2006, Squire 2009, Ceccorulli and Fanta 2013). The exclusive right to free movement for EU citizens may 'naturalize' the alienation of third-country nationals (Huysmans 2000a: 751). People who illegally cross borders may even be depicted as enemies under war-like conditions (Kahn 2013: 210), a discourse that terrorist attacks are likely to aggravate. While it is often the case that bureaucratic professionals rather than politicians are the actors voicing security threats, politicians are important in '(either authorizing, legitimizing, justifying, thwarting, dislocating or upsetting the enunciations of policy professionals' (van Munster 2009: 6). Such approaches are employed by several European politicians, which result in a more successful presentation of migration in security terms than if it was only conducted by the European Commission (Léonard 2010). Moreover, security does concern not only illegal behaviour but also people who may present a threat to state order, to society or to the welfare state via free movement (Huysmans 2006: 69).

Another controversial issue related to free movement is the migration of *ethnic and other minorities*. For example, many authors have critically observed discrimination with regard to the free movement of the Roma (Dietz 2003, Gehring 2013a, Mäkinen 2013, Balch, Balabanova and Trandafoiu 2014, Parker and Catalán 2014, Ram 2014, McMahon 2015). There is also arguably discrimination in the application of the right to free movement with regard to same-sex partners in certain countries (Roberts and Sakslin 2009, Schuster and Toniollo 2015). However, in such discriminatory cases, the question is primarily about the use of social security benefits, a highly contentious and complex issue with regard to free movement (Giubboni 2007). Sometimes, free movement may also bring additional rights for new arrivals compared to their compatriots who stay in their home country. For example, it is in some cases possible to utilize the rights of free movers in order to sidestep, for example, more stringent domestic family reunification rules in a certain country (Wagner 2015). The free movement of the Roma also comes up often in the discourses analysed in this study, while other groups are hardly mentioned. As the example of minority movement illustrates, free movement necessarily includes important normative questions, which have also been the focus of many studies.

1.3 Normative social science from a new perspective

Free movement entails many normative questions regarding who can move around in Europe and why and under which conditions. By combining a wide-ranging empirical analysis with an ambitious conceptual research matrix based on normative ideal types, the analysis here provides a new categorization of the general normative perspectives inherent in political discourses. I not only systematize the different types of utterances but also show that we can hardly talk of a single normative stance within the European Union in mobility issues. Although the European Union 'values' are nominally shared by all member states, these values are of little help when deciding who can freely move around the European Union.

Several existing strands of normative social science have inspired this book. Most generally, the contributions of *Normative International Relations*, an established subfield of IR scholarship, have focused on the normative assessment of existing global political structures and the ways these structures could be made more equal and just (Frost 1996, 2008, Cochran 1999, Smith and Light 2001, MacIntyre 2006, Dower 2007). It is the focus on the structural level of normative questions that links this study to the field of normative IR; to what extent do certain political structures rely on specific

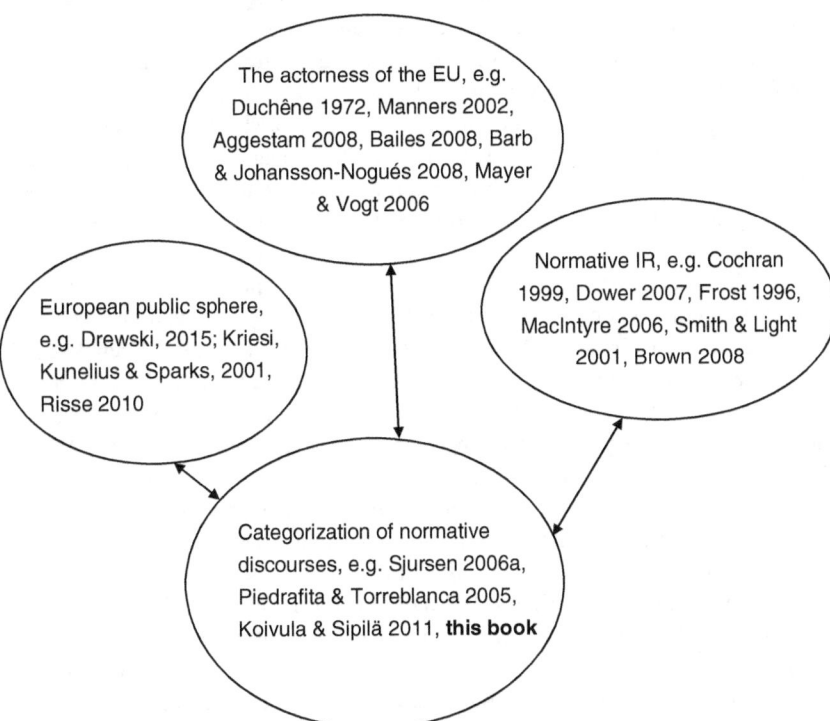

Figure 1.2 Normative research fields related to this study.

normative approaches? I do not take any normative stance on the goodness of the approaches, however; all the stances in the theoretical framework are equally 'ethical'.

Many books on normative IR also deal with the interests of the self and the interests of others, even distant individuals. Tim Dunne and Nicholas J. Wheeler, for example, argue that in ethical foreign policy, it is essential to place international order and human rights before economic or political interests, that is, to put collective interests before one's own interests (Dunne and Wheeler 2001). For Chris Brown, in contrast, interests and ethical action are not contradictory categories. A sense of responsibility towards one's own citizens and towards humanity forces us to reflect upon the nature of our interests and their ethical implications. The choice is between long-term, medium-term, and short-term definition of interests (Brown 2001: 26–7). Brown does not specify what 'ethical' means for him, but it is, apparently, something related to altruism.

The second strand deals with *the nature and values of the European Union as a political actor*. The Union's inherent values and its nature as an international actor have been a central theme in scholarly debates emanating from the 1970s discussion of the Union as a civilian power (Duchêne 1972) through the twenty-first-century debate about the EU as a normative power (Manners 2002).[4] In this literature, what I have found particularly intriguing is Lisbeth Aggestam's notion of an 'Ethical Power Europe' (2008). It refers to the Union's conscious efforts to promote good in the world, and it can materialize both in terms of civilian and military power as well as in terms of social and material power. The notion also changes the perspective from what the EU *is*, to what it *does*: it is not solely a role model but an active promoter of the global good. The EU as an ethical power has been discussed by researchers in different contexts, including security and defence policy (Bailes 2008), neighbourhood policy (Barbé and Johansson-Nogués 2008) and border conflicts (Pace 2008).[5] However, it is indeed a tricky question to what extent the free movement ideal can promote the good in the world.

The third strand analyses the *European public sphere* and its functioning through a number of empirical case studies (Kunelius and Sparks 2001, Van de Steeg 2004, Wessler et al. 2008, Kriesi 2010, Risse 2010, 2014, Kriesi et al. 2012, Drewski 2015); political talk on free movement can obviously be seen as a brick in the construction of a European public sphere. Public sphere refers to the Habermasian concept of the 'sphere of private people come together as a public' (Habermas 1989: 27), and European public sphere studies often regard the media as their object of study. The underlying premise is that a public sphere is worth pursuing: the studies often consider the European public sphere as a forum for practising citizenship and as an end in itself (Kunelius and Sparks 2001: 18). The European public sphere necessarily consists of several national public spheres, but harmonizing national public spheres could allegedly contribute to diminishing the democratic deficit of the Union. According to some authors, simultaneous discussion on the same topic testifies to a European public sphere, particularly if ideational cleavages are more significant than interstate cleavages (Eder and Kantner 2000, Kriesi et al. 2012, Drewski 2015). Other public sphere authors maintain that discursive convergence and European identification are features of a Europeanized public sphere (Van de Steeg 2004, Wessler et al. 2008: 25,

Risse 2014). Considering the material of this study, free movement discourses indeed seem to constitute a European public sphere to the extent that the topics are similar and political differences explain much of the variation, although European identification does not appear particularly strong. Public sphere literature seems to consider a European public sphere a necessary factor in the European transnational political community; a Europeanized public sphere could increase the legitimacy of the EU policies, such as free movement policies. However, one may argue that a true European political community would be necessary before a European public sphere can truly emerge.

Finally, there are a number of studies that focus on the *categorization of normative discourses*, in essentially a similar manner as the current work. The threefold classification of the various uses of discourses by Jürgen Habermas, that is, moral-practical, pragmatic and ethical-existential, is a typical example of these (Habermas 1994a, Sjursen 2002, 2006a). Another useful differentiation is found between the logic of appropriateness and the logic of consequentiality (March and Olsen, 1989; see also, e.g. Koivula and Sipilä, 2011), complemented with the logic of justification (Piedrafita and Torreblanca 2005, Heinikoski 2011) or the logic of moral justification (Sjursen and Smith 2004). One may also analyse discourses through a three-partite division in normative ethics: utilitarianism, deontology and virtue ethics (Manners 2008, Heinikoski 2013). Other possible categorizations rely on selected ethical theories (Huysmans 2000b) or Weberian modes of social action (Weber 1978: 24). Categorizing discourses or types of political agency – or the latter through the former (e.g. Sjursen 2012) – contributes to revealing how theoretical ideal types intertwine and overlap in reality. Successful categorization of normative discourses tells something about human nature itself: Which rational or value-based premises appeal to people and what sort of underlying normative premises do (political) discourses conceal? The categorizations do not suggest that the real world could be encapsulated in predetermined boxes but rather illustrate its fundamental importance for making sense of the world in social sciences (see also Onuf 1989, ÓTuathail 2002: 608). Imagining a number of extreme approaches and locating real-world phenomena in those categories is human. Similar to the framework introduced in Chapter 3, the above categorizations and classifications help in making sense of the complex discursive reality in which we live.

1.4 Research questions and the structure of the book

In the empirical analysis, I analyse a wide array of political documents – statements, addresses and speeches given by the heads of state and ministers of the interior of six large EU member states and by selected European commissioners.[6] By tracing the ways in which these politicians seek to regulate, promote and/or restrict free movement, with the help of a conceptual framework based on four philosophical approaches to reasoning, I shed light on the politically significant European perceptions of who should be entitled to free movement, on which grounds and through what kind of administrative mechanisms. The book also reveals people's underlying conceptions of Europeanness, of Europe's insiders and outsiders. Despite the philosophical–moral implications inherent in any analysis of justificatory argumentation, it is worth noting that in this study, philosophical ideas are used as a source of inspiration rather than as an object of scrutiny in and of themselves. The framework I develop is intended to assist in the discourse analytical interpretation of the empirical world in the field of free movement discourses.

In the discourse analysis, I postulate a discursive space of free movement (and perhaps of many other political phenomena as well) composed of two axes: rational thinking vs. sentiments of identification and value-based vs. instrumental mindsets. These two axes provide us with a fourfold categorization of the basic approaches to the justifications for the current European discourses on free movement (see Section 3.1). I have labelled these four classifications with the concepts of *agreement, community, utility* and *solidarity*. The four categories thus represent four elementary types of practical reasoning employed in the European free movement debates. While agreement discourses refer to commonly agreed upon formal duties and rules as the basis of action, community discourses focus on the identity of a certain community and reflect the perception of what is ultimately good for that community. Utility discourses focus on the consequences of an action, particularly on the most efficient ways of solving a problem, whereas solidarity discourses relate to maximizing mutual solidarity between different groups of people. I have classified all the free movement utterances that I have found in the document material under these four categories, in spite of the problems that this categorization necessarily entails in the complex real world.

Given the general context and the framework described above, the study answers the following four mutually related questions:

1. How can we theorize about free movement discourses in terms of practical reasoning? What are the implications of the conceptual framework and what kinds of subcategories does it require?
2. In what ways do EU politicians articulate and advance their views with respect to each of the four forms of practical reasoning? What types of argumentation prove particularly important?
3. How do the observed countries and the European Commission approach the question of European mobility and how can we explain the differences between their views?
4. What do these results reveal about the prevailing moods with respect to Europeanness, and the distinction between insiders and outsiders in Europe?

The second chapter deals with the research context: the evolution and the relevant aspects of the right to free movement and relevant research fields. It specifies the context of the free movement debates in Europe, analysing the political problematics observed in the history of mobility and in the legal evolution of free movement. The chapter is divided into three sections. In Section 2.1, the historical trajectory of regulation of mobility in Europe is outlined from the nineteenth century to the end of the Second World War. In Section 2.2, the right to free movement is shown to have originally evolved in terms of economic concerns but later encompassed features of a fundamental right. Section 2.3, in turn, introduces the issue of how security and rights-related concerns are intertwined in the history of the Schengen Area. The aim of the brief historical overview is to familiarize the reader with the general evolution of free movement and to assist the reader in contextualizing relevant political discourses.

In Chapter 3, I present the discourse analytical methodology and the empirical material. Section 3.1 introduces the conceptual framework based on four prominent categories of practical reasoning (encapsulated in the concepts of agreement, community, utility and solidarity). The section also introduces the classification criteria for the analysis and the discourse analytical method that I employ in examining free movement utterances given by (1) heads of state and ministers of the interior from Germany, UK, France, Italy and Spain; (2) prime ministers and presidents from Romania; as well as (3) European commissioners responsible for free movement-related matters.

In Chapters 4 through 7, I employ the conceptual framework of the justificatory discourses of free movement. Each chapter is based on one of the four categories of practical reasoning. I identify the contexts that possibly inform the differences and specificities in the form of the articulation of the analysed utterances. I mainly conduct my exploration at the all-European level, although the country differences are to some extent visible throughout the analyses. It is worth noting that I primarily treat the politicians as representatives of their respective countries (e.g. Berlusconi=Italy), but it is self-evident that these politicians equally importantly represent wider, European-level perceptions.

In Chapter 4, I demonstrate how the European discourses of free movement emphasized the duty to comply with rules, the duty of balancing between rules and security and the duty of better implementation. Many utterances highlighted the right to free movement as an inviolable fundamental right. Others, however, focused on the problems posed by people abusing that right. Although appealing to similar premises of practical reasoning, speakers may consequently arrive at diametrically opposed positions.

Chapter 5 discusses the typical manifestations of discourses springing from a sense of community. A significant number of utterances presented free movement as a fundamental part of the European community and a duty of younger generations, while other utterances took into account the alleged existence of a 'deep diversity' between nations. Again, community utterances can both promote and restrict free movement.

Integration and instrumental benefits are the focus of the utility dimension discussed in Chapter 6. I demonstrate how many European discourses, especially concerned with immigration across the Mediterranean, focused on the optimization of free movement with a common immigration policy. Other utterances emphasized the material benefits and costs of free movement. The overall line of practical reasoning was clear: free movement should serve European and national interests and thereby the populations at large.

Chapter 7 analyses how politicians sought to advance a sense of solidarity in Europe and in their respective countries through free movement. A few utterances emphasized solidarity as burden-sharing, whereas others focused on building deeper

Europeanness or promoting 'negative transactionalism'. There was a consensus that solidarity between European countries is a positive issue, but what that actually means for free movement remained undefined.

Chapter 8 provides a short overview of the migration histories of each of the countries, the aim of which is to set the scene for the country-specific discussion on the free movement discourses.

In Chapter 9, I focus on the relative importance of the utterances and the specific aspects of each country and the Commission. I also draw some tentative conclusions with respect to the factors that possibly inform the changes observed both within and between different countries.

The final chapter of the book provides further analysis of the overall discourses. It outlines which groups are encouraged to exercise their right to free movement and which are not. It also draws conclusions on the implications of the analysed discourses for European integration and practical reasoning discourses.

2

The context: The history of free movement in Europe

This chapter outlines the regulation of free movement in Europe from the nineteenth century to the present. At this point, a conceptual reminder is in order: free movement refers to both the right to free movement, originating from the European Coal and Steel Community (ECSC) in 1952, and to the Schengen Area without internal borders. The right to free movement applies to all EU citizens (only exceptions are the transitional restrictions after a country joins the EU), but not all EU countries are members in the Schengen Area: Romania is aspiring to become a member, together with Bulgaria, Croatia and Cyprus. The UK and Ireland, in turn, have an opt-out from the Schengen Area, but the right to free movement grants all EU citizens the right to stay in these countries and the right of the citizens of these countries to reside in all other EU countries. I take both aspects of free movement into account both in the following historical overview as well as in the discourses analysed in the book.

2.1 Historical overview of the regulation of people's movement

The extent of freedom of movement has fluctuated in Europe during the past centuries. Passports were in use already in the eighteenth century, but during the latter half of the nineteenth century, freedom of movement across borders was the rule, all the way until the beginning of the First World War (Lucassen 2001). As Michael R. Marrus has put it, 'up to the First World War "civilized" countries considered that no more formal arrangements were necessary to designate people moving from place to place' (Marrus 1985: 92). Before the 1850s, however, states restricted even domestic freedom of movement; domestic passports became then substituted by identification cards that people were supposed to carry with them (Geselle 2001: 215).

An early example of codified freedom of movement in Europe can be found from the Prussian-German state, which issued a law in 1867 guaranteeing freedom of settlement (*Freizügigkeit*) to its subjects (Gesetz über die Freizügigkeit). It was actually a case of the free movement of labour, as people had the right to work and trade, but municipalities retained the right to exclude poor people from entering their borders (Torpey 2000: 89). Interestingly enough, *Freizügigkeit* is also the German equivalent to the current 'free movement' within the European Union – sometimes current German politicians even refer to the freedom of establishment in English.[1] The Prussian-German state was also the first modern welfare state to introduce compulsory social insurance already in the 1880s (Steinmetz 1993: 5).

An interesting aspect of the Prussian-German policies is the fact that when becoming a nation state, the state liberated passport controls but simultaneously required that people have identification documents (Torpey 1998a). It was also required that all people entering Berlin have a passport or a pass-card (Deutsches Reichsgesetzblatt Band 1878). The nineteenth-century German state thus extended citizenship to the 'national' level, providing the lower classes the opportunity to move freely and even receive poor relief in new locations. As people were allowed to move more freely, it became essential to be able to identify persons; it was even more important than controlling mobility as such (Torpey 2000: 91–2). Indeed, although states started to abandon visa requirements and passport requirements due to rising number of travellers and problems of the passport systems, it was still necessary for people to carry some identification documents (Fahrmeir 2001: 233). Towards the end of the nineteenth century, passports also started to be required from certain foreigners entering the Prussian-German state, culminating in the border controls established during the First World War.

The German example aptly shows how the construction of the nation state coincided with the introduction of passports, which started to be regularly adopted during the First World War. In Germany, the approach towards Slavic immigrants, particularly Russian Poles, triggered the need to introduce passports in order to restrict immigration and protect the German nation from unwanted influence (Torpey 1998a, Zimmerman 2006).

We can also find other examples of immigration restrictions even before the First World War. In Britain, statistics were collected already in the nineteenth century about the country of birth, illustrating the need to discern people based on their origin. Pressured by the public opinion, the 1905 Aliens Act was the first British piece of legislation restricting the arrival of foreigners (Holmes 1999: 319), providing the basis for further restrictions later on (see also Section 8.4 in this book).

Wishes to control the movement of people, in both directions, also started to rise up at the end of the nineteenth century in other parts of continental Europe, as John Torpey has outlined. For example, Italy issued a passport law in 1901 with the aim to control the number of Italians leaving Italy, therefore escaping the compulsory military service and later the First World War. In the beginning of the twentieth century, France too made identification documents obligatory for all foreigners and introduced passport controls upon their entry. Passports made it possible to separate nationals from others, also in terms of access to voting, social services and the like (Torpey 2000: 103–21). Because of the war, European states introduced passports to prevent military-age men from escaping the military service (Marrus 1985: 92).

The passport, therefore, had several functions for both the passport holder and the state. The holder could move freely, prove one's nationality and identity, ask for assistance from an embassy or consulate and receive protection against expulsion. The state, in turn, could issue passports in order to prevent its citizens from leaving, stimulate its citizens to leave, control the entrance and movement of aliens and monitor the population (Lucassen 2001: 237). The emerging states in the early twentieth century sought to monopolize the control of people's movement, for example, by making it obligatory for people to have a passport in order to leave a state (Torpey 1998b). Passports and identification became to be seen as part of a bureaucratic administration with which people could be categorized into nationals and non-nationals (Torpey 2001: 270).

In contrast to the voluntary migration up to the First World War, the period from the beginning of the First World War until the end of the Second World War is characterized by forced migration, which created new problems for controlling people (Moch 2003: 163). After the First World War, a new type of passport was introduced, as stateless people originating from certain predetermined countries could receive a so-called Nansen passport issued by the League of Nations (Torpey 1998b: 253). It was only at the time when nation states were becoming the rule that the category of stateless persons for whom no state offered protection was created.

Already in the 1920s, there were attempts to remove passport controls that were set up during the war, and the newly established League of Nations also held a conference on this issue. However, the governments were prudent due to demobilization, unemployment, fears of Communism, monetary crises and the overall instability of the era, in addition to the concern over the welfare that states had started to provide for their citizens (Marrus 1985: 93). The suspicions created during the war thus did not come to an end even though the war did.

Originally, the League of Nations aimed at helping Russian-originating refugees with the Nansen passport arrangement. In 1921, the Russian government passed a decree which withdrew nationality from those who had been absent for five years and failed to register with the Russian Consul (Simpson 1938: 609), creating huge amounts of stateless people. The Nansen passport in itself did not grant rights of settlement or work, but it was later complemented with the 1933 Geneva Convention, which provided help for refugees in obtaining labour, admission to schools and other elements of nationality (Simpson 1938, Skran 1995). Furthermore, refugees were to be treated similarly as other foreign nationals in the newly established system.

At the same time in the 1930s, countries were suffering from economic recession and many decided to expel refugees from their countries. The League of Nations also addressed this issue, urging governments not to expel refugees that did not have a right to enter an adjacent country (Skran 1995: 134). In many ways, the work of the League became more difficult in the 1930s also due to the death of Nansen, economic recession and refugees fleeing from the Third Reich, which all countries did not welcome (Skran 1995: 194–5). The Nansen era, however, was crucial in creating the political will to help refugees, even though Nansen was not able to mobilize funds or obligate states to receive as much refugees as he planned (Marrus 1985: 120–1).

The Nansen passport was introduced in 1922, and approximately 450,000 such passports were issued during the inter-war period. The original passport included all information that is normally included in a passport and stated that the bearer was of Russian origin but has not acquired any other nationality. Fifty-three states adopted the passport in the first place and others followed suit. The passport was later also introduced for Armenian, Assyrian, Assyro-Chaldean, Assimilated (Syrian and Kurdish) and Turkish refugees (Sallinen 2013: 189–92). In the 1930s, some refugees originated even from Southern and other European countries, as the victims of fascism from Germany, Italy, Spain and Romania, among other countries, fled; many of them headed to France (Moch 2003: 168–9). The Nansen passport did not guarantee the refugees any protection, but it made their free movement easier across borders (Skran 1995: 122), granting them a right to free movement of sorts. Overall, the refugee arrangements of the League of Nations can be considered pivotal for the development of a universal refugee regime, despite the fact that the original arrangements were only reserved for specific, though expanding, groups of refugees.

While the refugee debate constituted a heated mobility discussion in the 1930s, some ideas were simultaneously presented about free movement of workers in Europe. For example, the International Labour Organization (ILO) proposed that a customs union, complemented with free movement of labour and protection for migrant workers, be established (Mechi 2013: 846). However, these ideas were soon forgotten in the middle of the economic recession of the 1930s.

During and after the Second World War, attention again turned to refugees, which grew into unprecedented numbers due to the war. The post-war European states were also in need of labour force, and the flow of workers included refugees from East to West and guest workers from South to North, with Southern European states signing guest worker agreement with countries such as France, Switzerland and Belgium (Stanek 2017: 17). In total, thirty million people were displaced after the war, many of them relocated from Eastern to Western European countries (Moch 2003: 171). In some Western countries, many of the people were classified as labour migrants, even though they were brought from the camp of displaced people (Ciupijus 2011).

It was only in the 1940s that political asylum became possible; before that, only stateless persons were considered refugees. However, after the war, people unwilling to return to their countries of origin (in the Soviet Union) also became considered as refugees (Janco 2014). Another legacy of this era is the prohibition to return refugees to the country of persecution, which became known as non-refoulement in the 1951 Refugee Convention (Skran 1995: 138).

In Europe, the period of strict passport and immigration controls lasted approximately from the beginning of the First World War to the 1950s, when certain groups of states started allowing free movement for their nationals. In the 1950s, Denmark, Sweden, Finland and Norway made an exceptional agreement in Europe, where the use of passports constituted the standard procedure: the countries abolished passport controls between them as well as the requirement for a residence permit for the nationals of the said countries (Torpey 2000: 145). In contrast, in the ECSC, the predecessor of the European Union, the countries merely allowed the free movement of certain workers, and it was only in the 1990s that the EU countries started to progressively abolish passport controls between them.

This brief history of movement controls illustrates that it is actually a very short period in the past when countries strictly controlled the movement of people across their borders. In this light, it seems peculiar how self-evident the 'sovereign' right to prevent people from entering a country appears in today's political debates. As will be illustrated in the next sections, the relaxation of border controls between European states has simultaneously been coupled with stricter control in the external borders of the European Union.

2.2 Free movement: From an economic principle towards a fundamental right

This section briefly outlines the evolution of the contemporary European free movement principle from an ideal serving the interests of the economy to the status of a fundamental right (see also Heinikoski 2017a). The European Union provides the primary context of the discussion, although the borderless Schengen Area also includes other European states (Liechtenstein, Iceland, Switzerland and Norway), and the citizens of the EEA countries too (Iceland, Norway and Liechtenstein) enjoy similar rights to residence in the area.[2]

In broad terms, free movement in the EU has evolved from an *economic* principle pertaining to workers, towards a right for all 'persons' holding EU citizenship. In other words, the free movement of labour was already a central premise of the Internal Market when it was launched in the 1950s, but from the 1960s onwards, the Court of Justice of the European Union (CJEU) has actively sought to turn this idea into a fundamental component of what, since 1992, has been known as European Union citizenship (Bellamy, Castiglione and Shaw 2006b: 10, Shaw 2007: 45). Free movement is also listed as a fundamental right in the Charter of Fundamental Rights that became legally binding along with the Lisbon Treaty (2007, in force since 2009).

Article 69 of the 1951 Treaty establishing the ECSC laid the foundation for free movement policies: 'The member States bind themselves to renounce any restriction based on nationality against the employment in the coal and steel industries of workers of proven qualifications for such industries who possess the nationality of one of the member States; this commitment shall be subject to the limitations imposed by the fundamental needs of health and public order.'

Workers' equal rights, irrespective of their nationality, thus constituted a central principle already in the early stages of European integration; however, maintaining public order and health was still seen as a legitimate reason for restricting people's mobility. Italian politicians of the time were particularly eager to support the adoption of the article, in order to make the emigration of Italian workers possible under the difficult conditions of Italy's post-war economy. However, Italian politicians had to acquiesce to the restriction clause of public health and order. It is important to note that the public health and order clause still justifies restrictions to free movement according to the Free Movement Directive 2004/38/EC (Maas 2007: 9, Recchi 2013: 42).[3]

The 1957 Treaty establishing the European Economic Community (EEC) mentioned the free movement of 'persons' in the title 'The Free Movement of Persons, Services and Capital', but it was evident that the people encouraged to exercise that right were primarily workforce (O'Keeffe 1998: 20-32). According to Article 48 of the Treaty, the free movement of workers:

> shall include the right, subject to limitations justified by the reasons of public order, public safety and public health:
> *a)* to accept offers of employment actually made;
> *b)* to move about freely for this purpose within the territory of the Member States;
> *c)* to stay in any Member State in order to carry on an employment in conformity with the legislative and administrative provisions governing the employment of the workers of the State; and
> *d)* to live, on conditions which shall be the subject of implementing regulations to be laid down by the Commission, in the territory of a Member States after having been employed there.

As is visible in the quotation, free movement only applied to people with an employment contract in another member state. However, the free movement principle later assumed a more comprehensive character in the 1960s. European politicians significantly enlarged its scope with regulation to cover all citizens of the member states and their family members (1612/68/EC).[4] As was already indicated, the role of the CJEU also became considerable in enlarging the right to free movement to all member state citizens in its case law. Gradually, the original principle, largely characterized by economic logic, began to resemble a fundamental right following the logics of freedom and equality.

The gradual expansion of the free movement principle culminated in 1992 when the Maastricht Treaty established EU citizenship, of which the right to free movement formed a crucial part. The linkage between the logics of economic development and freedom is clearly visible in the founding treaty of the EU (1992). Its Article B states that one of the main tasks of the EU is 'to promote economic and social progress which is balanced and sustainable, in particular through the creation of an area without internal frontiers, through the strengthening of economic and social cohesion and through the establishment of economic and monetary union, ultimately including a single currency in accordance with the provisions of this Treaty'.

The formulation seems to link free movement to economic and social progress, but the right is not unqualified. Whereas the principle of free movement inside a state represents a fundamental right – usually codified in the constitution – the principle of free movement in the EU is different in nature. Only in 2009, when the Lisbon Treaty entered into force, did the right to free movement become a legally binding fundamental right as it was codified in the Charter of Fundamental Rights.[5] Article 45 of the Charter, entitled 'Freedom of movement and of residence', provides that 'Every citizen of the Union has the right to move and reside freely within the territory of the Member States'. The second paragraph 45(2) complements the provision by stating that the 'Freedom of movement and residence may be granted, in accordance with the Treaty establishing the European Community, to nationals of third countries legally resident in the territory of a Member State'. For third-country nationals, the question is thus not of an automatic right, rather it depends on the immigration policies of individual member states. Only EU citizenship guarantees the full right to free movement. EU citizenship, in turn, is so densely tied to free movement that the entire citizenship can be considered dormant if a person resides in their home country (Strumia 2013: 102, Maas 2007: 64).

In addition to the EU treaties, free movement is regulated by secondary legislation, mainly directives, which often restrict the right to free movement with either economic or security arguments. For example, the Free Movement Directive 2004/38/EC stipulates that people exercising their right to free movement must be able to adequately provide for themselves. They must 'have sufficient resources for themselves and their family members not to become a burden on the social assistance system of the host Member State during their period of residence' (Article 7 of 2004/38/EC). However, there seems to be a contradiction here: member states may not restrict free movement on economic grounds, but there are economic conditions attached to those who want to stay in another country.[6] EU countries are, in theory, able to request that those EU citizens who are a burden on the local social assistance system leave the EU country in which they reside, but the decisions need to be made on an individual basis. It remains, however, very unclear on what basis EU citizens are asked to leave due to being a burden for the host member state, as the definition of being an 'unreasonable burden' differs from country to country (Minderhoud 2013: 209–26).

Another contentious issue in restricting freedom of movement is the possibility of establishing transitional restrictions for the workers of countries that join the Union.[7] Transitional restrictions concerning new member states have been in use since Greece, Spain and Portugal joined the Union in the 1980s, and these limitations may last a maximum of seven years.[8] It is also remarkable how unequally EU enlargements have seemingly treated foreign nationals in (old) member states. By way of example, in 2007, Romanians in Italy suddenly became 'co-nationals' while Albanians had to acquiesce to their old status (cf. Strumia 2013: 159–65).

2.3 Security and immigration intertwined in the Schengen Area

So far, I have discussed the evolution of free movement from a principle that primarily serves economic interests towards a fundamental right, but *security* concerns have also been crucial in the process. Security concerns are a comprehensive theme implicitly present in many a policy area. Here, the focus is on the explicit relationship between security, free movement and the migration of third-country nationals in EU policy.

In the 1980s, the connection between security and free movement became topical. Security aspects were high on the agenda when European countries began to plan Schengen cooperation in the early years of that decade – unavoidably, perhaps, as the resulting Schengen Agreement (1985/1990) abolished internal borders in continental Europe (UK and Ireland opted out).[9] At about the same time, the Single European Act (SEA, 1986) aimed at complementing the single market of the EU by abolishing internal border controls and strengthening the external ones (Huysmans 2006: 69). A few years later, the so-called 'Palma Programme' (1989) confirmed that 'an area without internal frontiers would necessitate tighter controls at external frontiers' (cf. Ette and Faist 2007: 6).

In the Schengen framework, which gradually came into effect during the 1990s, states were already allowed to impose temporary border controls for security reasons according to regulations. Article 2(2) of the Convention implementing the Schengen Agreement (1985) states:

> where public policy or national security so require a Contracting Party may, after consulting the other Contracting Parties, decide that for a limited period national border checks appropriate to the situation shall be carried out at internal borders. If public policy or national security require immediate action, the Contracting Party concerned shall take the necessary measures and at the earliest opportunity shall inform the other Contracting Parties thereof.

In practice, this has meant that the member states may check people at the borders, but they cannot restrict the mobility of EU citizens. In 2013, Schengen Borders Code were further specified in regulation 1051/2013 with regard to the rules for temporary reintroduction of internal border controls. Preamble 5 of the regulation explicitly states that migration should not be a reason for such controls, contrary to what took place in autumn 2015: 'Migration and the crossing of external borders by a large number of third-country nationals should not, per se, be considered to be a threat to public policy or internal security.'

The Schengen Borders Code was further specified with Regulation 2016/399, Article 29 of which allowed the Council to recommend certain states to carry out internal border controls for six months if the overall functioning of the Schengen Area is at risk. The recommendation can be renewed three times, and internal border controls were implemented in Germany, Austria, Sweden, Norway and Denmark between May 2016 and November 2017 on the basis of this article. Even though the rules normally allow the reintroduction of border controls for only six months, since autumn 2015, the five countries as well as France have upheld temporary internal controls that will last at least until spring 2020. The Commission urged the states to end them already in 2017 (European Commission 2017), but all the states have announced they will continue the controls, despite the fact that it is contrary to the Schengen Borders Code. This illustrates how EU rules may be sidestepped if domestic political concerns so require.

Going back to the early phases of Schengen, increased emphasis on security issues can also be observed at the basic treaty level. Towards the end of the 1990s, primarily due to the wars in ex-Yugoslavia, security and conflict issues gradually gained in importance on the EU's agenda. Accordingly, security concerns became explicit in the 1999 Tampere European Council and in the Amsterdam Treaty adopted the same year. The treaty established the European Area of Freedom, Security and Justice (AFSJ), which incorporated the Schengen framework.[10] Article B of the treaty recognizes the security risks of the free movement principle: 'The Union shall offer its citizens an area of freedom, security and justice without internal frontiers, in which the free movement of persons is ensured in conjunction with appropriate measures with respect to external border controls, asylum, immigration and the prevention and combating of crime.'

The Treaty of Lisbon, in force since 2009, abolished the previous three-pillar structure in decision-making[11] and simultaneously increased the Union's competence in criminal and police matters related to the Area of Freedom, Security and Justice. The treaty also introduced the aim that free movement policy be complemented with a common policy for asylum, immigration and external border control. In this policy, member states were to show solidary towards each other in immigration matters and act fairly towards third-country nationals, as defined in Article 67(1) of the Treaty on the Functioning of the European Union (TFEU), amended by the Lisbon Treaty: '[The Union] shall ensure the absence of internal border controls for persons and shall frame a common policy on asylum, immigration and external border control, based on solidarity between member states, which is fair towards third-country nationals.'

As the treaty provides, internal free movement is currently linked to common European immigration and asylum policies. However, the balance between free movement and migration control has not always been easy to determine, although the need for common immigration policies was acknowledged long before the entry at the treaty level. It is thus necessary to also examine how secondary EU law has discussed the connection of free movement and immigration controls. In the 1990s, along with the establishment of the Schengen Area, the entry of 'third-country nationals'[12] in the Union area became complicated; restrictive measures including tighter visa policies, border controls, strict conditions for applying for asylum and work permits in the Union came into force. As an illustration of the prevailing moods in the 1990s, the first criterion governing member states' labour migration policies in the Council Resolution of June 1994 declared that priority should be given to EU citizens: 'Member States will consider requests for admission to their territories for the purpose of employment only where vacancies in a Member State cannot be filled by national and Community manpower or by non-Community manpower lawfully resident on a permanent basis in that Member State and already forming part of the Member State's regular labour market.'

Member states have, in other words, committed themselves to privileging EU citizens over third-country nationals in employment decisions. The outlining of the free movement area has also resulted in other restrictions for third-country nationals moving in the Union area, thus contributing to the development of a 'Fortress Europe' (e.g. Talani 2012: 61–72).[13] As a sign of such fortress-building, European politicians have consistently established restrictions, although the rhetoric has sometimes been more open. For example, the conclusions drawn by the October 1999 Tampere European Council discussed the freedom of movement as a comprehensive principle:

> This freedom should not, however, be regarded as the exclusive preserve of the Union's own citizens. Its very existence acts as a draw to many others worldwide who cannot enjoy the freedom Union citizens take for granted. It would be in contradiction with Europe's traditions to deny such freedom to those whose circumstances lead them justifiably to seek access to our territory. This in turn requires the Union to develop common policies on asylum and immigration,

while taking into account the need for a consistent control of external borders to stop illegal immigration and to combat those who organise it and commit related international crimes.

Despite these eloquent words, third-country nationals still do not enjoy similar rights to free movement. Although the status of third-country nationals was already specified in Directive 2003/109/EC and enlarged in Council Regulation 859/2003 concerning social security, third-country nationals only have the right to short-term visits before five years of legal residence in another EU member state (Strumia, 2013: 96–9). The right to permanent residence in a member state may also be lost after six years of absence or when obtaining a permanent residence permit in another state, according to Article 9 of the Council Directive 2003/109 (cf. Strumia, 2013: 99). As the naturalization of immigrants is completely subject to national discretion, third-country nationals in different member states enjoy very different rights to mobility.

There has, however, been progress in establishing common immigration and asylum policies since the 1990s. The Dublin Convention related to the Schengen Agreement required that an asylum application must be handled in the first country to which the applicant arrives.[14] The 'Dublin II Regulation', the Council Regulation (EC) No 343/2003, replaced the first Dublin Convention. With the regulation, the EU also established the EURODAC system to compare the fingerprints of asylum-seekers and illegal migrants. Dublin III, in turn, came into force in 2013 with the Regulation (EU) No 604/2013, establishing the long-planned Common European Asylum System. Article 7(2) of the 2013 Directive includes the original Dublin provision: 'The Member State responsible in accordance with the criteria set out in this Chapter shall be determined on the basis of the situation obtaining when the applicant first lodged his or her application for international protection with a Member State.' The provision means that asylum-seekers should return, or be returned, to the first country – party to the Dublin arrangement – where they originally landed or registered. The return of people is not obligatory, and some countries (e.g. Germany in autumn 2015) have even declared that they would not send people back to the Mediterranean countries dealing with the largest share of immigrants.

Other progress in the field of migration has also occurred. The EU adopted a Global Approach to Migration and Mobility in 2005, which reached its second phase along with the Commission Communication COM(2011) 743. It provides a framework for more harmonization in immigration and asylum policies, but does not establish a common immigration policy. The Council also adopted the European Immigration and Asylum Pact in 2008, in which the member states, inter alia, committed to only conduct regularizations of irregular migrants on an individual basis. The member states promise 'to use only case-by-case regularisation, rather than generalised regularisation, under national law, for humanitarian or economic reasons' (Council of the European Union 2008).[15] This pact was pushed forward by France, in particular, as a reaction to the widespread regularization campaigns that had already taken place in Spain and Italy.

The plans to pursue common immigration policies seemed to reach their turning point in autumn 2015 when the great number of migrants coming to Europe made the question of 'burden-sharing' inevitable. In this burden-sharing, the needs and desires of the asylum-seekers seem to have a minor role, which is also demonstrated in the returns and transfers of such people. In 2001, a Council Directive on Temporary Protection in the Case of Mass Influx 2001/55/EC (Article 26(1)) outlined non-binding measures, where the transfer of people enjoying temporary protection from one place to another requires agreement from both the receiving state and the people concerned (see also Thieleman and Dewan 2007: 163–4). Despite this declaration, in the autumn of 2015, the Council decided to distribute asylum-seekers equally among EU member states (which was never properly implemented) and, in spring 2016, to conclude a much-criticized agreement on returning asylum-seekers to Turkey.

The ideal of free movement applies differently depending on the mover's citizenship, which has been illustrated in this contextualizing historical overview. The next chapter, in turn, elaborates how one can analyse contemporary discourses on free movement.

3

Conceptual framework and methodology

This chapter introduces a novel conceptual framework and the methodology of the analysis, which utilizes the concepts of the discourse-historical approach of Ruth Wodak (Wodak 2001, 2009, Wodak and Riesigl 2001). It also describes the empirical material of the book, consisting of political utterances.

3.1 A conceptual framework of practical reasoning

The political utterances analysed in this study can be seen as a form of practical reasoning, based on a number of premises and leading to a conclusion (Kratochwil 1989, Searle 2001). Scholars disagree, however, over how to *categorize* the different guiding premises of practical reasoning. In scholarly literature, the most traditional distinction is that between instrumental and value-based reasoning (Weber 1978: 1347, Walton 2007).[1] This distinction is based on the 'classical model' of practical reasoning (Searle 2001) and it resembles the most common division in the normative ethical discussion in philosophy; the instrumentalism-value-division can be seen to correspond to the ethical categorization into consequence-based and duty-based theories (see, e.g., Mackie 1984). Instrumental practical reasoning refers to an argument aimed at bringing about a certain goal or a state of affairs, whereas value-based practical reasoning refers to the individual's values (such as friendship) as the motivation behind their actions. John Searle, in turn, makes a similar distinction as he talks about desire-dependent and desire-independent reasons. For him, practical reasoning is ultimately based on desires: obligations may function as motivators for action, but even obligations ultimately only constitute grounds for desires (Searle 2001). For this book's analysis of political discourses as a form of practical reasoning, individuals' ultimate desires are hardly relevant, that is, I will not consider what their most fundamental hopes and motivations are. Behind the discursive level analysed in this study, there is a psychological level that remains a mystery to an outside observer.

The distinction between instrumental (or desire-dependent) and value-based (or desire-independent) reasoning does provide a useful starting point for my analyses. It is also noteworthy that unlike some scholars (Fairclough and Fairclough 2012: 247), I believe that values are separate from goals; one does not always choose one's form of action based on the expected consequences but based on what is in that person's view

Table 3.1 Practical reasoning types

Type of practical reasoning	Philosophical source of inspiration	Guiding reasons	Imaginary
Agreement	Jürgen Habermas	Collectively agreed rules	Rights-based Europe
Community	Charles Taylor	Communal values	Europe as identification
Utility	R. M. Hare	Costs and benefits	Europe that delivers
Solidarity	Richard Rorty	Solidary results	Europe of solidarity

Table 3.2 Theoretical framework of practical reasoning and examples

		Value-based reasoning		
	AGREEMENT		COMMUNITY	
	Duty to comply with rules		Duty to our community	
	Rules vs. security		Responsibility towards children	
Rationality	Implementation of rules		Deep diversity prevailing	Sentiment
	UTILITY		SOLIDARITY	
	Goal to maximize functionality		Close society as the goal	
	Maximizing benefits		Burden-sharing	
	Minimizing costs		Negative transactionalism	
		Instrumental reasoning		

the right and just thing to do. However, I deem that this dual distinction as such is insufficient and needs to be specified. In order to do this, I have complemented it with another distinction well known in normative philosophy: rationality vs. sentiment. 'Rationality' reflects rationally determined principles, while 'sentiment' refers to an emotional approach (Rorty 1999: 67–83). The rationality vs. sentiment discussion revolves around the method of finding the right moral principles and originates from the writings of Immanuel Kant (morals as a matter of reason) and David Hume (morals as a matter of sentiment) (Hume 1896: 470–6, Kant 1999, cf. Rorty 1999: 67–83). Simply put, the sentiment-based approach here refers to a need to separate between 'them' and 'us', while rationality refers to the effort to find the best course of action in 'universal' terms. The two axes – instrumentalism vs. values and rationality vs. sentiment – create the fourfold categorization of practical reasoning introduced and utilized in this study (see Tables 3.1 and 3.2).

Based on the fourfold conceptual framework, I divide value-based reasoning into two sub-categories: agreement and community-based categories. Agreement discourses rely on the *rational* duties of compliance related to formal treaties, authorities and rule-based premises. Community discourses, in turn, stem from *sentiment-based* duties concerning what is considered good for 'us' as a community. The goal-based discourses also contain two categories. *Rational* utility discourses focus on optimizing the cost–benefit ratios, whereas *sentiment-based* solidarity discourses emphasize the enlargement of solidarity between fellow human beings.

Table 3.1 illustrates the types of practical reasoning as well as their connections to my philosophical sources of inspiration (on these, see Chapters 4–7) and what I call *guiding reasons* and *imaginaries* in practical reasoning.[2] 'Imaginary' is a concept borrowed from discourse analysis, referring to a picture of a good society that an individual holds (Fairclough and Fairclough 2012: 104–8). The question is, in other words, what sort of imaginaries of an ideal Europe are present in the discourses and in which ways does free movement belong to them? The speaker may present his or her imaginary in either factual or desired terms. For example, politicians may discuss a Europe where everyone shares the equal right to free movement either as a desirable result or as a factual status.

The agreement dimension[3] relates to the *imaginary* of a rights-based Europe (Sjursen 2006b: 203–15), whereby citizens' rights reflect the commonly agreed-upon obligations of the state.[4] The right to free movement can manifest itself as a contractual norm guaranteeing equal possibilities for each individual within the EU or as a duty to protect member states' national security. The community dimension relates to the imaginary of Europe as an entity of identification (cf. Taylor 1993: 123), with a focus on communal values. The community utterances link the right to free movement to a sense of European community or to the duty to protect a community from outsiders. In contrast, the utility logic dictates that the rationality of actions depends on their overall costs and gains. It reflects the imaginary of a Europe that delivers and provides welfare (cf. Taylor 1993: 122), and as seen in this context, free movement should thus maximize the benefits of all actors. Finally, solidarity provides the grounds for deliberately extending the sense of 'us' and coming closer to others, be that a (pan-) European society or a smaller group of people. The solidarity discourse relates to the imaginary of a Europe of mutual solidarity (Rorty 2000a: 87–8).

The framework of analysis illustrated in Tables 3.1 and 3.2 can be employed to study different types of institutional and political utterances, and all four outlooks can be used for arguing both in favour of and against the right to free movement. Each dimension depicts a different normative stance and provides a novel perspective for the analysis of the discourses concerning the principle of free movement (see also Heinikoski 2015a).

3.2 The empirical material

The empirical material of this study consists of political documents from six European Union countries and the European Commission.[5] The countries include the five largest member states – they are also the most popular target countries for free movers in the EU – Germany, France, the UK, Italy and Spain as well as the country that has had the most mobile population, Romania.[6] The six countries represent ca. 343 million citizens of the European Union, which amounts to more than two-thirds of the total EU population, ca. 513 million. I have included the European Commission in order to be able to contrast the country-based views to the 'official' perspective of the European Union.[7]

The time period covered in the book spans the period from the start of the first Barroso Commission, in November 2004, to the end of June 2016 when the Brexit referendum was held. It is noteworthy that the year 2004 is the year when Free Movement Directive 2004/38/EC was adopted and ten new member states joined the EU. The year could also be said to have provided the starting point for the current free movement debates looked at from the target country perspective. The twelve-year time span allows me to observe to what extent different political constellations have had different agendas in terms of free movement and even whether, within a political constellation, views change considerably.

In the case of the five biggest member states, I included the speeches by the heads of state or governments (hereafter heads of state) and ministers of the interior, who have borne the prime responsibility for free movement policy in their respective countries.[8] The Romanian document sample proved sufficiently substantive by only including documents produced by the presidents and prime ministers, who have both represented their country in the Council of the European Union; there is still, in fact, some ambiguity concerning who should represent the country in EU matters. For the Commission, I have included the relevant commissioners' views. In all cases, the question is thus about the pervasive political view; I have not been interested in the intra-country cleavages and have therefore not included speeches from leading opposition politicians.[9]

Approximately 90 per cent of the documents are public speeches, statements and addresses; they represent views that the politicians have wanted to present publicly. In addition, the material also includes a number of newspaper interviews with more or less direct quotations from the politicians, which have been published on the official websites. The number of newspaper articles in the Italian case is larger; this is primarily due to Silvio Berlusconi's government (2008–11) publishing their interviews on the website of the prime minister and the minister of the interior. This, in turn, probably relates to the fact that Silvio Berlusconi owns much of the Italian print media and the published interviews were ergo uncritical of the government. Both the original speeches and the newspaper articles were available on the governments' websites. The majority of the documents are in the official language of the respective country. I have translated the quotations from the documents in English, but I provide the original language form in the endnotes.

I have included in the material the documents that made a distinct argument about free movement, on its negative or positive features, on its relevance in European or national contexts or on what should be done about it. I use the notion of *utterance* for referring to these arguments. In the selection process, I have had to use different selection strategies in different cases. In three cases (Germany, France and the European Commission), I did not have to review all the documents, thanks to database search functions at the official websites. In the other four countries (UK, Italy, Spain, Romania), I went through the entire archives of documents and first selected those that at the title level were somehow related to the context of free movement (e.g. immigration, official visits and EU summits).

While gathering the material, I initially made use of the classification software NVivo, which helped me in managing the large numbers of documents. The actual analysis entailed intensive reading of the texts, in which case NVivo proved to be of little use. Table 3.3 reveals the number of documents included in the analysis as well

Table 3.3 Empirical material of the study

Actor	Analysed documents (out of which media articles)
Germany	59 (4)
France	59 (9)
Italy	42 (16)
UK	54 (1)
Spain	40 (1)
Romania	53 (3)
European Commission	72 (0)
Total	**379 (34)**

as the number of media articles that the material collected from the official websites included. I present the table for illustrative reasons, while the focus of this study is on qualitative analysis. What the table reveals is that the number of primary analysed documents is within the same range for each country. The number of commissioners' utterances is somewhat higher as free movement has been high on the agenda within the Commission. The number of analysed German and French utterances is also slightly higher than that of the other countries; this mainly relates to the German and French leaders forcefully defending free movement before the Brexit referendum.

A few further notes regarding the material are in order. The material includes five joint statements, which are authored by politicians from two or more countries. Such utterances are included in the number of utterances of each country whose politician was involved in the statement. In the list of empirical documents in the end of the book, I list each document organized by the concerned politicians' surname (or in the case of joint statements, under the first author). I also do this even in the case of newspaper articles, in order to make it easier to trace the relevant sources regarding each person. I only cite a few utterances representing the overall discussion, but I list all the analysed documents at the end of the book. For a more in-depth explanation of my process, I briefly illustrate how I found the documents in each case in the Appendix.

In the case of several of the politicians, I could find only one relevant document on free movement; in other cases, only a few. I therefore cannot claim that these statements provide a complete picture of the overall stances of these persons, nor do I intend to argue that the utterances represent the perspectives of the 'nation'. The documents usually constitute carefully drafted speeches that reflect what people expect of the politicians as they aim to satisfy the audience and perhaps the voters, more generally. One specific feature of the utterances is that about a quarter of them were held abroad or during the visit of a European colleague, which may induce the politicians into talking about free movement matters. Alternatively, this may also account for the differences between the utterances of the heads of state and the ministers of the interior: while the heads of state often discuss European cooperation in foreign contexts, interior ministers tend to address domestic audiences and to also discuss the security concerns related to free movement.

3.3 Methodological underpinnings inspired by critical discourse analysis

My methodological underpinnings for analysing political discourses have been inspired by discourse analysis, particularly the discourse-historical approach outlined by Ruth Wodak. This approach enables one to look at both the linguistic means and practices of a text as well as to reveal the relationship between discourses and political structures by critically examining political arguments (Wodak, De Cillia and Reisigl 2009: 9). Wodak understands discourses as 'linguistic social practices [that] can be seen as constituting non-discursive and discursive social practices and, at the same time, as being constituted by them' (Wodak 2001: 66). In other words, discourses, social practices and knowledge are always interrelated and shape and are shaped by each other. On the linguistic level, she further defines discourses as a 'bundle of simultaneous and sequential interrelated linguistic acts, which manifest themselves within and across the social fields of action as thematically interrelated semiotic, oral or written tokens' (Wodak 2001: 66).

The discourse-historical approach includes three dimensions: topics, discursive strategies and linguistic means. *Topics* are the issues that are spoken or written about, while Wodak defines *discursive strategies* as a plan of practices 'adopted to achieve a particular social, political, psychological or linguistic goal' (Wodak 2009: 38–40). She specifies five different types of discursive strategies: referential, predication, argumentation, perspectivation and intensification/mitigation (Wodak 2001: 73, 2009: 40–2). Instead of trying to find all the discursive strategies identified in the approach, this book concentrates on identifying certain *argumentation strategies* that make use of justificatory *topoi*, that is, premises of an argument, which help in classifying the utterances in the categories of the conceptual framework. *Linguistic means*, in turn, are the manners in which these discursive strategies are constructed (Wodak 2001: 74, 2009: 38). Although linguistic means are crucial to constructing different discourses, I do not systematically discuss them in Chapters 4–7.

One of the reasons for focusing on the justificatory *topoi* is that the role of *topoi* is important in the practical reasoning literature; they 'function to legitimate a piece of reasoning' (Edmondson 2012: 113). According to Friedrich V. Kratochwil, *topoi* 'not only establish "starting-points" to arguments, but locate the issues of a debate in a substantive set of common understandings that provide for the crucial connections within the structure of the argument' (Kratochwil 1989: 219). From the discourse analytical perspective, Ruth Wodak, in turn, defines the *topoi* as 'parts of argumentation which belong to the obligatory, either explicit or inferable premises' (Wodak 2001: 74). In the present study, *topoi* refer to the starting points from which the discussants construct their different arguments. The list is certainly not exhaustive, but different *topoi* include those of usefulness/advantage, uselessness/disadvantage, definition/name interpretation, danger and threat, humanitarianism, justice, responsibility, burdening/weighting, finances, reality, numbers, law and right, history, culture and abuse (Wodak 2001: 74). I traced such *topoi* in the analysed utterances and often refer to them in Chapters 4–7. The use of *topoi* in terms of predefined lists has also been criticized for being arbitrary (Žagar 2010), but for the purposes of this study, such predefined *topoi* serve as useful tools for tracing the premises of argumentation and further specifying the utterances categorized under one of the four types of practical reasoning. Identifying the *topoi* of the utterances thus serves the purpose of discourse categorization.

A few notes about the actual analysis are in order. As previously mentioned, each document that I selected for the analysis included *only one* utterance discussing free movement. 'Utterance', in this study, means a proposition of one or more sentences that includes a stance on free movement; the length of an utterance varies from one sentence to several. The total length of documents, in turn, varied from short statements of less than one page to speeches of several pages. It is particularly important to note *that I decided to categorize each of the documents under just one of the four dimensions of the conceptual framework, as the free movement arguments were clearly built around one type of practical reasoning*. That said, documents focusing on the economic benefits of free movement did sometimes mention that free movement is also a fundamental right, while documents discussing the solidary aspects of free movement may also have mentioned its economic benefits; however, the dominant argument was nevertheless easy to determine.

I read the documents carefully, identified the *topoi* and classified each document into one of the four categories, after which I started outlining the general picture. I organized each empirical chapter around three broad groups that could be discerned from the material with the help of the theoretical ideas inspiring each of the four dimensions. In the agreement dimension, theories of constitutional patriotism inspired the classification, which included three types of duties: the duty to comply with rules, the duty of balancing between rules and security, and the duty of better implementation. The three groups of duties categorized in the community dimension, in turn, received their inspiration from communitarian authors, entitled: 'duty stemming from a fundamental piece of European community', 'duty stemming from responsibility towards future generations' and 'duty stemming from deep diversity: the nation as primary responsibility'. In contrast, the instrumental utilitarian dimension focused on three types of utilitarian goals: the maximization of functionality, the maximization of benefits and the minimization of costs. Finally, the instrumental solidarity approach included sentiment-related goals: of deeper Europeanness, of burden-sharing in immigration and of preventing negative transactionalism.

The empirical chapters (Chapters 4–7) weave together the conceptual framework and political reality observed at the discursive level. Theoretical and empirical dimensions thus intertwine, providing an overview on what sort of new issues arise in the material when utilizing the conceptual framework of practical reasoning. The discussion also considers the political contexts in which the addresses were made – the national politicians represent a certain state and a party – but the chapters are not organized around different political constellations. The multilevel nature of the material does cause some sort of difficulties for understanding in what kind of context a political actor operates. Whether a politician presents an utterance, for example, ahead of national elections, during an official state visit or in the national parliament, plays a major role in the content of the utterance. It should also be noted that the utterances may involve interests related to domestic politics, and differences between the major parties may relate more to electoral politics than to actual opinions. National perspectives may thus play a larger role in the material than they have in actual EU politics.

It is also worth mentioning that free movement seems to be considered a self-evident principle in major European countries. There were practically no utterances demanding the abolition of the said principle, but most of the utterances did, nonetheless, focus on some of the challenges related to free movement. Positive issues were, however, also mentioned when free movement was defended against criticism. Overall, the problem-focus of the material is fruitful in terms of analysing different types of practical reasoning – practical reasoning is indeed about finding the best course of action.

This chapter has introduced the conceptual framework, the empirical material and the methodology. The book might have looked different had I selected different material or utilized a different type of methodological toolbox to make sense of the discourses. I believe, however, that the selected theory-informed framework has proved sufficiently fruitful; it shifts the attention from *what* is said to *how* it is said, what sort of premises are utilized to back up one's arguments. Instead of conducting the analysis around the four broad categories, I could of course have chosen other alternatives. I could have treated different countries as case studies and compared them, but I might have missed the general European trends observed with my chosen approach. Further, I could have also let the material guide me and draw a historical timeline or focus on a few themes that stood out from the material, but such an approach would be less theory-informed. I might also have employed a quantitative methodology for analysing discursive strategies, for example, categorized all the linguistic means and discursive strategies. This, in turn, would have focused excessively on the linguistic form and less on content and justifications. Although no toolbox can provide an exhaustive picture of the complex phenomenon of free movement, I believe that the most important themes, historical trajectories, discursive tools and country-specific differences have received their due attention in the book as it stands now. Furthermore, the conceptual framework introduced in the study brings to light underlying assumptions related to duties, consequences, the presumed objectivity of political decision-making and the distinction between them and us.

Of course, as all research strategies, the research strategy adopted here has its limitations. It contains predetermined theoretical boxes into which reality must be condensed. Furthermore, placing each document into only one box necessarily simplifies the picture; and the breadth of the categories means that fairly different utterances can end up in the same category. A more quantitative methodology may have provided different results, but I doubt that having a greater amount of more precisely defined categories would have been able to reveal the essential nuances that this approach catches. The adopted framework is inclusive yet precise enough to reveal the grand lines of the discursive justifications for the principle of free movement.

I now turn to the empirical analysis. The analysis begins with the agreement dimension, as free movement agreements often represent the starting point for political debates. Furthermore, agreement utterances were, overall, the most common type of practical reasoning, relying on a *rationality-based duty* to hold onto free movement agreements. I continue with the *sentiment-based value reasoning* – 'community' – and finish with *the rationality-based and sentiment-based types of* instrumental *reasoning* – 'utility' and 'solidarity'. This order enables the reader to compare the differences inside and between the value-based and instrumental approaches.

4

Agreement dimension: Emphasis on common duties

The agreement utterances that are analysed below often refer to the status of free movement as a fundamental right of citizens. Many such utterances also present free movement as a potential threat to the collective order of the state. Furthermore, references to the European Union, the European Commission or the state as the principal authority that decides upon the application of free movement are also included here. In other words, the main topics in the ensuing analysis revolve around what the main duties are, who bears these duties and who should ultimately resolve problems related to free movement.

Before moving onto the empirical examples, I first introduce Jürgen Habermas's theory of constitutional patriotism, which represents an ideal type of agreement-based reasoning. One of the crucial questions of this chapter is whether and in which ways politicians in major European countries adhere to the basic principles of this ideal. The Habermasian framework includes different types of duties that need to be reconciled in the context of European free movement discourses: the duty to maintain equality across the continent, the duty to comply with common agreements and the duty to decide who can cross borders. The subsequent sections, then, deal with the different types of analysed discourses and with the manner in which agreement-based discourses have manifested themselves in the context of the free movement regime.

4.1 Agreement-based reasoning as a theoretical ideal: Equal moral worth

Jürgen Habermas's theory of constitutional patriotism provides the source of inspiration for the conceptual dimension of agreement-based discourses related to free movement. In the context of the free movement regime, constitutional patriotism could imply that all citizens should share an equal right to free movement. Indeed, constitutional patriotism, for the purposes of this book, culminates in the duty to guarantee equality and compliance with the agreed-upon rules. In Habermas's theory, the deliberative process of constructing constitutional principles is crucial for achieving equal and just rules. However, this procedural aspect of Habermasian thinking remains relatively unimportant, as I do not analyse the process leading to free movement agreements and rules. Instead, I regard free movement as an already established 'constitutional' principle and my focus is therefore on how leading European politicians approach this agreement on free movement.

A rational form of communication underlies the Habermasian deliberative processes, during which 'true' moral and legal norms should ultimately be determined; in these deliberations, freedom often plays a central role. The origins of the Habermasian discussion on communicative rationality can be traced back to Immanuel Kant (see, e.g., McCarthy 1994) who defined freedom as 'the one sole and original right belonging to every person by virtue of his humanity' (Kant 1999: 238). For Kant, this right is morally imposed on everyone and restricts the actions of both the legislator and any other individual who might violate an individual's freedom. The right described by Kant is thus a right of individuals against other individuals and the state, an innate right transcendentally known and granted to all.

In the world of politics, the idea of communicative rationality ought to materialize in terms of constitutional patriotism. Habermas has often discussed the European Union as a potential example of constitutional patriotism. According to Habermas, the sense of unity of a political entity – such as the EU – should be based on some sort of constitutional patriotism, that is, an identity founded on constitutional principles, established and reinterpreted in equality-based communication (Habermas 1994b: 135). Within the European Union, the individual member states can found their unity (in diversity) on common legal provisions; the member states can act within a sort of 'post-national self-understanding of the political community' (Habermas 1999: 119, Müller 2007).[1] Jan-Werner Müller (2006) has further divided constitutional patriotism into a 'protective' Sternbergerian variant intended to maintain stability (Sternberger 1963) and a 'purifying' Habermasian variant focusing on the public sphere. Both aspects of constitutional patriotism are visible in the discourses analysed in the ensuing sections.

The principle of constitutional patriotism arguably requires that people have the right to free movement (Tonkiss 2013a: 74–102). It further requires that citizens recognize each other as free and equal, and this equality justifies a comprehensive right to free movement. Katherine Tonkiss (2013a: 78) formulates this logic in the following way:

(a) Constitutional patriotism represents a deep commitment to equal moral worth, expressed as democratic political equality.
(b) Such a commitment, in the absence of strong, countervailing moral reasons to restrict membership, implies a commitment to the free movement of individuals across borders.
(c) Therefore, constitutional patriotism implies a commitment to the free movement of individuals across borders.

Tonkiss's formulation is, of course, idealistic and difficult to implement in practice. The most apparent contradiction in the idea of constitutional patriotism is that political orders should establish boundaries for themselves. From this perspective, it can be argued that constitutional and democratic states have a duty to guarantee their citizens the right to demand inclusiveness, and thus the right to exclude people who threaten that inclusiveness (Tonkiss 2013b: 499). In the words of Habermas, 'The right to democratic self-determination does indeed include the right of citizens to insist on the inclusive character of their own political culture' (Habermas 1999: 229). In the context of free movement, this may materialize, for example, as restrictions based on collective order, owing to the duty of political decision-makers to guarantee societal stability and maintain democratic legitimacy. The Habermasian framework can therefore justify enlarging citizens' right to free movement while at the same time restricting that right on the basis of democratic self-determination.

The idea of constitutional patriotism materializes in the European Union if we ultimately see the Union as a rights-based political actor (Calhoun 2002, cf. Fossum 2008).[2] In such thinking, the Union represents the idea of a 'rights-based post-national union' (Sjursen 2006b: 203-15). A perfect rights-based union relies on universal rights, the principle of constitutional patriotism as well as on the equal moral worth of all people. However, there are limits to this 'universalism'. First of all, Habermasian communicative rationality demands that everyone holding these rights can take part in the deliberation about moral truths. Nevertheless, people from outside the European Union are unable to participate in this deliberation, although it also affects them. Even more importantly, constitutional patriotism requires that people are equal before the law. In the context of EU free movement, however, only people holding European citizenship and sufficient financial resources are able to fully exercise the right to free movement.

The discussion above implies that common agreements lead to duties that require politicians and citizens to act in a certain rational manner. These duties, expressed in agreement utterances, are based on different types of *topoi*, such as a *topos* of law and right, a *topos* of justice or a *topos* of threat. In practical terms, the keywords of agreement premises include references to European agreements, to the European Commission as *the* authority above the member states, to the need to reform rules and to potential criminality related to free movement.

The ensuing sections analyse the relations between constitutional patriotism and national decision-making in official political discourses. Section 4.2 entitled 'Duty to comply with rules' focuses mainly on citizens' equal right to free movement, which is closest to the ideal of constitutional patriotism. Such discussions often relate to the free movement of the Roma and focus on the principles of equality and non-discrimination. Section 4.3, entitled 'Duty of balancing between rules and security', approaches free movement from the perspective of threats to security. Guaranteeing security is an important duty of politicians. In the empirical material, the politicians often called for more and wider measures to tackle certain unwanted phenomena related to free movement. However, they usually required European-wide measures, which implies that security issues were assumed to be best addressed at the EU level in line with constitutional patriotism. Section 4.4, entitled 'Duty of better implementation', discusses demands for the improved enforcement of free movement rules. The third aspect also considers how much leeway member states should have in implementing EU rules. This aspect thus balances between supranational constitutional patriotism and national decision-making.

4.2 Duty to comply with rules: Free movement of the Roma

In this section, I discuss those agreement utterances which emphasize compliance with the existing commonly agreed-upon rules. This duty stems from the ideal of constitutional patriotism and it requires the equal guarantee of citizens' right to free movement and the prevention of discrimination against people entitled to the said right. Equality is a key concept in constitutional patriotism, and many of the discursive *topoi* were based on justice and equality, with which politicians seek to argue for people's equal treatment in similar situations. Another *topos* is that of danger and threat, based on the argument that if there are certain threats, some actions should be taken to counteract the threat (Wodak 2001: 75).

This section focuses on the free movement of the Roma, a focal point in the discourses emphasizing equality between different types of people (see also Heinikoski 2016a, 2017b). Here we observe that politicians often approach the movement of this minority group from a value-based agreement perspective, by referring either to a duty to guarantee mobility rights or to a duty to protect national collective order. Whereas some politicians maintain that it is unlawful to take measures against the Roma, others have determined that mobile Roma communities violate EU rules in one way or the other.

Many politicians argued that *compliance* prevents discriminatory practices among citizens. Compliance, as defined here, relates to adherence to commonly agreed-upon rules and the prevention of rule abuse, whereas non-compliance means the neglect of rules and their abuse. Compliance was a central element in the discourses on the free movement of the Roma. The Roma's equal right to free movement was often weighed against its consequences, such as perceived threats to collective order or security. The Roma issue provides a good example of discourses where rules are utilized as the argumentative premises, regardless of which side of the dispute one stands.

There were differences, of course, in the perspectives across the case studies: The commissioners paid more attention to ensuring that the right to free movement could be equally utilized by all groups, including the Roma. For their part, French and Italian leaders justified their restrictive measures targeting the Roma in 2007–10, while German, Spanish and British politicians balanced between EU rules and national discretion. Romanian politicians, in turn, demanded assistance from the European Union in order to integrate the Roma. Romania was constantly pushed by the Commission to improve the situation of the Roma prior to the 2007 accession (Papadimitriou and Phinnemore 2008: 79). However, EU accession based on the free movement principle gave Romanian politicians, in some way, a further excuse to not improve the integration of the Roma. In practice, this meant that Romania could not be kicked out of the Union and that the Roma could then seek better living conditions in other states.

The repatriation of the Roma from France in summer 2010 was an issue that generated strong statements from the European Commission, which claimed that France was violating EU rules. The commissioner for justice, fundamental rights and citizenship, Viviane Reding, was the fiercest defender of free movement and she emphasized the authority of the Commission. According to her, the principle of free movement represented an individual right and was not related to one's ethnic origin. Her utterance utilized the *topos* of justice, emphasizing citizens' equal rights:

> This is a situation I had thought Europe would not have to witness again after the Second World War. ... This preliminary analysis stressed, inter alia, that France would be in violation of EU law if the measures taken by the French authorities in applying the Free Movement Directive had targeted a certain group on the basis of nationality, race or ethnic origin. (Reding 2010)

Although her reference to the Second World War aroused criticism for being somewhat controversial (see below), the reaction of the Commission did not lead to any formal sanctions; the amendments France was forced to make to its legislation proved sufficient (Gehring 2013b: 143–74). The measures undertaken may not have corresponded with the level of determination in the utterance, but Ms Reding manifested a strong commitment to the equal rights of citizens and demanded that states ensure that they uphold such rights. Commissioner Reding's overall emphasis on (EU-centred) equality-based discourse also appeared in her other utterances. For example, she did not consider European citizens living in other countries as 'immigrants', but simply as EU citizens exercising their Treaty right:

> I want to make it absolutely clear: Free movement is a fundamental right, and it is not up for negotiation. Let language not betray us: European citizens exercising their right to free movement are not 'immigrants'. European citizens have all the same rights. Let me also be clear that Roma people are EU citizens and as such have the right to free movement. (Reding 2013a)

The French discussions during this time (around 2010) presented the Roma as abusers of the rules of free movement. President Sarkozy considered the EU rules valid, although he felt that they were not always complied with, a discourse type that was particularly common during his presidential term.[3] He never seemed to question the principle of free movement as such but often referred to non-compliance when balancing free movement against some other principle. Balancing with security seems to have been the argument he used when restricting other fundamental rights in France.[4] Mr Sarkozy justified the French measures by employing the *topos* of danger, that is, the notion of rules violation committed by, for example, the Roma:

> At the same time, I hope that we begin an important reform in order to enhance the fight against irregular immigration. Every year, about ten thousand irregular migrants, including the Roma, leave voluntarily with state aid. And the following year, after they have left the country with the state aid, they come back illegally to ask for more state aid to leave. That is called 'abuse of the right to free movement'. (Sarkozy 2010)[5]

It is intriguing that President Sarkozy calls the mobility of the Roma 'irregular immigration', although admitting that the people have the right to free movement. Contrary to Commissioner Reding, he is referring to the EU citizens as not only 'immigrants' but also 'irregular' ones. He seems to aim at restricting the sphere of EU citizens allowed to move freely by labelling the Roma as irregular immigrants abusing the right to free movement. In this manner, President Sarkozy emphasized the generosity of the French state, whereas the Roma, among others, were characterized as abusing the right to free movement when they allegedly entered France in order to collect return aid. If this issue was an actual problem, one should ask why France continued granting the said aid. Nonetheless, the subsequent Socialist-led government abolished return aid, which has not stopped Roma from coming to and being repatriated from France (Parker and Catalán 2014: 385).

During Mr Sarkozy's presidency, there were also certain legal measures aimed at alleviating the 'Roma problem'. In 2011, an act was passed that allowed the repatriation of EU citizens who posed a threat to public order by, for example, begging or illegally occupying land (Parker and Toke 2013: 366). Instead of appealing to the European Union, as Spain and Italy did (see below), French politicians thus aimed at dealing with the issues nationally; Mr Sarkozy also defended the right of the member states to re-establish border controls even before 2015. The national stance seems to have dominated the discussion, at least if the finding that the Commission's decisions were also strongly affected by member state pressure is correct (Gehring 2013b: 143-74). Expulsions of the Roma from France also continued during Mr Hollande's presidency (Mäkinen 2013: 201-18, Parker and Catalán 2014: 385).

The abuse of rules was a recurrent theme in French UMP politicians' discourses, although it should be noted that some socialist politicians also made similar comments. For example, Manuel Valls, who was interior minister during Mr Hollande's first presidency, demanded law abidance from people (especially the Roma) who utilized their freedom of movement. He maintained that the state should create a balance between the rights of 'travellers', free movement and the travellers' responsibilities as citizens. Minister Valls reiterated that it was unacceptable to illegally reside on public and private land, thus practically banning travellers' residence in France. In his view, the crux of the matter was not that France limited free movement, but rather that the travellers obey the law (Valls 2013b). Indeed, it seems evident that the attitudes towards the Roma did not improve substantially after the Socialists stepped in as people were still banned from setting up camps (Parker and Catalán 2014: 385-6).

Italian politicians were also worried about Romanian, and particularly Roma, migrants, who had already come to Italy in large numbers before Romania joined the European Union. In 2007, a Romanian Roma killed an Italian woman named Giovanna Reggiani, which further worsened the attitude of many Italians towards both Romanians and the Roma. In the same year, the EU Free Movement Directive (2004/38/EC) was incorporated into Italian legislation in a more extensive form than stipulated in the directive. The Italian legislation required, for example, EU citizens to fulfil the conditions of minimum wage, adequate housing and not burdening Italian society, measures which were later cancelled due to remarks from the European Commission (di Martino et al. 2013). An expulsion measure on the basis of threat to the public order – for example, not being registered with local authorities constituted a threat – was also introduced into Italian legislation after Ms Reggiani was killed (Cetin 2015: 384).

In Italy, legislative measures targeting the Roma were justified under the *topos* of danger as they were intended to prevent criminality. Silvio Berlusconi's later government (2008–11) was mostly responsible for such legislation. Italy has traditionally been one of the most pro-European countries (Conti 2016); however, Mr Berlusconi's utterances were not very pro-European or pro-immigration. The European Commission also criticized his government for introducing legislation that allowed the collection of fingerprints from Roma children and made the expulsion of EU citizens easier. It was the so-called Security Package (*Pacchetto Sicurezza*) (see also Domnar 2009: 36), which addressed the alleged 'nomad emergency' of the time. Despite considering the launch of an infringement procedure, the Commission did not ever take any formal measures against Italy, arguably due to pressure from the other member states who themselves did not want to accommodate Roma migrants (Gehring 2013b: 169). In an interview for *Unione Sarda* in September 2008, published on the government website, Berlusconi referred to the European Commission as an actor legitimating the Italian measures towards the Roma. Utilizing a *topos* of danger, he claimed that the purpose of the legislative package was to prevent criminality. According to Berlusconi, 'In the end, all the lies were revealed: The European Commission found the norms we established "non-discriminatory", indeed, "completely in line with the EU law", including the norms concerning the fingerprints of Roma children, with the only intention to protect them from exploitation and from parents who would rather send them to steal than to school' (Berlusconi 2008).[6]

Silvio Berlusconi was not the only person in his government making these types of comments. It seems that the Commission and the EU were utilized as a legitimating factor for the Italian discriminatory measures. For example, when accused of discriminatory practices towards the Roma, Italy's interior minister, Roberto Maroni, claimed that the EU has approved the introduced practices (Maroni 2008b). Minister Maroni also lamented the possibility of the Commission launching an infringement procedure against Italy and claimed that the state had the right to appeal to the 'imperative reasons of public order' (Maroni 2008c).[7] Although EU rules do indeed mention public order as a valid reason for restricting the right to free movement, one can question whether those reasons were actually imperative.

Many leading Italian politicians of the time supported French expulsions and perceived the Roma as being in violation of the rules of free movement. EU-level rules thus presented premises for the claims of Italian politicians that their actions were just. Minister of the interior Maroni stated that expulsions of EU citizens should be possible, but only for those who violate European rules. He stated that many Roma do not fulfil the conditions of the Free Movement Directive, such as meeting minimum wage and housing requirements. In other words, these Roma acted illegally, and their repatriation was therefore justified (Maroni 2010b). It should be noted that there is not actually any EU directive that sets minimum wage or adequate housing requirements, rather those are conditions set by Italian legislators while implementing the EU Free Movement Directive 2004/38/EC (see also Cetin

2015: 385). The directive only stipulates that persons should not become a burden on the social security system after the initial 90 days of unlimited residence.[8] Despite the legal ambiguity, the fact that Minister Maroni relied on the EU directive as his source of justification implies that the EU law was considered a sufficient authority for the legitimization of political decisions. Mr Maroni thus hoped that people could be expelled if they did not fulfil conditions, and expulsions would require better implementation of the existing rules. Here we can see that certain Italian politicians employed EU rules as a justification for their measures both when the Commission did not intervene and even when it did.

Reactions towards Roma expulsions in other countries varied considerably. Regarding the French expulsions, Spanish Prime Minister Zapatero made some carefully measured statements. In 2010, when asked about the expulsions, Prime Minister Zapatero emphasized that he would stand by what is in accordance with EU rules. He made the assertion that all the decisions that Spain had made related to free movement were done in a manner favourable to living harmoniously and to integration, especially regarding the Roma, with whom they were working intensely. Mr Zapatero's use of agreement-based utterances was deeply tied to European law; he was happy to grant the Commission the task of deciding whether the repatriations were in fact unjustified. In other words, he appeared unsure of the duty that determined the nature of the action and therefore refused to take a stance. The justice of the matter depended, in Mr Zapatero's view, on legal compliance with stated norms. Some scholars, in turn, have argued that Spain was actually quite supportive of the French measures (e.g. Gehring 2013b: 162). In short, Mr Zapatero did not take a stance towards Roma repatriations, but argued that Spain would respect the judgement on whether France has acted wrongly, relying on the *topos* of justice:

> But we have to be careful, which in my case, means the feeling of responsibility for what the European Commission – which is the one who has the responsibility to supervise European directives, because the question is whether European directives are violated – declares. And, of course, I will stand behind what the European Commission says. If [France] has acted wrongly, I will criticize it, if not; logically I will not criticize it. (Zapatero 2010b)[9]

British and German politicians were more careful in their Roma-related utterances and they emphasized the importance of non-discrimination and equality. However, politicians in the two countries were also critical of the comments made by Commissioner Reding that drew comparisons to the Second World War. Prime Minister David Cameron's utterance relied on equality and compliance with rules as the premises of action:

> But I think the principles are clear that you should of course have the right to remove people from your country if they're there illegally, but it should never be done on the basis of membership of an ethnic group and the point I also made at the lunch is that members of the Commission have to choose their language carefully as well. (Cameron 2010)

German Chancellor Angela Merkel also utilized rule-based discourse with the *topos* of justice, arguing that just actions must be based on the equal application of European Treaties. Reference to EU Treaties also appeared as a way in which the politicians could avoid taking a position on the movement of the Roma or any questions of discrimination:

> We had then a discussion that was closed on the question of the Roma and the discussion that was between France and the European Commission. On this matter, we agreed on four points that I think are also important in order to reach a clarification on this theme, namely first that it is the right and the duty of the Commission to examine whether the member states comply with the community law. Second, we were all informed of the clarification that the President of the Commission gave yesterday in the name of the whole Commission. Third, we agreed once more that it is important to have respect between the Commission and the Council, because it is the basis for successful cooperation. Fourth, we stated that the Roma question will be once more dealt with in the Council meeting in October. (Merkel 2010c)[10]

In Romania, in turn, equality with regard to the free movement of its citizens was seen to be endangered with repatriations, and the priority of Romanian politicians was on compliance that would not allow any room for discrimination. In addition to the actual right to free movement, the Schengen Agreement was usually discussed in relation to compliance, that is, in terms of Romanian demands for being accepted in the agreement.[11] For example, in the annual reunion of Romanian diplomats in 2010, President Băsescu claimed that some states hoped to block Romania's accession into the Schengen Area due to problems concerning the free movement of its Roma minority. The French expulsions of the Roma – which took place in the same year that the speech was held – may have strengthened the perception that the Roma issue affects other decisions related to Romania. It is apparent that for the Romanian leaders, the matter that needed to be addressed revolved around access to the Schengen Area, and not the rights of the Roma. Rather, the Roma were seen as the problem that 'ruined' the reputation of honest Romanians willing to work abroad in the Schengen Area. Mr Băsescu did not consider any linkage between the unsuccessful negotiations concerning Romanian accession to the Schengen Area and Roma mobility to be legally justified, and thus relied on the *topos* of justice. According to him, 'There are some states that try to set the problems of free movement of the Roma minority as a burden for our accession into the Schengen Area, an issue which for me appears incorrect and is not in conformity with the Treaty' (Băsescu 2010c).[12]

In Romania, the main concern regarding linkages between potential issue with the Roma and Romanian citizens was that all of the country's citizens could be discriminated against because of the reputation of a minority group. Romanian politicians typically only made cursory references to the Roma and emphasized that they did not represent the majority; most Romanians in this parlance worked hard and benefited the host societies. In relation to emigration to Germany, in the German newspaper *Frankfurter Allgemeine Zeitung* in 2013 (available on the Romanian government website), Prime Minister Victor Ponta emphasized that the elimination of transitional restrictions would not result in a massive migration flow to Germany as most Romanians emigrated to Italy or Spain. He also stated that Romanian immigration was beneficial to Germany, and that his government had tried to keep its people in Romania. Prime Minister Ponta acknowledged the need for Roma integration in Romania, but he argued that the 'Roma problem' was not a national but rather a European one. He considered that encouraging qualified workers to stay in Romania was an issue that had to be solved at the national level, whereas Roma integration was something that the European Union must help to resolve. The utterance also illustrates that he was concerned about qualified people wanting to move abroad, although it did not matter if the Roma were to leave; the European Union should help Romania if the other countries wanted to decrease Roma mobility. Mr Ponta acknowledged that social security systems may be abused, but, in accordance with the *topos* of justice, Romanian citizens should not be discriminated against compared to other European citizens:

> In addition, most Romanians that wanted to go to Germany are there already: they are primarily well-qualified young people, who work hard and pay taxes. They are useful for the society in which they now live. For Romania, their leaving is a loss: we will work in this regard in order to be able to keep these people here. ... The solution in the long term consists of integrating the Roma here in Romania. For this, we need financial support and a strategy for ten, fifteen years. It is legitimate that Germany wants to combat the abuse of the social system with new laws. We understand and support this work. All we ask is that there be no discrimination of Romanians against the citizens of other European countries. (Ponta 2013b)[13]

Utterances related to equality and constitutional rules-based ideals were indeed very common throughout the debate on the mobility of the Roma. This may also relate to the sensitive nature of the issue: a reference to rules seems like an objective stance, although, as we saw in this section, rules can be exploited for different purposes. An unsurprising unequivocal support for free movement rules was detectable in the utterances with a strong emphasis on non-discrimination and tackling rule abuses. The commissioners seemed, in general, to rely on the view that free movement is a right that should not be questioned and referred to it as a duty accepted everywhere in Europe. National politicians, in contrast, were more critical of free movement. French, Italian and Romanian politicians wanted to take measures to prevent abuse of rules. Spanish, British and German leaders, instead, vaguely emphasized the need for rules to be followed and thought that compliance with rules thus determines the just nature of an action. It seems that a reliance on compliance was also a way of evading responsibility, as it is easy to not take a position by simply insisting that rules must be followed. In contrast, measures targeting the Roma were defended with the claim that the Roma did not obey EU rules. The practical reasoning manifested in this section relied on supranational rules as legitimizing certain actions in the vein of constitutional patriotism.

4.3 Duty of balancing between rules and security

In this section, I demonstrate how European politicians argued that more should be done to prevent people on the move from threatening security. Their concern over collective order is visible in utterances emphasizing the notion that there is a duty stemming from the need to control threats. Some politicians were prepared to consider revisions to the right to free movement and, for them, free movement did not appear as an unqualified fundamental right and was subject to security concerns. Indeed, the main *topos* found in this section is that of danger and threat; different types of threats require action (Wodak 2001: 75). Unlike in the discourses presented in Section 4.2, the following utterances primarily addressed general criminal groups or other people who were in violation of the right to free movement. This means that the central principle of constitutional patriotism, equality, was not considered to apply to people who constituted a security threat. It is noteworthy that protection from threats is also an important part of constitutional patriotism, particularly of its 'protective' variant (Sternberger 1963, Müller 2006).

In addition to questions about compliance discussed in the previous section, the Italian 'Security Package' presented in 2007 spurred discussion about the balance between security and free movement. In the commissioners' utterances, only one commissioner considered these measures justified due to security concerns. At the European Parliament in 2007, European commissioner for justice, Franco Frattini, discussed free movement as an EU-wide norm that should be balanced with security concerns. Relying on the *topos* of threat, Commissioner Frattini argued that member states have the right to protect citizens from criminality:

> Measures should be taken to strike the right balance between the right to free movement and the duty of each Member State to react in the interests of honest citizens when the legal conditions to stay are not fulfilled. ... Finally, as much as the Commission is not prepared to tolerate any form of discrimination or intolerance of its citizens, we equally will support Member States who lawfully protect their citizens from criminality, whether they are nationals or citizens of the Union in general. After all, freedom, justice and security go hand in hand. (Frattini 2007a)

Mr Frattini justified the legislation adopted by Prime Minister Berlusconi's government.[14] In a sense, Commissioner Frattini's discourse is not very different from the domestic discourses of Italian politicians who promise to guarantee the security of their citizens, although Mr Frattini's utterance revolved around security concerns related to *EU citizens*. In most cases, however, the Commission coupled security with the arrival of third-country nationals and the lack of external border controls (see Commissioner Malmströms utterances below).

With regard to EU rules and security, EU employment commissioner, Vladimir Špidla, took a critical stance on the discrimination of Romanians in Italy in the late 2000s. He emphasized the notion that expulsions should only be conducted on an individual basis as they limit a fundamental Treaty right.[15] This was one of the few instances where Employment Commissioner Špidla discussed free movement as a fundamental right and not as a workers' right. His approach to the Italian situation was very different from Commissioner Frattini's, which sought to legitimize the exclusion of EU citizens in terms of security. According to Mr Špidla, the Commission would ensure the right of free movement was respected, emphasizing the authority of the Commission in monitoring compliance with the law. Nevertheless, he stated that expulsions are justified in the case of an actual real threat:

> Romanians are citizens of the Union. They cannot under any circumstances be treated less favourably than the other citizens of the Union, and the Commission will ensure that their rights are respected. ... The rules on free movement are not made to benefit criminals. The Directive allows the exclusion of people whose behaviour represents a genuine, current and sufficiently serious threat to the fundamental interests of society. The fight against crime must be done with full respect for the rule of law. A decision to exclude can only be made on a case-by-case basis and the procedural guarantees and basic conditions must be respected. In the case of immediate exclusion, the urgency must be duly justified. The exclusion of citizens of the Union is an extreme measure. It is a limitation of a fundamental freedom of the Treaty. (Špidla 2008a, EU translation)[16]

One could conclude that for the Commission, the right to free movement appeared to constitute a right of Europeans who should also be protected from people crossing European external borders – a view that has also been singled out and criticized in scholarly literature (Mitsilegas, Monar and Rees 2003). Examples of this logic can also be found in later discourses. In 2011, Home Affairs Commissioner Malmström did not question the principle of free movement but rather proposed new measures enabling temporary internal border controls (later adopted in Regulation 1051/2013 of the European Parliament and of the Council).[17] The utterance below shows the exclusive nature of the freedom of movement: free movement is arguably strengthened by more effectively controlling external and internal borders from outsiders. 'Pressure' (instead of 'people') is a particularly noteworthy word here, as it seems to dehumanize migrants. The *topos* of threat related to 'unexpected pressure' appeared as the justification for introducing border controls:

> The free movement of people across European borders is a major achievement which must not be reversed, but rather strengthened. That is why the Commission has already proposed a better evaluation mechanism to ensure that the external borders are effectively controlled. To safeguard the stability of the Schengen area, it may also be necessary to foresee the temporary re-introduction of limited internal border controls under very exceptional circumstances, such as where a part of the external border comes under heavy unexpected pressure. (Malmström 2011)

Discourse similar to Malmström's obviously became more attenuated in autumn 2015 with the increasing numbers of asylum-seekers. For example, in December 2015, Commission President Jean-Claude Juncker stated that

> I announced plans for a European Border and Coast Guard and here we are. The Commission has now agreed those plans, and I call on the Parliament and the Council to treat them as a matter of urgency. We have no time to lose when it comes to preserving the Schengen area of free movement. For this, effective management of our external borders must be a priority. (Juncker 2015b)

Physical free movement of European people seemed possible to safeguard only where external borders are 'managed', that is, the entry of third-country nationals is controlled.

Whereas the protection of external borders was mainly discussed without explicating the threats, Migration Commissioner Avramopoulos also explicitly referred to the threat of terrorism and said that Schengen needs to be protected, there are threats at Europe's external borders and that data exchange systems must be used to prevent terrorism. In his utterance in a press conference after a meeting of ministers of home affairs on 25 January 2016, he referred to a more apparent *topos* of threat than most other commissioners:

> I have stated since the beginning that Schengen is EU's biggest achievement and we need to protect it. But in order for us to maintain free movement within our internal borders, we need to better manage our external borders. The Commission has come forward with a very bold and much needed proposal for a new European Border and Coast Guard. I am happy to see that the Presidency has also taken it up as a priority and is committed to moving ahead. We need to quickly agree in order to address the challenges posed by the migratory crisis and the security threats at Europe's external borders. And since we're talking about security in Europe, I would like to bring to your attention a few important points which we have discussed today. In order to keep our citizens safe and reduce the terrorist threat, it is essential for the Member States to use the systems that are in place, I clearly underlined this point with Ministers today. Databases like the Schengen Information System and Europol systems need to be fed and fully used. (Avramopoulos 2016g)

A similar logic was also visible in the country discourses, for example, in relation to the above-mentioned regulation 1051/2013 of the European Parliament and of the Council on temporary border controls. For example, Spanish Prime Minister Zapatero did not look at security from the Spanish perspective but reported that the European Council decision on specifying the Schengen rules was fully supported by Spain (in 2011, the European Council had called on the Commission to specify the mechanism for temporarily establishing border controls in the Schengen Area). Regarding the decision, Prime Minister Zapatero discussed the 'necessity to preserve the fundamental right to free movement of persons in the entire area of the European Union', but he also reiterated that the safeguard clause for re-establishing border controls was an exceptional measure only undertaken in cases of uncontrollable movements of people:

> The European Council has affirmed, with full support from Spain, of course, the necessity of retaining the fundamental right of free movement of people across the whole area of the European Union and, more specifically, of the Schengen Area. In no case can the exceptional safeguard mechanism, which we have today approved and which is to be developed by the Commission, be used to arbitrarily restrict this liberty, since its objective is limited to guaranteeing the effective control of the external borders in exceptional situations of uncontrolled movement of people. (Zapatero 2011)[18]

Romanian utterances also referred to problems related to balancing between security and valid legislation. The main concern, however, appeared to be that Romanians might be discriminated against as they were not part of the Schengen Area. After the Charlie Hebdo attack in January 2015 – when the office of the satirical French newspaper was attacked and 12 people were killed – Romanian President Iohannis reported to the press that he had discussed the balance between free movement and security in an informal European Council meeting with other European leaders. The issue that was apparently seen to be particularly important for Romania was that there would not be any separation between the Schengen and non-Schengen countries. Although President Iohannis emphasized that there was also a threat against the 'security of our citizens', the main *topos* arose from the fear of the Romanian state being treated differently in comparison to the Schengen signatories:

> I highlighted the necessity of maintaining an equilibrium between fundamental freedoms, such as upholding the principle of the free movement of people in the Union, valid legislation and our duty to guarantee the security of our citizens. I argued that our actions must not create new barriers, the measures that we will decide must be applied coherently inside the borders of the European Union, without differential treatment between Schengen member states and non-Schengen member states. (Iohannis 2015b)[19]

In Italy, in addition to relating security to the question of Roma migrants, worries arose over foreign fighters – potential terrorists – who were EU citizens and thus able to move freely. In 2014, Interior Minister Angelino Alfano, a representative of the New Centre-Right party, cited terrorism as a problem in an interview he gave to the newspaper *Corriere della Sera*, published on the Ministry's website. He linked collective order and free movement, and suggested that European Union citizens might include terrorists and foreign fighters in their ranks. In order to tackle the threat, he was reported to have made a collaboration proposal to the EU. Although security threats were typically addressed by employing national measures, Minister Alfano emphasized the need for European interventions: 'This position [EU presidency] makes us even more responsible for proposing solutions at the Union level … The problem is that these individuals, the "foreign fighters" move freely in Europe, since they are Union citizens' (Alfano 2014b).[20]

Also during and after the so-called migration crisis, Minister Alfano expressed his concern over the balance between free movement and security. He emphasized the need to make free movement safe, and the only manner to make it safe seemed to constitute the control of external borders. He did not directly state who was supposed to be responsible for making free movement safer, but obviously Italy was not able to change free movement rules alone. For example, in an interview he gave for *Il Piccolo* in December 2015, also published on the Ministry's website, he argued that 'It is necessary to show that free movement is also safe movement: security is an essential part of our liberty, the attempt is to combine freedom and security in movement. There is a risk of confusing terrorism and free movement, but people are afraid' (Alfano 2015a).[21] In January 2016, he stated in an interview for *Il Messaggero*, again published at the Ministry's website, that Schengen can only be saved with stronger control of the external border, which appeared to be a European duty to be fulfilled by 'us'. According to him, 'Movement needs to be free and it also needs to be safe, and the way to reconcile these two issues is by strengthening the controls at the external border, because only in this manner are we able to save Schengen' (Alfano 2016).[22]

Italian concerns thus related to both EU citizens and people coming through the external borders, while French politicians were more worried about the abuse of free movement by both individuals and employers. However, politicians in almost all countries referred to free movement and security in 2015–16, as a result of the increasing number of asylum-seekers and terrorist attacks. In light of the fact that there were several terrorist incidents in France in 2015 and 2016, it seems surprising that the issue was rarely connected to free movement. Despite the rhetoric, it is noteworthy that France introduced temporary internal border controls immediately after the 13 November terrorist attacks and continued these controls with the justification of a terrorist threat at least until the end of October 2020. The connection between the protection of external borders and free movement also became clear in an utterance of President Hollande in March 2016:

> France and the Netherlands share the same principles: the free movement of people in the Schengen area and the right of asylum in welcoming those women and men who flee from regimes or fear for their lives. We also have the duty to protect our external borders and to ensure solidarity with regard to the countries that face tragedies. That is the case of Turkey, Lebanon but also Jordan and I do not forget Greece in this situation. (Hollande 2016f)[23]

German politicians also talked about the protection of the external borders after autumn 2015, but the discourse was less security-oriented; Chancellor Merkel, for example, wanted to reduce the number of refugees in order not only to save the common market but also to find legal ways for people to enter Europe. Overall, the protection of the refugees did not seem to be in the focus when talking about free movement during the migration crisis, but the protection of external borders, free movement and the common market were in the limelight, that is, the protection of European institutions. Merkel also criticized national solutions and the reintroduction of border controls within the European Union, such as introducing border control in

Brenner, in the Italian-Austrian border. However, Germany itself reintroduced border control in the German-Austrian border in September 2015, and the controls are still upheld in 2020. In a speech held at a German family business event on 10 June 2016, Chancellor Merkel also summarized her account of the situation:

> Also when we look at Italy, the question arises: is a European solution a solution at Brenner? I would say: no. We also need to try to find a solution at the external borders of the Schengen area and not in some place inside the Schengen area, otherwise it is not a European solution. My thesis is – and that is why it was right to wait but still to work towards reducing the number of refugees – that a common currency and a common internal market can only function when we really protect the external borders and uphold internal free movement. That is in our most profound economic interest; and that is why it worked and still works. At the same time, we must fight the causes for fleeing and find legal ways for people to come here – but decided by the states and not through ways determined by smugglers. (Merkel 2016b)[24]

In Britain, the discourses differed to a certain extent from those in other countries. British Prime Minister Gordon Brown's utterances presented 'EU migrants' as a group that potentially abuse social benefits or conduct criminal behaviour.[25] With regard to EU movers, this contributes to the creation of a picture of the EU as the 'Other' and of 'welfare chauvinism' (Huysmans 2000a: 751). In such thinking, non-nationals are not considered entitled to benefits; in Prime Minister Brown's utterance below (2008), the two problems related to free movement included social benefits and criminality. Mr Brown expressed his view about the justification to limit free movement in the following way:

> Where the rules allow us to limit migration within the EU, we will also use them where appropriate – as we have imposed restrictions on migrants from Romania and Bulgaria, in particular their access to our labour market. And we will make sure that where EU citizens do come to Britain they are exercising not an open-ended right but their treaty right which is a right to work – we are able to remove EU citizens if they come here but are not employed after three months or are not studying or self-sufficient. ... The British Government will review access to benefits for EU migrants, and what more can be done to disincentivise and punish criminality – developing proposals to put to our EU partners later this year. (Brown 2008)

Later British leaders were also afraid criminality related to free movement. Terrorism was very rarely mentioned, but a few ministers of the interior referred to terrorism in connection with free movement in the later utterances (e.g. Italian Minister Alfano above). In a similar vein, the British Home Secretary May mentioned already before the 'migration crisis', in March 2015, that passenger name records (PNR) should be more effectively exchanged inside the European Union in order to prevent terrorism. According to her, 'the UK will push for progress on intra-EEA PNR and press for more effective information exchange, in order to counter the opportunities that free movement within the EU provides for terrorists' (May 2015b). May thus presented free movement as providing opportunities for terrorists, which is not a very positive presentation of the principle, added with the simultaneous discussion on 'welfare tourism' by Prime Minister Cameron.

For the most part, British Labour politicians wanted to ease the potential security threats of free movement with European-level measures, but Conservative politicians, in power since 2010, were more concerned with national interventions in cases of welfare abuse. Indeed, the two major British parties drew the picture of free movement very differently during these years. The Labour government assured the public that it could control free movement, but the principle in itself was not questioned. In contrast, the Conservatives depicted free movement as something that makes the abuse of social security in the UK possible. The critique of the status quo of the European policy principles became more common towards the end of David Cameron's first term as the prime minister (2010–15); free movement no longer appeared as an unqualified fundamental right but something that the member states should be able to restrict. Restricting free movement was also one of the four central demands in the renegotiation of the British EU membership in spring 2015 (Cameron 2015i). However, as we know, the settlement on restricting EU citizens' benefits (see, e.g., Sangiovanni 2017) was not sufficient to convince British voters to remain in the EU. The British utterances before the Brexit referendum will be mainly analysed in the following chapter, as they primarily dealt with the alleged economic costs of free movement for the UK.

What can be considered noteworthy in the utterances related to free movement and security is that the security threats were usually very vaguely defined. Most politicians only talked about criminality or about protecting the external borders in general, without specifying what the borders are protected from. The protection of external borders was, in any case, considered a necessary factor for, again, protecting the existence of the Schengen Area. The perceived threats seemed to mainly consider the Schengen Area, that is, the fact that people may cross the internal borders unnoticed. However, the agreement duties discussed in the previous and the following sections are more related to the *right* to free movement and especially to social benefits related to it.

4.4 Duty of better implementation

In this section, I demonstrate the ways in which European politicians relied on agreement-based reasoning that demanded better implementation of rules. While the discursive strategies in the previous sections were based on addressing specific occurrences of non-compliance or security threats, here, the emphasis is on the ways in which the EU as a whole sought to better implement the existing rules. The main topos of this section is that of law, that is, the responsibility to act as the rules prescribe (Wodak 2001: 76). The utterances below subscribed to the ideas of constitutional patriotism in the sense that rules should be equally applied to all citizens in all corners of Europe, while more national discretion also appeared to be another necessary feature. Some politicians, in other words, acknowledged that state-specific actions were needed in free movement policies to guarantee better implementation, although this may lead to different policies in different countries.

In Romania, the duty of better implementation was connected to the need for the reform of free movement policies. The politicians wanted all restrictions for Romanian workers seeking employment abroad to be abolished, although they simultaneously aimed at preventing qualified Romanians from leaving. For example, in 2007 – in a meeting with the president of the German Bundestag, Norbert Lammert – PNL Prime Minister Popescu-Tăriceanu reassured his German counterpart that state actions would be taken to decrease emigration. Popescu-Tăriceanu's aim was not, however, to limit free movement but to remove the existing restrictions that Germany, the venue of the speech, still had in place:

> As the Romanian citizens are freely moving in the EU, as European citizens, it is important that the employment restrictions disappear since they encourage illicit work, situation we want to avoid as soon as possible. The Government of Romania does not want to encourage the migration of workforce from Romania and through the actions we are carrying out, we search solutions to boost the number and quality of jobs in Romania. (Popescu-Tăriceanu 2007)

It appears that being a full-fledged member of the European Union was more important for Romania than gaining material benefits from Brussels. This conclusion is also supported by previous findings that suggest that Romania had few real EU priorities to pursue. For example, Papadimitrou and Phinnemore have found in their analysis that despite cross-party support for membership, Romanian politicians were unable to clearly specify their policy priorities and conditions during the process of joining the European Union. A post-accession strategy was published just two weeks before accession, and it only contained 'very vague statements of intent' (Papadimitriou and Phinnemore 2008: 153, fn. 50; Government of Romania 2006).

Sometimes, implementation discourses referred to the assignment of responsibility to others, that is, someone else must put forth the effort to truly realize the right to free movement. For example, it was insisted that the free movement of Romanian citizens should not be restricted due to problems with individual cases. During a visit in 2008 hosted by Italian Prime Minister Silvio Berlusconi, Prime Minister Popescu-Tăriceanu commented on the Italian Security Package. The Romanian prime minister painted the image of the honest and working Romanian citizen who meets the standards of free movement being employed by 'Eurostars' (Favell 2008), that is, high-qualified EU citizens moving around Europe for employment purposes. Free movement appeared to be a principle that must be totally adhered to as one of the fundamental principles of the Union; Prime Minister Popescu-Tăriceanu requested that other states comply with free movement legislation and continue welcoming Romanians:

> It is in the Romanian interest that the image of our country and the efforts of honest Romanians who work hard in Italy are not affected by some individual cases. Romanians knew how to integrate, and currently more than 1 per cent of

the Italian GDP is provided by Romanians who work in this country ... One of the fundamental principles of the European Union is free movement and this principle must be respected. (Popescu-Tăriceanu 2008)[26]

Romanian politicians also brought up the need to retain the social security of workers in other EU countries before the Brexit referendum. Romanian Prime Minister Cioloș seemed to consider that the European Parliament had the same view as the Romanian government and thus hoped the parliament would defend its position against the European Council. In line with the *topos* of law, the premier referred to the treaty and to the need to accommodate the British views in that. On 16 February 2016, the prime minister stated in a joint press conference with the president of the European Parliament, Martin Schulz, that free movement and social rights need to be maintained:

> As Mr President also said, I have stated that we have similar viewpoints with regard to the relation between the UK and the EU especially in the issue of social rights of workers, solutions which we see converge with the requests of Great Britain ... or viewpoints on the solutions that we consider to converge, an issue that I have become very convinced, because one of the Romanian questions is how we will be able to maintain the rules of free movement of workers and the social rights in conformity with what is stated in the treaty and I have stated that this parliament has the same viewpoint, thus in issues in which the decisions of the European Council will arrive to the parliament, I understand that the parliament will support the viewpoint that Romania has. (Cioloș 2016b)[27]

In the Commission, better implementation was strongly connected to the non-discrimination against different groups of people. Particularly during the last year of the second Barroso Commission, President Barroso was forced to defend the principle of free movement time and again as critical voices became more vocal. The speech, which Mr Barroso held in the European Parliament plenary session in 2014, presented free movement as, inter alia, a fundamental principle, a core element, an indispensable ingredient, a popular freedom and an indispensable pillar of the single market. Barroso's utterance strongly called for complete compliance with historically evolved free movement rules, in line with the *topos* of law. He also emphasized that there should not be citizens of first and second class in Europe:[28]

> So, let's be clear about free movement. The European Commission as the guardian of the treaties will uphold this principle: it is a historic achievement, a civilisation progress, a true agreement on freedom, democracy and the rule of law. It cannot come as a surprise to anybody that the principle of free movement exists and that it is applicable throughout the Union, without discrimination, because we don't want citizens of first class and citizens of second class in Europe. Free movement is the result of decades of negotiations and agreements between the Member States and also this Parliament, it is in our law and we should respect our common law. (Barroso 2014b)

EU rules about free movement include a number of seemingly surprising incentives that encourage people to be mobile. One such issue is the fact that EU citizens utilizing their right to free movement are entitled to bring their third-country spouse to the host country more easily than nationals in certain EU countries, for example, in Denmark and the UK (Wagner 2015: 43–62). In this regard, the EU has also taken steps to tackle sham marriages, which the Commission argued would strengthen free movement (Reichters 2014). Similar logic appears in several utterances made by both commissioners and national politicians: preventing the abuse of migration rights or the right to free movement helps maintaining free movement inside the Union. The movement of the insider group thus requires that outsiders be excluded as effectively as possible, which appears to be an efficient manner for ensuring the proper implementation of the principle of free movement.

Another aspect related to better implementation concerned more effective realization mechanisms for member states. Italian minister of the interior, Roberto Maroni, called for 'the Union' to convince the Commission of the need for member states to be able to provide sanctions for violations of EU rules. In his thinking, apparently, the Council of the European Union was the organ that he hoped could convince the Commission. It seems that when Mr Maroni agreed with the Commission, the Commission represented the entire EU. In contrast, when he disagreed with the Commission, the EU had to convince the Commission that its opinion was correct. He generally referred to the EU as consisting of 'us', the member states, but when there was disagreement in the policies, the EU and especially the Commission constituted the 'Other' for his country. The utterance below reflects the *topos* of law, whereby there was nothing wrong with rules themselves; they just were not implemented properly:

> This is the topic of the dispute with the European Commission, with whom we started negotiations a year ago, a position supported and shared by France, and I hope that in this case, the Union could make an effort and succeed in convincing the European Commission that it is right to establish rules, but the Member States must be provided with instruments to effectively implement these rules. (Maroni 2010c)[29]

In his several utterances concerning the insufficient implementation of EU rules, Mr Maroni did not solely discuss the expulsion of EU citizens; he also considered 'illegal immigration' in the Mediterranean, which he cited as a challenge that required better border control measures (Maroni 2010a). He suggested that the enhancement of surveillance at the external borders was necessary as it concerned the whole continent. Although he insisted on having more national tools regarding internal borders, he simultaneously called for European cooperation in managing external borders. This was certainly in Italy's (long-term) interest. When thousands of migrants arrived to the Italian Lampedusa Island in 2011, other European states seemed to consider it an issue that should be solved by Italy alone (McMahon 2012: 1).[30]

Spanish Prime Minister Mariano Rajoy, representing the conservative People's Party, also called for better implementation of free movement rules. Mr Rajoy seemed to be more concerned with free movement issues than other Spanish politicians, especially in 2014 as a reaction to UK Prime Minister David Cameron's criticism towards the right to free movement in the EU. Rajoy often discussed free movement in the context of all the four freedoms. The utterance below illustrates Rajoy's view on who should be responsible in free movement matters: the European Union and its institutions, rather than individual member states. Prime Minister Rajoy stated that the EU should thus create a real, internal market and implement the four freedoms effectively: 'The European Union and its institutions must do more, more rapidly and more effectively in order to create a real internal market that guarantees, in an effective manner, the free movement of persons, services, capital and goods' (Rajoy 2014i).[31]

Fighting the abuse of free movement was another widespread theme in the research material. Politicians in many countries requested better implementation to prevent people from exploiting free movement principles without a just cause. Before the Brexit referendum, many British discourses also included calls for better implementation of free movement rules. The home secretaries, in particular, often referred to people who allegedly claimed benefits in an unfavourable manner. For example, in 2007, Home Secretary Jacqui Smith from the Labour Party requested a better EU-level approach for removing people who 'are seeking to take unfair advantage of the right of free movement' (Smith 2007). Smith would have wanted to introduce legislation to allow the exclusion of European Economic Area (EEA) migrants from the UK before their arrival. More generally, it seems that British home secretaries tended to think that many problems originated from inside the EU, while ministers in other countries often referred to third countries in that respect.

Although the British Conservative party has generally been divided on EU and migration matters (Tonkiss 2013a: 116, Startin 2015), David Cameron and Home Secretary Theresa May presented very similar stances that were critical of free movement. In the following example, David Cameron calls for a Europe-wide settlement in enhancing the free movement regime: 'It is time for a new settlement which recognises that free movement is a central principle of the EU, but it cannot be a completely unqualified one. We are not the only country to see free movement as a qualified right: interior ministers from Austria, Germany and the Netherlands have also said this to the European Commission' (Cameron 2013).

In the utterance above, David Cameron referred to a letter sent by the ministers of the interior from the UK, Austria, Germany and the Netherlands to the president of the European Council, Alan Shatter. According to the letter:

> As responsible Ministers we are committed to protecting the rights of those Union citizens who exercise their right to the freedom of movement in line with the common European regulations. However, we are equally committed to protecting the rights and legitimate interests of the citizens of our countries who have to shoulder the burden caused by the immigration of European citizens who actually fail to meet the requirements governing freedom of movement. And we are equally committed to preventing and combating the fraudulent use of the right of free movement by Union citizens or by third country nationals abusing free movement rights in order to circumvent national immigration controls. (Mikl-Leitner et al. 2013)

As visible in the utterance above, the ministers utilized the term 'immigration' for both EU and extra-EU mobility, willing to tackle the abuse of free movement rules by the said migrants. In the British discourses, despite the generally critical mood towards EU mobility, EU and non-EU citizens were treated differently. The latter were considered the more dangerous group, at least in the discourse of Home Secretary Theresa May. The attitude towards EU mobility was, however, also critical, and British citizens appeared as the most important in all considerations. Although the UK is not a member of the Schengen Area, Home Secretary May expressed her concern about the liberalization of visas with non-EU member states in 2014. For her, it would be alarming to allow non-EU nationals entrance to the area: 'We will call for the EU to consider the role that Schengen visa liberalisation with non-EU Member States can play in creating opportunities for immigration abuse, including the abuse of free movement rights by non-EU nationals' (May 2014e).

Germany was one of the signatories of the above-quoted letter to Alan Shatter, and the abuse of free movement also seemed to be a recurring theme in Germany, though it was always mentioned that free movement as a principle shall not be questioned. Some of the agreement-related utterances of the German politicians seemed to revolve around economic matters, albeit dressed up as a question of the abuse of rules. The said rule abuse was mainly argued to consist of the claiming of benefits in Germany, which the politicians wanted to avoid (see also Minderhoud 2013: 209–26).

In Chancellor Merkel's later government, Thomas de Maizière took over the post of the minister of the interior in December 2013. In 2014, he stated that 'we want to keep free movement and secure its acceptance in the society' while fighting abuse of child benefits, for example (de Maizière 2014). In early 2015, he reiterated the same problem: 'We have had problems in the social system with migration from the EU – keyword: poverty migration – and we must make sure that free movement means that one can freely choose one's workplace in Europe, but not that one matches the choice of residence to where the child benefit is highest' (de Maizière 2015b).[32]

Beginning from the Alan Shatter letter, Chancellor Angela Merkel also discussed the need for better implementation of free movement policies. She did not question the right to free movement, but argued that it could be seen only as a general principle or starting point; cutting back on social security benefits for EU citizens should also be possible. However, the assessment of the principle should be made among the EU member states together instead of allowing for more national discretion. In a joint press conference with Prime Minister Cameron, Ms Merkel emphasized her view that the principle of free movement should not be questioned, but the exploitation of free movement should be fought with legal means:

> We do not have any doubt about the issue that the principle of free movement should not be questioned. It is valid. But we also have to fight abuse. In this, we have collaborated closely. We follow the jurisdiction attentively. We want to point to those who are concerned in the municipalities and villages: abuse must be fought, whereby free movement as a principle can also be assessed. (Merkel 2015b)[33]

Merkel made several similar utterances in 2015 and 2016 before the Brexit referendum, and they were content-wise close to those made by the French President Hollande, though Hollande also made several community-based utterances (see next chapter). Their key message was clear: free movement cannot be questioned but must be implemented in a similar vein as the other three freedoms are. What is interesting is that the utterances of both Chancellor Merkel and President Hollande immediately after the Brexit referendum had almost identical contents with regard to free movement; if the UK wants to be part of the internal market, they also need to accept free movement associated with it. On 28 June 2016, Chancellor Merkel (2016a) stated that 'free access to the internal market can be obtained by those who accept the four European basic freedoms: of people, of goods, of services and of capital'.[34] In a similar vein, President Hollande uttered on 29 June 2016 in line with the *topos* of law that

> If the United Kingdom wants to access the internal market, which was the privilege of being a member of the European Union, the greatest advantage that the United Kingdom was able to obtain in the European Union, if outside the European Union, the country wants – like Norway, for example – to be entitled to access the internal market, the United Kingdom will have to respect what are called the four freedoms: the free movement of goods, the free movement of services, the free movement of capital and the free movement of people, and the country cannot have any dispensation. One cannot take three liberties and reject a fourth one, notably the free movement of people. (Hollande 2016d)[35]

Hollande also referred to the need to have the Schengen rules firmly in place, in line with the *topos* of law. He also supported the proposal of Commission President Juncker of establishing a European border and coast guard:

> We also need to reinforce what is called the Schengen area. Questioning the free movement of people by reinstating internal borders would be a tragic error. But demanding that Schengen, in its current manner of operation, should be able to face the pressure within it would be another error. Effective control of the Union's borders requires more assistance for the frontier states, for the concerned states and putting in place a European corps of border guards, of coast guards, like the President of the European Commission has proposed. (Hollande 2015c)[36]

Based on the analysed agreement utterances, it seems to be important for politicians to state that free movement is not questioned in principle. However, French politicians did not consider the repatriation of Roma being against the principle, and the German and British politicians wanted to fight the abuse of the right to free movement. All these utterances relate to the compliance with rules: the politicians suggested that poor migrants do not follow either the domestic rules (such as the Roma in France) or the free movement rules in general as they 'abuse' the rules ('poor' migrants in the UK and Germany). Even though all the politicians were unanimous of the importance of the principle of free movement, they did not seem to consider that poor people should make use of the right, assuming that they were not working or studying but collecting welfare benefits. Whereas the commissioners and Romanian leaders discussed the equal right to free movement of all citizens, the politicians of the largest member states had a more exclusive idea of the right.

4.5 Rights-based Europe: Mobility justified by common rules

Most utterances in this chapter referred to free movement as based on agreements and formal duties to be complied with by member states. However, the material also included utterances belonging to the other part of the agreement dimension, namely the question of preventing the abuse of the right. Most of the utterances still acknowledged the primary authority of European legislation in free movement issues, but many argued that the rules should be amended or better implemented.

In all country discourses, free movement as such appeared as an unquestionable right, but for many politicians, the rights of their citizens seemed to be threatened by illegal migrants, poor migrants, criminals and groups conducting improper behaviour (such as in Roma camps).[37] Although no politician was willing to give up the right to free movement altogether, the politicians saw problems in free movement and wanted to solve these problems in order to make the right to free movement better justified.

No major changes during the period have been made in the internal free movement policy, but surveillance at the external borders of the Union has been reinforced and the exchange of information between the member states has improved. These have also become possible due to the alleged existence of threats at the borders of the EU, a discourse that was reinforced by both the member states and the European Commission.

One crucial theoretical question remains: whether free movement as a fundamental right has an intrinsic or instrumental value. Those who support the maintenance of domestic discretion tend to think instrumentally (see also Tonkiss 2013a: 88), while free movement could be argued to have intrinsic value as an EU citizen's unqualified right. The discourses in which free movement resembled an intrinsic value were clearly evident in this chapter, where the most important issue proved the equal realization of the right across Europe.[38] It is still controversial that there is the possibility to restrict the principle of free movement by appealing to public order, a principle that has existed ever since the Treaty establishing the European Coal and Steel Community came into effect. This suggests that the founding states considered free movement subordinate to collective order from the very beginning, although they discussed it as a right.

Table 4.1 shows the wide variety of the differences of emphasis of each of the countries with respect to the different types of discourses that belong to the category of the agreement dimension.

The European Commission emphasized the importance of the right to free movement as a contractual duty. Some commissioners' utterances also related the concepts of security, ('illegal') immigration and organized crime (see also Mitsilegas, Monar and

Table 4.1 Agreement-related discourses on free movement

	Europe-wide constitutional patriotism emphasized	Domestic society emphasized
States → ensure free movement	Commission, Romania	
EU → implement rules	Spain	Italy
EU → restrict abuse		France, UK, Germany

Rees 2003: 49). The Romanian discourses, by contrast, included a somewhat more critical tone, as the right was not fully enforced. Politicians in Spain appealed to the EU rules in their discourses; they could thus employ the EU as a justification for both why their national measures were legitimate and why they refused to take a stance on certain issues (e.g. Roma expulsions). Italian politicians, in turn, emphasized national discretion in the better implementation of EU rules, such as those related to expulsion. The idea of European constitutional patriotism was present in the sense that the body making free movement rules, the European Union, should also be the institution setting the limits. In the UK, France and Germany, calls were made for the European Union to implement its rules more effectively to prevent abuse, although socialist French politicians were not as worried about the abuse of the social system as were President Sarkozy and the representatives of his party.

Let me finish this chapter by employing analogical thinking. The analogy of a *court* depicts well the European Union as an entity that seeks to guarantee the equal realization of the rights of EU citizens; European politicians are ultimately committed to the legal interpretations made in the EU. Moreover, some politicians referred to the Union as a sort of 'scapegoat', with which one can legitimate national decisions, which the public does not necessarily like. Although a few politicians seemed to require more national discretion in free movement implementation, they did not as such question the authority of the 'court' in free movement matters.

The Romanian discourses, in particular, support the analogy as the country's politicians appealed to the EU to guarantee that rules were equally applied and that Romania would be able to enter the Schengen agreement under similar conditions offered to other countries. Romanian politicians sought to achieve the recognition of the country and its citizens as good Europeans, trustworthy enough to be granted complete freedom of movement in the Schengen Area.

To conclude, all observed politicians argued that European and national rules were to be followed, but many were also willing to restrict the existing regulations. The analysed discourses revealed that the right to free movement does not enjoy a fully acknowledged status as an each-and-every citizen's right, but it was understood as the right to work in another EU country under certain conditions, not to claim social benefits. One can even wonder whether the existing framework of various kinds of conditions for the right to free movement makes it possible for the politicians to argue for further restrictions in the framework. Although intimately connected to EU citizenship, long-term residence in another EU country has never been or become an unquestionable right. Then again, if we look at the national picture, neither do all politicians acknowledge the right of national citizens to claim benefits without studying or working, so why should they accept it at the European level?

Constitutional patriotism, as discussed in this chapter, is not, however, the only possible framework for Europe's free movement discourse. In the following chapter, we look at value-based reasoning from a more sentiment-based perspective.

5

Community dimension: Reproducing the community of the European Union

Free movement materializes in community utterances through two contradictory viewpoints: either as the politicians' duty to guarantee free movement in the European Union in order to continuously recreate the existing value community of Europeans or as their duty towards *national* citizens to restrict free movement and thereby protect national values. For Jef Huysmans, among others, the EU member states constitute a communitarian community, 'because they share an identity, or better, the identity of individuals is constituted in and through the community rather than being externally given to them' (Huysmans 2000b: 161). The problem with this kind of a concept is, however, that it may provide legitimacy for the exclusion of non-EU citizens from the community and therefore from free movement.

According to Charles Taylor, a communitarian sentiment prevails in an 'institution that identifies' (Taylor 1993: 132), which I discuss in this book under the label of 'Europe as identification'. If the European Union was an identifying institution in the communitarian sense – as opposed to the utilitarian 'institution that delivers' (see next chapter) – it should represent a pole of identity, a site within which important values can be defined (Taylor 1993: 123). After the theoretical introduction, the analysis examines whether such an image of Europe exists in the free movement discourses.

5.1 Community-based reasoning as a theoretical ideal: Focus on 'our duty'

Community thinking, as intended here, is inspired by theories of communitarianism, where the emphasis is on people's moral duty to preserve their community and on the collective sense of 'us' related to that community. Communitarianism is originally grounded on Aristotelian virtue ethics and focuses on the norms each *polis* necessarily constructs as well as on respecting the idea of a good life (*eudaimonia*) for each community (MacIntyre 1982). In the current study, community references can be employed in order to claim that free movement threatens 'our community' or in favour of free movement inside 'our community' as an elementary aspect of it. The community dimension thus implies a number of duties that politicians face with respect to inclusion and exclusion in their society: who is, or should be, included in the community?

As the academic discussion on communitarianism is vast, we need to only concentrate on a very limited number of its aspects, with a focus on duties towards one's own community. The idea of community in this chapter is largely inspired by the multicultural communitarian theory of Charles Taylor (1994), possibly the most prominent contemporary communitarian moral theorist. While Taylor recognizes the existence of common norms between different communities, he deems that different cultures are ultimately incommensurable. The notions of sentiment and self-preservation thus become central in Taylor's communitarian ethics.

Taylor has also suggested that cooperation between different communities is possible without them having common or universal norms. He argues that 'a convergence on certain norms from [sic] out of very different philosophical and spiritual backgrounds' (Taylor 1999: 137) can be achieved in a cross-cultural dialogue among separate communities. Such cooperation does not necessitate shared norms or values; however, it is unlikely to result in a unified community. Furthermore, according to Taylor, if individuals are able to claim individual rights from the society without having to heed the common good, this may decrease the level of collective identification (Taylor 1985: 229, 1999: 124–44). What is also important for the present analysis is that communitarian theory may provide grounds for limiting the scope of free movement or claiming an individual right to free movement in the first place. Taylor argues that some freedoms are only realizable 'within a certain form of society'; this means that not even the right to free movement can exist if societies (or states) are unable to guarantee that right (Taylor 1985: 229).

Another important concept in Taylor's writings is *deep diversity*. In deep diversity, the profound differences between different communities and the 'plurality of ways of belonging would ... be acknowledged and accepted' (Taylor 1993: 183). A European manifestation of deep diversity would mean more focus on national traditions and less on binding norms for all Europeans; states would be considered diverging communities that only cooperate in a 'community of interests' (see Walzer 1994: 78) and would not strive for deeper unity. Indeed, at least on the surface, the European Union seems to represent a prime example of the idea of deep diversity. Many researchers, politicians and citizens consider the EU too vast and too diversified to constitute a single community (de Beus 2006, Risse 2010).

However, in reality, the picture may be more complex than he proposes. Although the ultimate pursuit of the EU appears to be a sort of a communitarian unity, the Union simultaneously strives to maintain diversity. John Erik Fossum has examined Taylor's concept of deep diversity in the context of the European Charter of Fundamental Rights. In his view, deep diversity refers to a society that contains different collective conceptions, the existence of different collective goals is acknowledged and those who feel different strive to maintain the diversity (Fossum, 2003: 233; cf. Weiler, 2002). However, he fails to find distinct expressions of deep diversity in the Charter. Based on his operationalization of the concept, the following features should have been observed for the Charter to reflect deep diversity: 'a) the pursuit of distinct collective visions and group-based rights, b) opposition to a Charter that would have a binding effect,

c) demands for exemptions from the provisions in the Charter, and d) the settling of standards is considered a national concern' (Fossum 2003: 234). Indeed, despite the recent talk about the increasing importance of national interests in European politics, it seems that other logics may still be more pertinent. Perhaps the ideas of constitutional patriotism are more important in contemporary Europe, after all (Fossum 2003).

Be that as it may, with respect to the politicians' duty to guarantee the right to free movement, one can argue from both the perspective of deep national diversity and a unified European community. In this regard, a final note before moving onto the analysis is in order: states have several types of duties regarding free movement. These include both formal obligations and communitarian-type moral responsibilities. First of all, in the sending country, people should be able to leave that country, that is, to have the necessary information, potential contacts and resources to do so (although usually these are not provided by the state). Thereafter, the receiving country must allow these people to enter and reside in the country if they fulfil established conditions. The right to free movement thus presupposes two simultaneous rights: the right to exit and the right to enter a country. In addition, the right to reside in a country is a separate right, which is crucial for the right to free movement to function (Bauböck 2013: 350). In the free movement regime of the EU, the right to residence is the most exclusive of these rights as technically anyone can cross the internal borders of the Schengen Area; however, only EU citizens possess the full-fledged right to reside in another EU country, and only on the condition that they have sufficient economic resources for doing so.

In the following sections, I discuss three approaches that can be identified in the community discourses. The first section deals with the ideal of free movement as a fundamental part of European community because free movement represents an intrinsic value stemming from the community. This is the approach that comes closest to the communitarian ideal of a community 'in which we define important values and hence the possible poles of identity' (Taylor 1993: 123). The subsequent section discusses free movement as a responsibility towards future generations, whereby free movement appears as a family-type duty to one's children. Taylor has also presented family as the prime example of an institution that constantly generates processes of identification (Taylor 1993: 122). The last empirical section, in turn, provides an example of what deep diversity could mean in the free movement context. In that approach, the EU does not really appear as a community and the primary responsibility lies at the national level.

5.2   Duty stemming from 'a fundamental piece of European community'

A fundamental piece of European community' is an approach that represents free movement as a crucial feature of the European Union. In such a view, free movement primarily holds an intrinsic value instead of serving as an instrument towards further gains. The utterances in this section represent prime examples of a sentiment-focused, value-based discourse. The main *topos* is that of definition (Wodak 2001: 75), that is, an object is designated as having certain features. Free movement, for example, may represent an essential and defined part of the European community.

European commissioners, in particular, often referred to free movement as a fundamental piece of the European community. For them, free movement was something without which the European Union could not really exist. For example, in 2011, Commission President Barroso compared free movement to the foundations of buildings, which is why the principle could not be removed. His utterance made use of the *topos* of definition delineating free movement as essential for the entire project of European integration: 'To put it plainly, ladies and gentlemen, free movement is to Europe what foundations are to buildings. Remove it and the whole structure is undermined' (Barroso 2011a).

To look at another example from 2014, EU Justice Commissioner Viviane Reding referred to free movement as part of 'our Union' and opposed the questioning of this right due to local concerns. The community approach is imminent: the EU becomes the EU through its common values such as free movement. The *topos* of definition materialized in her list of the different features of the right: 'It is not only a fundamental freedom, a legal right, but also a common European value on which our Union is based. In short: it would be the wrong response to question the right to free movement in order to address local challenges' (Reding 2014).

Similar comments also became more common after autumn 2015. For example, in spring 2016, Migration Commissioner Avramopoulos hoped that countries would give up the internal border controls they had established. Speaking at the Bavarian Parliament, he outlined free movement as the 'backbone' of the European Union. The utterance also aptly reveals that despite the Commission urging the countries to end the controls before the end of 2016, they are still in place at the time of writing (at least until spring 2020):

> However, border controls are no long term solution. And they cost us far too much as you know. Not just economically, but also – if not more – socially. Internal free movement is one of our greatest achievements; it is the backbone what we are as a European Union. Let me be clear: our ultimate purpose is lifting all internal border controls no later than the end of the year – even if this may require in the meantime that we allow the extension of temporary border controls at specific points within the EU. I have presented on 4 March a 'Back to Schengen' Roadmap and I hope that Germany will participate in the measures aimed at restoring the proper functioning of the Schengen area as soon as possible. (Avramopoulos 2016c)

In addition to the Commission, several national leaders have also regarded free movement as a fundamental piece of the European community. One of the most active supporters of free movement was Spanish Prime Minister Mariano Rajoy. For example, Rajoy referred to free movement in a list of 'values and innate principles of the European Union' in July 2015 (Rajoy 2015a). On that occasion, he wanted to point out the common support of Spanish and Romanian leaders for European integration, as President Iohannis was visiting Spain. On another occasion, he seemed to be concerned that the UK would discriminate against other EU citizens, which, he considered, would 'destroy one of the most important principles of the Union, which is the free movement of people' (Rajoy 2015b).[1]

He also wanted to save the integration project and 'the basic pillars of our project, including the free movement of workers' (Rajoy 2015d).[2] Furthermore, in early June 2016 before the Brexit referendum, Prime Minister Mariano Rajoy stated that the European Union is constructed on the basis of free movement, making use of the *topos* of definition. He stated: 'Because of this, I want the United Kingdom to stay here; but, of course, Europe has been constructed on the basis of free movement of people, capital, goods and services. If the United Kingdom leaves Europe, the worst affected will be the British citizens who cannot move freely and who cannot transfer capital, goods nor services' (Rajoy 2016b).[3]

Free movement was also referred to as a fundamental piece of the European community in several French utterances. President François Hollande presented himself principally as a firm supporter of free movement. In 2013, he made use of the *topos* of definition by arguing that the European political project is based on, among other issues, the free movement of people. He wished to see the European Union return to the essence of the European project: 'We have to return to the very purpose of the European project, which is a political project founded on values and the movement of persons, knowledge, ideas, works, culture and creation' (Hollande 2013).[4]

In 2015 and 2016, the community utterances of President Hollande became more numerous, mainly related to the refugee crisis and the Brexit referendum but also without reference to these phenomena. For example, in June 2015, he emphasized that 'I am a European leader and I am attached to the principle of Europe. Free movement is one of the choices we wanted several decades ago when making Europe' (Hollande 2015i).[5] Hollande utilized community utterances to criticize those countries, which tried to control the entry of asylum-seekers in autumn 2015. On 29 September, he argued that 'We can see others at the moment, demanding that free movement applies for their nationals and in particular for working – besides, it was one of the foundations of the Union – and who close their doors today, erect walls against refugees who flee war or persecution' (Hollande 2015e).[6] France too reintroduced internal border controls in its borders in November 2015, but justified it on the basis of the threat of terrorism, unlike the other five Schengen countries (Germany, Austria, Denmark, Sweden and Norway). Given that France still upholds the controls in 2020, it seems a bit peculiar that Hollande argued in February 2016 that internal border controls will mean the end of Europe: 'It means that from the moment the internal border is restored, one can also reintroduce internal currency, then internal law and finally, Europe breaks up' (Hollande 2016h).[7]

Most fiercely Hollande seemed to defend free movement before the Brexit referendum. He commented on the Brexit referendum on 22 September when he reported having told British Prime Minister Cameron

> that it is Europe's interest, that it is the UK's interest that the forthcoming referendum can result in a yes but it is not a conditional yes, it is not a yes to be promoted to the detriment of Europe. It has to be a yes that will strengthen

the principles of the European Union, especially free movement and social rules. (Hollande 2015f)[8]

In January 2016, he further emphasized that Britain will have to respect the principles 'which have founded the European Union, notably free movement' (Hollande 2016a).[9] In a similar vein, in February 2016, he said that the willingness to maintain the UK in the EU should not question the founding principles of the EU such as free movement (Hollande 2016g). He reiterated in his speech in late May 2016 in Verdun that it was there François Mitterrand and Helmut Kohl showed their sign of friendship and initiated the process of free movement of people and goods in the 1980s (Hollande 2016i). Finally, after the Brexit referendum on 28 June 2016, Hollande reminded that Britain had received concessions in free movement, which is the founding principle of the Union, but that 'it is precisely this argument that was not able to convince the Brits and that they rejected with a majority' (Hollande 2016j).[10] These numerous community utterances illustrate the commitment to the principle of free movement, defending it against internal border controls and British criticism. Interestingly enough, Hollande did not conflate the French internal border controls and free movement or migration but apparently regarded them as antiterrorist measures, which was the official justification for the controls.

A similar approach, but less often appearing one, was also apparent in one of the utterances from the German community. In 2008, Chancellor Merkel talked about the European Union in a very eloquent tone at the European National Forum in Dublin. She referred to mobility as an integral part of the Union; free movement came straight after the objectives of stability and peace in terms of importance. Arguing from the *topos* of definition, Europe in this utterance equalled free movement and free movement could not be abolished without abolishing the entire European Union. Adherence to community thinking becomes clear: Merkel's words rely on the view that common values existed all the way from the founding of the EU and united the whole continent:[11]

> Today, the European Union has a great significance for all members and individuals. Europe, it is stability and peace – for us it is also already self-evident, but it can never be too highly appreciated. Europe, it is free movement and a framework that does not restrict but protects. Europe, it is plurality of languages – a Europe that also enjoys about the differences of the individual members. Europe, it is living together and mutual exchange, without having to give up one's home, traditions and roots. In addition, Europe is a declaration of common values, which unite us all. I am convinced that the political unification of Europe would not have been conceivable, if the European project had not been grounded from the beginning on fixed, indispensable values. (Merkel 2008)[12]

In February 2015, the German Interior Minister de Maizière also referred to free movement as a 'core element' of the EU and hoped that free movement would also fully function between the EU and Switzerland. He stated: 'I support Switzerland remaining as close to the EU as possible, and I support the full enforcement of free movement, which is a core element of the EU' (de Maizière 2015c).[13] Otherwise, community utterances were rare in the German discourses.

A few Italian politicians also connected free movement and the principle of freedom to the core of Europeanness. Prime Minister Renzi stated that we should not shut ourselves 'in fortresses in the name of security' (Renzi 2015),[14] and even Minister of the Interior Alfano referred to free movement in a similar manner. Alfano mainly discussed the relation between free movement and security (see Section 4.3) and also considered free movement as an achievement of liberty that should not be given up due to fears. In his interview in *Corriere della Sera*, published on the Ministry's website, Alfano referred to free movement in duty-based tone: 'The [Schengen] agreement is an achievement of liberty: if one thinks that in order to break down fear freedom should be diminished, we would find in a few years even greater fears, having repressed the freedom of movement' (Alfano 2015b).[15] This, of course, may relate to the will of Italian politicians to enable the further movement of migrants arrived in Italy to other European countries.

Above, I have explored several utterances from different countries, all emphasizing the fundamental importance of free movement for the European Union. The statements referred to free movement as the foundation that the European project is based on. Such utterances justified the *existence* of the principle, representing free movement as an intrinsic value. It was possible to find, however, also other types of community utterances in the analysis.

5.3 Duty stemming from responsibility towards future generations

Responsibilities towards future generations constitute the second significant viewpoint on preserving the community, observed in the utterances coming from the French, Spanish and Italian lead. Their utterances made use of the *topos* of responsibility, representing an actor responsible for certain circumstances with the duty to act (Wodak 2001: 75). The politicians below justified the need to improve free movement policies with family-type responsibility towards the young. The discourses were value-based, but this value-based duty concerned only a specific group of people rather than the European Union as a whole.

For example, the conservative Spanish Prime Minister Mariano Rajoy discussed free movement as a young workers' right. He limited the mobile group to workers, but considered free movement as a principle protected by the entire European community. He also stated that Europe must be a space of opportunities for 'our citizens' (*nuestros ciudadanos*), utilizing the *topos* of communal responsibility.[16] Prime Minister Rajoy was strongly in favour of mobility and felt that the right to free movement should thus concern young workers in particular:[17] 'Europe has to be an area of opportunities for our co-citizens, especially for the young, protecting the freedom of workers to move freely, reside and work in any European Union country' (Rajoy 2014f).[18]

In a similar vein, Italian politicians referred to future generations in their community-preserving free movement discourses. For example, Prime Minister Matteo Renzi (PD) stated in 2014, with a highly pro-European tone, that the generation of his children must have more 'Europe' than his own 'Erasmus generation' had encountered. The utterance made use of a *topos* based on the responsibility of the European community to represent a source of hope for the younger generations:

> The theme of Europe is to say each of us to say to ourselves and to others and, allow me, then for our children – we who are the Erasmus generation have to have something more for our children – whether it is possible or not to imagine that the Europe in which my grandfather fought, shooting someone else in France, could be, for my child, a place in which there is not only interaction and dialogue, but there is the institutional dimension able to represent hope, already hope. (Renzi 2014)[19]

Sometimes the politicians seem to have conflated the right to free movement and the Schengen Area, presenting Schengen as a factor ensuring the free movement of citizens. For example, in March 2015, French Interior Minister Bernard Cazeneuve said that 'Schengen works because it ensures the free movement of students within the internal area' (Cazeneuve 2015d).[20] Furthermore, President Hollande presented free movement as a fundamental piece of the European Union and as an important opportunity for students in his speech in October 2015: 'Now, Europe, it is mobility, it is free movement. It is also the possibility to access more widely the ERASMUS processes, which – for many young people, not only students because we have wanted to enlarge it to trainees and even to those who will be in their first jobs – can be a discovery and an experience' (Hollande 2015d).[21]

These French, Spanish and Italian *topoi* of responsibility justified the facilitation of free movement for younger generations and were less focused on the general status of free movement within Europe. French, Italian and Spanish politicians were the only ones that referred to young people from a primarily value-based rather than a utilitarian, benefit-incurring, perspective. This may reflect the fact that all countries have suffered from high youth unemployment, which has made young people seek work and study places from abroad. In contrast, in other countries, such as Germany, young workers from other countries were considered a labour market resource that provide a number of utilitarian benefits.

5.4 Duty stemming from deep diversity: The nation as primary responsibility

The final community-preserving aspect observed in the analysis focused on deep diversity, manifested in utterances promoting the national rather than the European community. These points of view mainly make use of a topos of culture, where 'culture' refers to something essentialist and stable (Wodak 2001: 76–7).

Deep diversity was present in the Italian discourses, although there were also more EU-centred utterances as we observed above. For example, the minister of the interior representing Silvio Berlusconi's *Forza Italia*, Giuseppe Pisanu, assured the public in an interview given to *La Giornale*, published on the Ministry's website, that Italy supported France in its decision to re-establish border controls after the 2005 terrorist attacks in London.[22] He made a value-based claim that Italy must back its neighbour, although the country did not make the same decision herself. This arguably represents an ideal case of deep diversity, where different communities make their own choices while respecting those of others. Mr Pisanu also justified open borders with the responsibility to maintain free movement for 'our' citizens. The duty to back France thus appeared to be less important than the national duty, as argued from the *topos* of culture:

> We will support, as it is our duty – he says – the decision of France to suspend the Schengen agreements. And for our part, we prefer to strengthen the surveillance of the borders with Austria and Slovenia [...] We cannot restrict the freedom of our citizens in order to combat the enemies of freedom. If we did that, we would let them win. (Pisanu 2005)[23]

Some form of deep diversity also appeared in German utterances, whereby the cultural differences in Germany and Europe were in focus. In 2011, German Interior Minister Hans-Pieter Friedrich (CDU) referred to common duties in a joint interview held with the French Interior Minister Claude Guéant, where he emphasized responsibility towards Europeans rather than non-Europeans.[24] Minister Friedrich argued that Europe was a large job market 'for us all', and Europe should predominantly provide work for unemployed Europeans rather than importing labour force from outside Europe. This could also be cited as an example of 'regional nationalism' (Tonkiss 2013a: 52–5), where responsibility towards Europeans is greater than towards non-Europeans.[25] In addition, minister Friedrich argued that 'we' should know our cultural identity, apparently referring to the German cultural identity. Such an utterance reflects the *topos* of culture in the sense of deep diversity, whereby each culture has a specific identity that needs to be maintained. He also implied that there were some core foundational ideals and values that were not shared with immigrants from outside Europe, who therefore needed to be integrated into European ways of thinking:[26]

> I see Europe as a large job market for us all. In this job market, there are currently more than 22 million unemployed people. It is our duty to first give these people work, before we bring more labour force from outside Europe to, for example, Germany ... Some years ago, in Germany, there was a false idea of a multicultural society. Many leftists thought that it was be possible that different cultures could live side by side – so not together, but next to each other. But living side by side leads to tension that harms social cohesion. That is why Chancellor Angela Merkel also talks today about the failure of multicultural thinking. We need to recognize our cultural identity. This identity also involves tolerance that we human beings

must foster with other cultures. This acceptance of our ideals and values is a precondition for successful integration. (Friedrich 2011)[27]

In 2012, French President Nicolas Sarkozy also expressed an utterance resembling deep diversity thinking about Europe and its external frontiers. The EU did not seem to represent a community-based commitment for President Sarkozy, but rather it consisted of cooperation between sovereign partners who must be committed to controlling their common external borders. Mr Sarkozy was particularly worried about the border between Greece and Turkey, an issue on which the EU concluded an agreement with Turkey in spring 2016. Interestingly, President Sarkozy chose not to discuss people crossing the border, but stated that the border is wide open (*ouverte à tous les vents*). In the same speech, he made several demands: national politicians should govern the Schengen agreement, migration policies should be harmonized and countries that do not control their borders in Schengen Area should be excluded. After this, he declared that France would leave Schengen if these conditions were not realized within a year. The strict tone of the statement may be explained by the upcoming 2012 presidential elections, which Mr Sarkozy lost – and the demands remained unrealized.[28] The utterance of President Sarkozy made use of a *topos* of culture based on deep diversity; all countries should retain their sovereignty while jointly committing to controlling external borders:

> As we have made Europe, it is in order to become stronger, not weaker! And as we have made Europe, it is in order to exercise our sovereignty with others, not to renounce the exercise of our sovereignty. I have demanded, and I have warned: we have agreed to control our borders with our European partners, but on the condition that they really control theirs. We cannot accept that the border between Greece and Turkey, 115 kilometres long, is wide open, not regulated or controlled by anyone. (Sarkozy 2012)[29]

Free movement as reflecting deep diversity was also apparent in Britain. Indeed, the aspect of deep diversity and minimum common norms is particularly well reflected in the British utterances concerning the EU. As argued by Tonkiss, British cooperation with the EU is accepted in the case of necessary common provisions, but without the need for deeper unity (see also Tonkiss 2013c: 35–48). There was practically no talk of a European community in the UK – national unity was the focus of attention and the interests of the EU and the UK were presented as competing.[30] However, there was also some sense of duty towards the European Union. In 2009, Prime Minister Gordon Brown appealed to 'obligations to our neighbours in the European Union' in the context of migration. Other Europeans were regarded as neighbours towards which there was a duty not to restrict immigration. Obviously, the UK was not able to set any quotas for EU citizens.[31] The approach towards the European Union was duty-based, but there were also economic grounds for not restricting immigration:

> So we reject the views of those who argue for an inflexible, arbitrary quota or cap on immigration. It would deny British business flexibility; it would prevent them from

getting the skills that they need; it would prevent employers from filling vacancies; it would overturn our obligations to our neighbours in the European Union; it would damage our economy; it would hurt our public services. (Brown 2009)

Labour Prime Minister Brown appeared concerned over what Britain's neighbours in the EU would think. His Conservative successor, in turn, presented a stronger articulation of deep diversity. David Cameron was concerned about British employees being sidestepped because of a stream of more motivated and qualified people from the EU. For Mr Brown, duties towards fellow Europeans were a relevant matter, while David Cameron's discourse progressively went in the opposite direction, constructing more juxtaposition between the EU and the UK (e.g. Cameron 2014a). In 2011, Cameron argued that the government should take actions because some employers preferred recruiting people from abroad rather than selecting workers from among unemployed people in the UK:

> Now, I completely understand this from the employers' point of view. Confronted by a failing welfare system, shortcomings in parts of our education system and an open-door immigration system they were able to choose between a disillusioned and demotivated person on benefits here in the UK or an Eastern European with the get up and go to come across a continent to find work. Or they could choose between an inexperienced school leaver here or someone five years older coming to Britain with the experience they need. But that situation is simply not good enough and we do have to change things ... Not discriminating against those from other countries, but making sure that the British option with the local knowledge that an employer needs is once again the best option. (Cameron 2011)

Instead of regional nationalism (see Friedrich above), the British Conservative leader thus emphasized national interest in employment matters, reinforcing the special duty towards co-nationals. In another speech from 2014, Mr Cameron implied that Brussels was trying to prevent Britain from getting what it needs, while he presented himself as the person who could stop such bad intentions. He considered it to be a negative thing that people were recruited from abroad and that there were more immigrants than 'we wanted'. This illustrates the *topos* of culture based on preferences for the desires and needs of the national community:

> Employment agencies signing people up from overseas and not recruiting here. Numbers that have increased faster than we in this country wanted ... at a level that was too much for our communities, for our labour markets. All of this has to change – and it will be at the very heart of my renegotiation strategy for Europe. Britain, I know you want this sorted so I will go to Brussels, I will not take no for an answer and when it comes to free movement – I will get what Britain needs. (Cameron 2014a)

In Romania, ideas of deep diversity rather than a sense of belonging to the European community also seemed to prevail. In the country's discourses, national interests were regularly emphasized, and special attention was paid to the joint community of Romanians and Moldovans. Both countries share the same language and roots; President Băsescu had even expressed his wish to unite them.[32] Further, a great number of Moldovan citizens have applied for Romanian passports on the basis of their Romanian ethnicity, which would provide them access to the entire European Union. Moldova is not likely to join the European Union any time soon, but due to holding Romanian passports, many Moldovans already have the right to free movement.[33]

The Romanian utterances reflected a view that Moldovans belong to the same community, but that community was hardly the EU community (see also Heinikoski 2015b). In 2009, President Băsescu stated that Romania would continue to acknowledge ethnic Romanians in Moldova, even though not all EU countries were supportive of this position. This community utterance was directed at 'us' as ethnic Romanians, who should all enjoy the benefits of free movement. President Băsescu justified this claim under the *topos* of culture: it was not acceptable that Romanians on the other side of the river were deprived of the right to free movement:

> We will continue to provide our support for persons from the Republic of Moldova who consider themselves Romanians and feel Romanian, for them to maintain their identity. We cannot accept that Romanians on the other side of the river Prut be isolated from the rest of Europe. We cannot accept that especially the young generation would not have the chance to move freely and study in our country and in other European countries. (Băsescu 2009a)[34]

In addition to Moldovans, Romanian politicians also called for some form of deep diversity as they raised concerns over Romanian citizens abroad. In 2009, Romanian associations in Italy had reported that there were dysfunctionalities with the legal rights of Romanian citizens related to the free movement of labour (Italy only lifted its transitional restrictions on Romanian workers in 2012). Prime Minister Boc's quotation below is the only one that was critical towards Romanians moving permanently abroad or, in the very least, his statement expressed the hope that they would return home as 'their place is at home in Romania'. In a bulletin published on the prime minister's website, he seems to regard the Romanian community as permanent; it cannot be dissolved by European integration:

> The representatives of the Romanian associations in Italy have also signalled certain dysfunctionalities with regard to ensuring good consular services and obtaining European health insurance cards, and also aspects related to the rights of Romanian citizens as regards the free movement of workers. The Prime Minister specified that these problems would be analysed in order to identify solutions that are enforced, and he informed the Romanians who live abroad that 'sooner or later, the place of each of us is at home in Romania. (Boc 2009b)[35]

In this section, we have observed that free movement as part of the European community is not as self-evident as the previous sections suggested. Free movement was also connected to regional nationalism, national interests and the view that citizens of a single country should eventually return to their home country. Nevertheless, Britain was the only country where politicians argued that free movement might be directly detrimental to its national needs and interests. These utterances thus made use of the *topos* of culture to justify the exclusion of people deemed as outsiders from enjoying specific rights or benefits.

5.5 Europe as identification: 'Our' mobility justified with values

The community-related utterances were relatively few in the material, and more than half of them reflected the idea of 'Europe as identification'. The small number of community references may be due to the fact that Europe went through several crises during the observed period, from constitutional and financial to the migration crisis. In this context, politicians may not be inclined to emphasize an emotional approach towards supranational activities, particularly as the analysed period witnessed increasing support for populist Eurosceptic and anti-immigration parties. The idea of 'Europe as identification' materialized in utterances where people's mobility was justified with European integration history, and those were particularly common in the period before the Brexit referendum. Duties to future generations also required the facilitation of free movement, while references to the ideals of profound diversity between the member states, in contrast, implied that the duties towards the EU were not the primary obligations.

A mismatch between national and European duties may exist if the transnational social relations between EU states have been unable to become complementary (rather than contradictory) to national duties (cf. Recchi 2013: 192). The conclusions drawn from studies on European mobility argue that migration and transnational identity formation do not always go hand in hand (Recchi 2013: 212). Rather, there are some indications that negative experiences with EU movers in the host countries deleteriously affect attitudes towards the entire European project (Messina 2014); this may have happened in some of the analysed countries, too. European policies also involve questions of identity, and if there is a perception that the affairs of a single country have been unjustly interfered with by a group of other states, it is no wonder that the feeling of the EU as the 'Other' might become stronger. As an implication of the importance of deep diversity, researchers have also argued that national pride is still a relevant topic in essentially all European Union countries (Dimitrova-Grajzl, Eastwood and Grajzl 2016).

The individualistic tendencies of today may also challenge the communitarian mode of thinking. Transnational activities sustaining people's aspirations such as educational exchange programmes are *individual* undertakings, which may mean that the idea of trying to uphold a *collective* sense of Europe faces difficulties (Recchi 2013: 210–11). Some communitarian authors have also argued that (liberal) human rights pose a threat to community thinking. They warn about the individualistic tendency of people to enjoy rights in their community, without having any duties towards it (e.g. Taylor

Table 5.1 Community utterances on free movement

	Community	Diversity
Duty towards historical achievements	Commission, France, Germany	
Duty towards future generations	Spain	Italy
Duty to one's own nation		UK, Romania

1999). Human rights are intended to provide rights for everyone regardless of where they live, but there are also people without a community from which to claim rights. For example, refugees are de facto stateless persons and may not be able to claim those rights (Benhabib 2004: 66). This relates to the writings by Hannah Arendt on the 'right to have rights' (Arendt 1951: 296), a right which is very exclusive in the European Union, particularly with regard to free movement. Although rights and duties usually go hand in hand, it is doubtful whether Europeans think that they have duties towards the European Union, though they can enjoy the right to free movement.

I finish this chapter by summing up how different countries and the Commission approached community duties in their discourses. Table 5.1 loosely summarizes the results. We see how history, future and nation were the most important reference points, while the emphases on community and diversity varied.

Duties towards historical achievements and to the future implied the existence of overarching, European-level duties. The Commission presented itself as a moral actor of sorts whose role was to take care of all European interests without any national biases. Spain, France and Italy, in contrast, were the only countries where the leaders explicitly connected free movement to the responsibility for future generations. French President Hollande forcefully defended the right to free movement as a founding principle of the EU. German politicians, however, rarely discussed free movement as an element of European identity, although Chancellor Merkel did draw a parallel between 'Europe' and the right to free movement.

The expected distinction between the political left and right was observable in the French and British discourses; the left-wing politicians made use of community-emphasizing utterances, whereas the right-wing leaders were more concerned with national duties. The Romanian utterances, in contrast, remained more consistent over time; the Romanian community utterances seemed to be directed towards Romanian nationals, which also included Romanians residing abroad and Moldovans. Out of all the countries, French and Romanian politicians employed community utterances in (somewhat) larger numbers than their colleagues in other countries did (cf. Chapter 9 and Appendix).

It is also important to observe how the nature and frequency of the community utterances varied over time. Whereas the German and Italian utterances mostly originate from before 2010, the utterances of French and Spanish politicians and of the commissioners tended to be more recent. This may also reveal something about the attitudes towards free movement in general as French and Spanish politicians and the Commissioners Barroso, Reding and Malmström began to forcefully defend free movement only after the criticism expressed by David Cameron in the early part of the decade and during the so-called migration crisis. In the UK, the differences can be better accounted for by party-political rather than temporal changes. In Romania, the focus on Moldovans was present throughout.

Let me conclude this chapter with the analogy of the family, the basic unit of any society. It may help to understand the differences between countries; it is also often used in communitarian literature (e.g. Taylor 1993: 122). In the discourses of the analysed politicians, there seemed to exist a general sense of responsibility towards the entire European family. The European Union does not perhaps provide an object of identification as strong as the family, but obligations towards the other Europeans certainly did matter. Some politicians, however, appeared to only care about their own children's future. For example, the French supported free movement as a European ideal but sometimes criticized the housekeeping manners of their relatives. The commissioners and Italian and Spanish politicians also wanted to reinforce the principle of free movement. The British and Romanians emphasized the most immediate family and duties towards them.

Overall, the European Union can hardly be regarded as a community proper, although there are certainly views that create – and continuously seem to recreate – such an impression. The 'Europe as identification' is still in many respects a distant ideal, in spite of the fact that free movement was often connected to duties towards the community. The duty towards the community did stem not only from formal historical agreements and treaties but also from the foundational status of the ideal of free movement and from the need to take care of future Europeans.

6

Utility dimension: Optimizing concrete benefits

I have categorized the utterances in this chapter on the basis of their instrumental nature, placing particular focus on how the speakers seek to optimize tangible benefits. In other words, if free movement is discussed in terms of its concrete positive and negative consequences, an utterance is included in the utility dimension. After examining the data, there proved to be three distinct groups of utility utterances: the first group focuses on the necessity to complement free movement with more EU policies; the second group aims at maximizing the benefits that free movement can generate; and the third group discusses the costs and problems associated with free movement. Before turning to these categories, I first introduce the Harean utilitarian theory and a few other relevant theoretical viewpoints, primarily related to functionalism. In contrast to the value-based reasoning discussed earlier in Chapters 4 and 5, in which existing agreements and obligations should not determine actions, here, the main emphasis lies on expected results in an instrumental manner.

6.1 Utility-based reasoning as a theoretical ideal: Strain or gain?

The utilitarian moral theory of R. M. Hare (1981) is the theoretical source of inspiration in this chapter. I decided to rely on Hare's account of utilitarianism because it is, arguably, the most comprehensive contemporary utilitarian theory.[1] In utilitarian thinking, consequences are the key to determining the correct course of action. The theory relies on rationalism: individuals should base their moral action on critical deliberation. In many respects, Hare draws from traditional utilitarian theory – most prominently outlined by John Stuart Mill in the early nineteenth century (Mill 2000) – but Hare has also incorporated distinct Kantian elements in his theory, such as the demand of universalization concerning moral principles.

According to Hare, moral statements are not descriptive sentences in the sense that their 'meaning completely determines their truth-conditions' – the words 'truth' or 'rightness' should not even be used with regard to moral statements (Hare 1981: 212–13). In Hare's vocabulary, the sentence 'no EU citizen should be prevented from moving and residing in the EU area' is a moral imperative: 'do not prevent EU citizens from exercising their right'. Still, this imperative may conflict with other imperatives, such as preventing people from incurring costs for the host country while residing in it. Hare argues that an imperative requires a separate critical and rational assessment in each specific situation.

This version of utilitarianism also appears under the label of 'two-level utilitarianism', as it differentiates moral principles at the critical and the intuitive levels (Hare 1981: 60). Hare claims that rights in general belong to the class of intuitive moral principles, which everyone should intuitively know and always respect. However, in a situation where there are different rights operating simultaneously, one needs to employ critical thinking to determine which of the rights override the others. The only universal and overriding right, according to Hare, is the 'right to equal concern and respect' (Hare 1981: 154). This implies that rights should be applied in a manner that (broadly) promotes the interests of all relevant actors. In the case of conflicting rights, we need to make the decision 'on the score of their acceptance-utility, i.e. on the ground that they are the set of principles whose general acceptance in the society in question will do the best, all told, for the interests of the people in the society considered impartially' (Hare 1981: 156).

The consideration of everyone's interests relates to another central idea in Hare's theory, namely, universalization: because the core of Harean moral thinking is the need to pay due attention to other people's preferences, the changing of 'I' and 'you' makes no difference in the universal properties of a moral sentence (Hare 1981: 122–3). In other words, in moral deliberation, the changing of a person's position (or changing the person) should not affect the end result of the process. Moral principles should therefore apply to all people universally regardless of their background.

In Hare's theory, critical thinking helps to locate the overriding principles of morality in any given situation. This entails consideration of the situation's properties and its potential future course of development; this ought to make it possible to form a universal principle according to which the individuals should be ultimately willing to act, whatever role they may have to play in the situation (Hare 1981: 44). An individual should be treated in the same way in virtually all similar situations irrespective of his or her identity or interests in that situation.

How does all this, then, theoretically relate to the free movement context within the European Union? The classical European integration theories (neo-functionalism and liberal intergovernmentalism) seem to subscribe to a sort of utilitarian approach to integration. A prime example is Ernst Haas's spill-over theory (Haas 1968). Haas's theory can also describe the evolution of the right to free movement, which seems to have progressed in accordance with an institution-led functional logic. What was originally only meant to cover the movement of cheap labour gradually became an all-encompassing right that concerns not only EU citizens but even, to some extent, 'outsiders'.[2] The spill-over logic does underpin the position of some politicians, as we will see. There are European politicians who would like to adopt more far-reaching common policies based on free movement. There are also those who would like to turn the objective of free movement towards a more nation-centred political framework.

Utilitarian thinking also underpins another central tenet of EU integration theory, namely liberal intergovernmentalism (Moravcsik 1998). It places the economic interests of states and the ways in which these interests have been formed in the focus.³ In this context, the benefits of free movement will have to be assessed at the national level and then negotiated at the European level.

Both Haas's and Moravcsik's theories have been criticized in the free movement context. In Willem Maas's view, for example, spill-over theory cannot account for the creation of free movement and EU citizenship rights as the evolution of rights has been episodic rather than consistent (Maas 2007: 7). States have de facto controlled the development of rights instead of being victims of the institution-led spill-over logic. Jef Huysmans, in turn, considers that the spill-over theory better describes the development of the EU's internal security field along with free movement (Huysmans 2004: 295). Maas also challenges Andrew Moravcsik's intergovernmentalism: national interests fail to explain why the creation of free movement rights, citizenship and political community would have taken place if the states were only 'interest-driven' (Maas 2007: 7). Espen D. H. Olsen finds evidence of such state-centredness in the evolution of European citizenship but contends that there are also cosmopolitan features in it (Olsen 2014: 348). Similarly, Parker and Catalán (2014: 382) contest the rational nature of the overall development of free movement, which they seem to consider a haphazard evolution rather than a teleological story.

In political discourses in general, the utility dimension is, by and large, based on a means–goal premise (or calculation), whereby a certain mean is expected to provide a certain goal (Fairclough and Fairclough 2012: 89). Free movement should represent an instrument aimed at a concrete and measurable target, such as economic, income-based benefits or the prevention of negative consequences, for example, in terms of job security for host nation residents. However, many utterances exploit the existence of free movement as an argument for a common immigration policy, while others simply focus on economic benefits and the costs that free movement might incur. Utility utterances include the *topoi* of usefulness/advantage, uselessness/disadvantage, burdening/weighting and finances (Wodak 2001). The keywords with which utterances were identified as utilitarian include 'because of/due to/thanks to free movement', economy, employment, workers and costs.

As mentioned in the outset, the chapter includes three sets of utilitarian discourses. Section 6.2 introduces utilitarian utterances that focus on free movement as a justification of their call for a common immigration policy in the Union. Discourses in Section 6.3 aim at promoting workers' movement specifically because it is believed to be highly beneficial in the utility-maximization vein. Finally, the discourses in Section 6.4 argue that less movement could be economically more beneficial, emphasizing national interest in the liberal intergovernmentalist manner.

6.2 Goal of maximizing functionality

In this section, I argue that many European politicians sought to promote a common European immigration policy as a necessary complement to the right to free movement. The often-implicit goal of deeper integration can be achieved by the means of a better-functioning free movement regime. The main *topos* proved to be that of advantage, wherewith a certain course of action was deemed useful (Wodak 2001: 74). There was also an alarmist concern over third-country migrants moving freely, a concern that sprang from a *topos* of reality that called for a common immigration policy (Wodak 2001: 77, Fairclough and Fairclough 2012: 143).

In the below utterances, several politicians assessed the results of free movement. These consequences, they thought, required a common immigration policy that would reduce illegal immigration and thereby benefit their countries. In addition to a spill-over logic of sorts (Haas 1968, cf. Huysmans 2004), this first discursive approach brings to mind the Harean universalization principle where actions are considered from a wide-ranging perspective. It should be noted, however, that the benefits were thought to be only EU-wide at best.

Focus on a common European immigration policy can be observed in French President Sarkozy's utterances during his presidential term, but not during his term as the minister of the interior. The promotion of the policy during the presidential term also reflects his position as a head of state charged with handling European matters (cf. Marcussen et al. 2001: 108). Free movement in the EU seemed to constitute a self-evident matter for President Sarkozy; he even referred to the free movement of persons as a postulate (*postulat*), which necessarily requires a common immigration policy. Instead of justifying free movement as such, President Sarkozy employed free movement in defence of his other political views related to restrictions on immigration policies. Mr Sarkozy's approach was centred on the European perspective, and on several occasions, he relied on utterances that utilized the similar goal-based *topoi* of advantage. According to Sarkozy, the need for a common immigration policy was self-evident in any area of free movement. He asked: 'How can we imagine that Europe, in which the majority of the countries are in the Schengen area, which asserts the free movement of people and goods as a postulate, could continue without creating common principles for the elaboration of a common immigration policy?' (Sarkozy 2008b).[4] Sarkozy stated this in the year when the European Pact on Immigration and Asylum was concluded as an initiative of Sarkozy himself. The Pact, however, seemed to be insufficient for agreeing on common principles during the so-called migration crisis.

President Hollande also called for a common European immigration policy in August 2015, when the so-called migration crisis was in an acute phase. He justified the existence of a common asylum and migration policy with the existence of the Schengen Area and free movement, making use of the *topos* of advantage:

> We also need to establish a unified asylum system, because it is a precondition in an area of free movement such as Schengen, so that there cannot be countries, which receive more people than other countries in proportion to their population. We also need to have a common migration policy with common rules and thus verify that this harmonisation actually takes place. (Hollande 2015h)[5]

It is possible to find similarities between the French and Spanish utterances concerning a common European immigration policy. The politicians from both countries seemed to attempt to upload their respective national agendas to the

European level. French politicians wanted to ensure that the conditions for accession into the free movement area would not be overly loose. Spanish politicians, in turn, wanted help in addressing (illegal) immigration across the Mediterranean. Particularly in the early 2000s, Spain was active in trying to put immigration on the EU agenda, requesting European Agreements of Return, more resources for the EU border agency Frontex and European labour offices in the countries from which new immigrants came (Zapata-Barrero and Witte 2007: 89). The European Union has also served as a legitimating actor by validating the stricter immigration policies employed by Spain, making use of the impression that everything emanating from the Union is positive (García Juan 2015).

Prime Minister Zapatero's (2008) utterance below reflects a strong Spanish commitment to European integration, while simultaneously justifying extra-European immigration on utilitarian grounds. He seems to be open to EU movers in particular (Parker and Catalán 2014, McMahon 2015), but his demands for a common European immigration policy would probably mean restrictions on immigration originating from outside the EU. Indeed, Mr Zapatero clearly expected that a common European immigration policy would decrease the number of irregular immigrants in Spain. He also acknowledged that Spain has needed foreign labour. Indeed, the country has even opposed zero immigration schemes and preferred controlled immigration (see, e.g. González-Enríquez 2009). Prime Minister Zapatero argued, utilizing his goal-based *topos* of advantage, that a common immigration policy should become a European policy due to the area of free movement:

> We have promoted a policy in the European Union. Immigration should become a European policy, given that there is the free movement of persons in the EU area. But we have to remember one thing: half of the economic growth we have had in the recent years is the result of immigration. What immigrants contribute to social security is equivalent to the amount paid to almost a million retired Spanish people. (Zapatero 2008)[6]

As the numbers of immigrants across the Mediterranean grew after the so-called Arab spring in 2011, Spanish utterances on the necessity of a common immigration policy became more numerous. The country's appeal to free movement in terms of a common immigration policy was increasingly based on the view that there were people coming from outside Europe who might exploit this principle. Therefore, states should collectively decide whom to let move freely in the EU. Further, Spanish utterances also demanded the strengthening of external borders, which could be facilitated with more integration in immigration matters.

In almost every utterance on free movement, Prime Minister Rajoy reiterated the call for a common immigration policy in the EU. In the example below, he contends that it is '*absurdo*' to have different norms in an area of free movement and that people must be helped in their country of origin, instead of just trying to stop them from coming to Europe. Given the rising numbers of immigrants and asylum-seekers in Spain, Prime Minister Rajoy's utterance reflects a *topos* of reality in favour of drafting a common immigration policy:

> What I have put forward and will continue to put forward is that immigration requires a common European policy; it requires similar rules in a lot of issues, i.e. provision of the same rights, of the same obligations and similar rules on repatriation, since, if we are in an area with free movement of people, it is absurd to have different norms; and, above all, it requires decisive action with funds to help the countries where these people come from, because it is evident that if people cannot lead a dignified life in their own country, the rational and logical thing to do is to try to lead it in another country. (Rajoy 2014e)[7]

In Italy too, a few demands for deeper integration were made. Italy tried to cope with large migration flows from North Africa, supporting their motivation for creating a common immigration policy. In many respects, however, the national context remained at least equally important to the European one as the Italians apparently did not want other countries to dictate what they should to do regarding immigration. For example, the utterance of the Northern League minister of the interior, Roberto Maroni, resembles the above utterances of Mr Sarkozy and Mr Zapatero, emphasizing national interest in their demand for more integration. Roberto Maroni represented the Northern League Party, which usually resists deeper European integration; the party seems to have a rather controversial approach to the EU and opposes EU institutions while still identifying with Europe (Huysseune 2010). It is noteworthy that the only Italian politician who proposed deeper integration was the minister of the interior. Mr Maroni's utterance was based on the *topos* of advantage. He seemed to assume that if there were a common immigration policy, then other EU countries would be obligated to help Italy with African migrants:

> However, this [having separate immigration policies] contradicts the principle of free movement in the countries, at least in the Schengen area. Hence it is convenient that starting from this phenomenon – which, I repeat, does not only concern, as I have always said and I emphasize, undocumented migration, but mass movements that have not yet been manifested in their complexity – Europe takes the opportunity to transform the system of 27 immigration policies into a European system. (Maroni 2011b)[8]

Roberto Maroni was the only Italian politician who explicitly called for a common immigration policy in the free movement context, and it cannot be concluded that Italian politicians would have extensively supported such policy. Commission President Barroso also mentioned in the analysed material that having a European immigration policy would be in order. In the selected material, however, Mr Barroso only made two calls for a common immigration policy, which possibly indicates that he expected the political push to come from the member states.[9] In 2006, Mr Barroso defended the creation of a common immigration policy, because separate national policies did not make sense in an area of free movement (Barroso 2006c). Two years later, his wording was equally outspoken in favour of common policies: 'A common European approach to immigration, integration and asylum is another priority. Within a common space and free movement of people it does not make sense that each Member States has its own immigration and integration policy' (Barroso 2008). Other commissioners also referred to the need for common policies, especially after the so-called migration crisis. Commissioner Avramopoulos stated in February 2016 that 'Without a functioning Common European Asylum System, free movement within the Union will continue to be at risk. The two go hand in hand' (Avramopoulos 2016f).

Although all the EU's five largest member states accepted the Pact on Immigration (2008), it is peculiar that only French, Spanish and Italian leaders apparently discussed the issue of a common immigration policy within the context of free movement. Out of the three countries, Spanish utterances were the most utility-based, and instrumental utility discourse was by far the most common and most emphasized type. In Italy, *left-wing* politicians were apparently more reluctant towards a common policy and stayed silent about free movement as a justification for a common immigration policy. Based on the analysis, the Spanish politicians' approach towards the right to free movement and towards European integration in general appeared more positive across the major parties than in France or Italy.[10] Whereas common immigration policy was justified on functional utilitarian grounds, the following section emphasizes benefit maximization through workers' movement.

6.3 Goal of maximizing benefits

In this section, the utterances focus on economic benefits resulting from workers' free movement, which was seen to create a win–win situation for the host states, sending states and movers themselves; these benefits are seen as undeniable. The main *topos* utilized in this context was that of finances, where a causal justification in terms of costs and benefits was the key (Wodak 2001: 76). Furthermore, the *topos* of advantage based on common interests was also present (Wodak 2001: 74). The focus here is predominantly on the benefits of states hosting other EU citizens. Such utilitarian thinking, on the one hand, undermines the status of free movement as a fundamental right, but, on the other hand, it may increase the general level of acceptance of the use of this right.

One beneficial issue that German politicians repeatedly discussed was circular migration, which was considered to unquestionably benefit everyone. German immigration policy has traditionally been based on the idea that people may come to Germany to work for a limited period of time (Ellermann 2015), which is clearly visible in the analysed material. The idea of circular migration resembles the *Gastarbeiter* policy that was applied in (West) Germany, especially in the 1960s and 1970s, in which it was assumed that migrants had *not* come to stay and thus they did not need citizenship or special social protection (O'Brien 1988, Malik 2015, Klekowski von Koppenfels and Höhne 2017). Although it has since then been acknowledged that some people move permanently to Germany, at least in the opinion of the Minister of the Interior Schäuble given in 2009, circular migration would be the most beneficial option for Germany.[11] He relied on the *topos* of advantage while listing the benefits of such 'triple-win' migration: 'It [circular migration] creates, in the words of migration experts, a "triple win" situation, from which the host country and the country of origin and the migrants themselves benefit. Its objective is that jobseekers from other regions of the world enliven our job markets with temporary migration and further qualify here with us' (Schäuble 2009).¹²

Chancellor Merkel discussed a few times the importance of free movement, and she mostly did this in relation to the free movement of workers. Accordingly, she assured the German people that free movement from the new member states should not be avoided because there were also educated people, that is, potential labour force for the German economy, who were willing to relocate to Germany. In general, Ms Merkel presented herself as a firm supporter of free movement, explicitly arguing that the removal of transitional restrictions would have a positive impact on the German labour market. As visible in the quotation below, a minimum wage was also to be introduced to prevent potential 'wage dumping'. Although Chancellor Merkel was originally worried that free movement might move jobs away from Germany (see Section 6.4), she nonetheless looked at this right mainly from the perspective of how it could benefit employers in need of labour force, relying on the *topos* of finances:

> Free movement in Europe is not a threat at all, but something, which many Germans in other countries undeniably benefit from. In addition, it is no longer the case that millions of Eastern Europeans only wait to come here. Against eventual wage dumping, minimum wage will be fixed for the particularly affected fields, and also for temporary work, minimum wage will be provided. Many fields that seek labour force urgently will soon acknowledge the new free movement as an opportunity. (Merkel 2011)¹³

German politicians in Merkel's government indeed seemed to be unanimous in their view that movers had already benefited the German economy. In many of her utterances, Ms Merkel stated that additional labour force should be attracted, and minimum wage systems should prevent the aforementioned wage dumping. Chancellor Merkel also referred to the importance of language skills, with which the other heads of state were not explicitly concerned; she was willing to attract foreign workers and students, but she deemed that there may be linguistic barriers preventing more students from coming to Germany (Merkel 2012b).

German politicians were in a fortunate position in the sense that the country had the strongest economy in Europe, and free movement was easy to justify by referring to its benefits for economic growth. Work-based migration was necessary for the country's economic development. At the national level, some utterances also referred to the 'employment insurance thesis', according to which EU mobility was able to fill in the labour shortages in specific sectors and thus enhance growth and productivity (Recchi 2008, 2015: 45). Indeed, mobility inside the EU has had positive economic effects and Germany may have been even better off by having chosen not to apply transitional arrangements in 2004 (Elsner and Zimmerman 2013: 17). Free movement was related not only to the right to free movement in Merkel's utterances but also to the Schengen Area, as she outlined in a press conference with the Singaporean prime minister in February 2015: 'We know the principle of free movement. It means that everyone from a European Union member state, who finds a job in Germany, can work here, without a need for a special permit or purpose. It is of course for us a possibility to receive well-educated labour force, when we are ourselves experiencing a demographic change' (Merkel 2015g).¹⁴

The commissioners also often praised the undeniable benefits of the free movement of workers. Particularly after the beginning of the financial crisis, German politicians and commissioners actively defended free movement with economic benefits. For example, Employment Commissioner Vladimir Špidla often emphasized the role of free movement both as a fundamental freedom and as a boost for the economy. His approach focused on the movement of workers, which is of course understandable given his position as the employment commissioner, citing, for example, that 'mobile workers move to where there are jobs available, and this benefits the economy' (Špidla 2008b). In a similar vein, Employment Commissioner Marianne Thyssen cited in 2015 that 'Mobility can be an opportunity both for workers and the host economies. This has been shown by previous enlargements. The Commission is fully committed to facilitating labour mobility, while ensuring it is fair for all' (Thyssen 2015c).

Commission President Barroso also paid great attention to the relationship between free movement and economic results, such as the benefits of free movement for Europe's competitiveness. Indeed, he presented his argument by utilizing the *topos* of finances: better structures, training and cooperation would facilitate free movement, which 'in turn would help raise the competitiveness of the region' and facilitate cooperation between administrators (Barroso 2010).¹⁵ Often, instead of giving preference for any group of people exercising their right to free movement, Mr Barroso chose the group of beneficiaries based on the audience he was addressing (Barroso 2012a, 2012b, 2013). In such cases, he strongly linked free movement to economic growth and material well-being, which was something any audience was likely to receive warmly. In a similar vein, commissioner for home affairs, Cecilia Malmström, referred to free movement as, for example, 'one of the greatest achievements' that has benefited all Europeans; she also regretted, however, that free movement was not respected everywhere (Malmström 2010).¹⁶

The commissioners seemed firm in their faith in the economically beneficial nature of free movement. In 2014, Justice Commissioner Vivine Reding admitted that although there may be local challenges related to free movement, free movement should not be questioned as it was beneficial for Europe (Reding 2014). Along the same line, the commissioners seemed to be convinced that free movement provided a solution to unemployment in the 'employment insurance' vein (Recchi 2015: 45). On another occasion, Commissioner Reding also cited recovery from the financial crisis as one justification for the enforcement of free movement as a beneficial principle (Reding 2013b). European commissioner for justice, Věra Jourová, in turn, brought up that free movement brings economic benefits for individuals who move and that states may protect their public finances against abuse. In her speech in September 2015, she made use of the *topos* of finances from the perspectives of both the individual and the receiving state:

> It brings numerous personal and economic benefits brings. Citizens benefit fully from the opportunities of the Single Market to travel, study, work, or do business in another EU country. Let me also stress that EU law includes robust safeguards

Member States can use to protect their public finances against any abuse of our free movement rights. The Court has confirmed this in a series of important judgments. (Jourová 2015)

Often, references to benefit maximization through free movement remained implicit or were made in the context of some other essential rights. In Italy, for example, the technocrat government led by Mario Monti, the successor of Silvio Berlusconi's government, did not often address issues related to free movement but rather focused on its primary political task, economic reforms. PM Monti was strongly in favour of going forward with the single market of services, of which free movement was one aspect. Mr Monti thus connected free movement closely to services and economic benefits, relying on the *topos* of finances:

> Well, going forward with the single market of services is a fundamental pillar of the single market, but what does it mean for individual countries? It means making openings, liberalizations at home in services, not only respecting the aspects of free movement, free services, free establishment, and in this matter the Senate in Rome yesterday approved in a vote the liberalization and competition package, which concerns for the vast majority precisely services, from gas distribution services, to financial and banking services, to free professional practice, and a wide range of economic and interest solutions that have to be made in order to make room for more active and more efficient service markets. (Monti 2012a)[17]

In France, as we saw in the previous section, the presidents promoted a common immigration policy to complement the free movement regime. President François Hollande also praised the historical role of free movement in European integration, usually in the community discourse vein but also sometimes related to economic benefits. It is to be noted that he talked about free movement of *persons*, not about the movement of workers, the usual utilitarian point of reference in the analysed material. Mr Hollande's utterance from 2014 reflected an instrumental approach towards free movement as an achievement as such, relying on the *topos* of advantage: 'Cities have been rebuilt, the standard of living has increased tenfold, the removal of borders has ensured the free movement of persons and the multiplication of trade has favoured the return to prosperity' (Hollande 2014).[18]

In the UK, the benefit-emphasizing approach was mainly visible in the early utterances of Labour prime ministers (see also Heinikoski 2016b). Tony Blair's Labour Government decided not to impose any transitional restrictions for the 2004 accessing countries, and PM Blair defended that decision on several occasions afterwards. Prime Minister Blair deemed free access economically beneficial, and instead of only perceiving it as a benefit for the British employers, he hoped it would be a 'two-way traffic'. In the utterance below, made in a joint press conference with the Slovakian prime minister, Mr Blair emphasized the *topos* of advantage for people:

> I think probably it is an awful lot easier for people to move between Slovakia and the UK than it was before because we have got free movement, not just of people,

but of workers now with the European Union membership. And I think, is it 35,000 Slovaks who are working in the UK – some testament to that. Obviously though people have got to make sure that the proper procedures are gone through. Look, I think in time this will settle down. I think the most interesting thing is that Britain was one of the very few countries to say let's have free movement of workers as well as people. There were many predictions of catastrophe that accompanied this decision, but actually it has not worked like that at all, people have benefited enormously, and I am sure and I hope it is a two-way traffic. (Blair 2006)

Another example of the economic utility type of reasoning can be found in the utterances of Prime Minister Gordon Brown. Before the 2010 general election, he emphasized migration's economic contribution to the British economy; he deemed it positive that (eastern European) EU citizens pay more than their share of taxes. In this case, Prime Minister Brown's approach appeared to be in favour of free movement, justified by the fact that EU movers did not seem to be a burden on the British society, as visible in the utterance below. PM Brown did not consider it unfair that the migrants contributed more to public services than they utilized. However, if the statistics appeared to demonstrate the opposite effect, then this would have been unfair to British society, as stated in some British utterances analysed in the following section.

There have been disagreements in the past – for example over whether to impose temporary restrictions on eastern European migrants in 2004. But recent research published by the institute of fiscal studies has the first detailed analysis of the contribution to our economy of the eastern Europeans who came to Britain in the last few years – showing that in every year their net contribution was positive – and that even after 5 years here they are over 50 per cent less likely than British people to receive benefits or tax credits and over 40 per cent less likely to live in social housing. They pay 5 per cent more than their share of tax, and account for a third less than their share of the costs of public services. (Brown 2010)

EU mobility was also a central theme in electoral campaigning in Britain, which seemed to further polarize the different perspectives. Before the 2015 general election, Mr Cameron's utterances focused on the national interest in which he maintained that free movement should exist *because* British people benefit from it:[19]

Well I don't think that the right answer is for Britain to leave the EU. I think the right answer is for EU reform and then a referendum. And I've set out very clearly the changes in terms of immigration and welfare that need to take place; and they don't, I think, break the principle that there should be free movement because, of course, many British people benefit from moving inside the European Union to live and work in other countries. (Cameron 2015)

In Romania, it was a widely held view that a free movement area that covers Romania would benefit all actors. Romania *not* joining the Schengen Area would thus be costly for the other EU countries, as claimed by Prime Minister Victor Ponta in

2012. He stated that entering the Schengen Area was not particularly important for Romania itself, whereas the continent of Europe had a lot to lose, in line with the *topos* of disadvantage – an argument that indeed appears questionable: 'After all, Europe has much more to lose than Romania in that we would have free movement' (Ponta 2012b).[20] Of course, easier transport to and from Romania could facilitate trade in the EU, but it is unclear whether the other European countries stand to lose something in the current situation.[21] A similar line of thinking vas visible in President Iohannis's comment in May 2016, when he stated that Romanian accession in the Schengen Area would increase security: 'Our place is in the Schengen area, as a member state with complete rights. The accession of Romania will consolidate its security and send, in a pivotal moment, a strong political message in support of maintaining the principle of the free movement of people' (Iohannis 2016a).[22]

President Klaus Iohannis also praised the value of free movement from the perspective of Romania and Romanians in his speech on the Europe Day on 9 May 2016. He stated that: 'Furthermore, the advantages of Romania belonging to the European Union are being felt positively in the lives of each of us, whether we refer to the free movement of people, or to the economic or educational opportunities' (Iohannis 2016).[23]

The utterances of Iohannis's predecessor, President Băsescu (PDL), were also positive towards free movement, although many Romanians were simultaneously leaving the country. He acknowledged that it was good to take advantage of the opportunities provided by the free movement of labour. His approach was individual-centred: free movement was beneficial for the individuals who strove for more. President Băsescu also explicitly stated that the country had to choose between having free movement and keeping its educated graduates in Romania. He thus relied on the *topos* of advantage in arguing that Romania is not losing due to free movement: 'We have to decide between: "we want free movement of workers" and "we do not want it because we want to avoid losing young graduates". I can tell you that Romania does not lose from the free movement of workers' (Băsescu 2009e).[24]

Referring to economic benefits was particularly tricky during the harshest years of the financial crisis in the late 2000s, when there was apparently a shortage of qualified workers in Romania. In addition to the brain drain, the Romanian economy was badly hit by the economic crisis, when the GDP fell by 6.6 per cent in 2009. The crisis resulted in around 315,000 unemployed people from industry, commerce and construction (Stan and Erne 2014: 35). But it may also have been beneficial for the country to have people working abroad rather than being unemployed in Romania. Although this aspect was not visible in the analysed material, in the British *Daily Mail*, Romanian President Băsescu even thanked Romanians working abroad for not claiming social security benefits in Romania (*Daily Mail Reporter* 2010).

In February 2016, Prime Minister Cioloş, in turn, praised the Romanian diaspora, which, also thanks to free movement, had become an intellectual and economic force. He, however, did not specify what he meant with being an economic force: for the receiving countries or in terms of sending remittances. Interestingly, while Romanians were often cited in other countries as mobile EU citizens who could be a strain for the countries' social security system, Romanian leaders in the 2010s seemed to appreciate the fact that people went abroad and there was much less debate about the brain drain that some previous leaders were concerned about. Prime Minister Cioloș made use of the *topos* of finances when praising the value of the Romanian diaspora throughout history:

> The Romanian diaspora has become not only an intellectual force, especially in the post-war years and during the communist period, when, in particular, those people left who decided that they did not share certain values promoted by the state leadership of the time. As a result of this, in many countries, the Romanian diaspora was above all represented by these intellectual values, but the Romanian diaspora is at the moment also an economic force, as also stated by the Chair, after the massive migration, especially in the period preparing the accession of Romania into the European Union and post-accession, when many Romanians have benefited from the right to free movement of people and workers. (Cioloș 2016a)[25]

Most Spanish utterances referred to free movement as maximizing functionality, but there were also occasions in which the focus was more on economic benefits. For example, in January 2015, President Rajoy reminded that 'I have said it many times, but I would like to emphasize it here in front of you: one of the most important core ideas in the European Union is the creation of the borderless area of shared prosperity' (Rajoy 2015f).[26]

The discourses in this section have justified free movement mainly from the state perspective, arguing that free movement is good not only for public finances but also for European economy and security. Justifications that focus on finances may provide a picture that European policies should be supported only if they benefit the national economy, which may provide too narrow a picture of the possibilities inherent in the free movement of people.

6.4 Goal of minimizing costs

In this section, I focus on the discourses that appear to present migration as a zero-sum game where one's gain is another's loss. The emphasis in the following section is on utility calculation. The main *topos* found in this section was that of burden, according to which burdens should be alleviated (Wodak and Boukala 2015: 261). In addition, politicians utilized the *topos* of disadvantage, that is, negative expected consequences (Wodak 2001: 74). The approach was thus thoroughly utilitarian, but the emphasis was on the national context, instead of the universal Harean framework.

German politicians made use of utility calculation concerning workers' free movement in its current form. For example, Chancellor Angela Merkel worried in 2006 that the new Central and Eastern member states might move jobs away from Germany, which is why she opposed the minimum wage in Germany at this stage (but later came to support).[27] The most important issue for Chancellor Merkel was to create more jobs in Germany by attracting workers from countries where the wage level was lower, instead of moving jobs abroad. For her, free movement seemed to constitute a question of labour force, which must be harnessed to benefit the German economy. Although Chancellor Merkel was worried about the challenge Eastern European workers posed for the German labour market, her solution was not to demand changes in free movement policies but to transform the German employment conditions. This is clearly different from the approaches observed in the other states, where politicians demanded that EU policies respond to the problems resulting from free movement. Ms Merkel relied on the *topos* of disadvantage in her utterance opposing minimum wage:

> I turn to the theme of minimum wage. I stand openly on the opposite side of this discussion. I know that in connection with the Service Directive, we will also have situations – not today and not tomorrow but in 2011, when complete free movement inside the European Union is achieved – where we have states, in which the wage level is clearly below ours, which is why we have to consider: How do we react to that? For me the overall discussion on minimum wage has one criterion: In the end of this discussion, we should not have less jobs in Germany, but we must have more jobs in Germany. (Merkel 2006a)[28]

Another perceived problem caused by free movement was that of false asylum applications, which contradicted 'natural' free movement inside the European Union. The utterance of Chancellor Merkel below suggests that some asylum-seekers came to Germany to seek asylum if their applications had not been accepted elsewhere. She reiterated that free movement was connected to the expectation that migrants come to Germany to work and not just to submit their asylum applications. She thus took a critical stance towards the exploitation of the system with invalid asylum applications. The positive features of her speech related to free movement arose from its beneficial impacts and not from its nature as a fundamental right as such, especially not for non-EU citizens. The *topos* of burden was in use: free movement was not supposed to burden but benefit the state:

> I think, on one hand, that inside the European Union we naturally have free movement – that I must say – but I think that free movement is connected to the expectation that one also works here and does not come with the intention to submit an asylum application, if the conditions of an asylum application are not fulfilled. (Merkel 2013c)[29]

Another *topos* of burden in Germany related to claiming social benefits, which Merkel considered that EU citizens should not do. Even though she insisted that free movement could not be questioned, she hoped that the social benefits of EU citizens should not necessarily equal those of native citizens. In her utterance in January 2016 – before the new compromise settlement for the UK agreed in February 2015 – she was sympathetic to the calls of the UK and German SPD politicians to fight the so-called abuse of free movement:

It is not the intention of the free movement provision; which is that one can work anywhere in Europe. This intention does not mean that one could also receive the same social welfare benefits from the first day anywhere in Europe. That is why I find the thought interesting, which both Ms Nahles and Mr Scholz have expressed. Their thoughts are to a certain extent similar to the hopes of the United Kingdom for a specific regulation. (Merkel 2016f)[30]

As a result of the initiative of German SPD Labour Minister Andrea Nahles, a policy was adopted in 2016, which allowed to exclude those EU citizens that had resided in Germany for less than five years from subsistence-level support (Roos 2019: 643). Merkel herself did not discuss this particular reform, but expressed her support for the principle of free movement. In January 2016, Merkel referred to free movement as a necessity for an area with common currency, and according to her, 'the common market would massively suffer' (Merkel 2016e),[31] if one did not have an area where it is easy to cross national borders. The European commissioners considered free movement beneficial for the most part, but they were also aware of the challenges related to mobility. The Commission approves the reintroduction of transitional restrictions if countries consider them economically necessary; the EU rules thus enable the reintroduction and it can be made on an economic basis. However, as soon as the host state has formally removed all restrictions, economic ends cannot justify restricting free movement.[32] In 2011, Spain decided to reintroduce transitional restrictions for Romanian workers, which it had lifted two years earlier. Employment Commissioner Lázló Andor regretted the decision, but expressed his sympathy to the unemployment and financial situation in Spain. He made use of the *topos* of burdening as the justification for the Spanish measures:

This decision has been taken because of the very specific employment situation in Spain. As a rule, I am convinced that restricting the free movement of European workers is not the answer to high unemployment. We should rather focus on creating new job opportunities. From the start, Spain has always had a very open policy to workers from other countries, including the new Member States, which the Commission has always welcomed. However, the Commission understands why, at this particular juncture – because of the dramatic employment situation and the very complex financial environment – the Spanish authorities wish to step back from full free movement. The Spanish request is supported by factual evidence and the Accession Treaty does allow the re-imposition of temporary restrictive measures in such cases. (Andor 2011)

Whereas Commissioner Andor justified the restriction of free movement based on economic arguments, Migration Commissioner Avramopoulos tried to convince the member states that it is economically costly to reintroduce internal border controls. He listed not only the negative impacts for transport and tourism but also the political cost of reversing a 'major achievement of European integration' in a speech in May 2016:

> Our objective is to return to a normal functioning of the Schengen area with no internal border controls as soon as possible, and within six months at the latest. Because the costs of internal border controls are already visible. We see transporters complain about increasing delays and cost. We see the tourism industry in some Member States suffer. And this is only a fraction of what would happen if border controls were re-established systematically. But the political cost of non-Schengen would be much more important still: it would be a highly symbolic reversal of a major achievement of European integration. (Avramopoulos 2016a)

In a similar vein, in his speech on 14 June 2016, Avramopoulos referred to the *topos* of burdening, while stating that 'However, temporary border controls not only hamper the free movement of our citizens, they also come with significant economic costs. According to our estimates, a full re-establishment of border controls within the Schengen Area would generate immediate direct costs for the EU economy of between €5 and €18 billion annually' (Avramopoulos 2016b).

British politicians also wanted to ensure that free movement would be beneficial for their country. In 2006, Labour Home Secretary Reid assured the listeners of his speech that EU mobility would be managed, and public services would not be endangered. He aimed at tackling the concern that EU movers exploited British social security in an 'unfair' manner.[33] He expressed both concern and praise for Polish migrants, who have been the most numerous in the UK after the 2004 enlargement of the EU. Mr Reid assured the audience, employing the *topos* of burdening, that over-demand on public services would be prevented:

> The Polish people who have come recently have brought doctors, they've brought dentists, badly needed, they've brought plumbers, they've brought a host of skilled labour to this country. So, we recognise, most sensible people do, that migrants can bring great skills to the United Kingdom but they also want to be assured that immigration will be properly managed and their own public services and benefit systems, schools, hospitals, and other public services, will be protected from misuse by those who come not to contribute but to use and to leave, and at best will be protected from over-demand which means that there is some, in their view, unfair access by citizens of this country. (Reid 2006)

Although not necessarily a reflection of the real situation, the potential for new immigrants to place an unfair burden on social services was the most common argument against free movement in Britain (cf. Gifford 2016). Home Secretary May was eager to bring up the issue of free movement in the meetings with her European counterparts. The G6 meetings of the European interior ministers seemed to only start to address free movement issues in 2012, when Home Secretary May declared that she had introduced the theme. She even criticized the European Union Court of Justice, which protected the right of European citizens to employ their right to free movement. Ms May implied that free movement was not a fundamental right but a principle that must be abolished if its results failed to be beneficial (May 2013c). The approach was thus similar to that of Prime Minister Cameron, who expressed his satisfaction for the

Council settlement agreed in February 2016. In 2015–16, while campaigning for the renegotiated EU deal and for people to vote for the 'remain' side in the referendum, PM Cameron's arguments followed the same lines: I support free movement, but the scale of it is just too much. For example, in his speech in Denmark he emphasized the 'pressure' of free movement on the British public services:

> I support the principle of free movement and I greatly value the contribution that many make when they come to Britain. But the challenge we've identified is the scale of movement we've seen from across Europe to Britain over the last decade and the pressure that has put on public services. Now these are problems that we can share. For example, I know as we've just heard that in Denmark you have concerns about paying child benefit for children not living here. And that's why the reforms I'm seeking can benefit other countries too. I've now secured a commitment from the commission to address this. So the text the Council has put forward shows real progress in all 4 areas, including on protecting the legitimate interests of non-euro member states, which of course is so important to Denmark too. (Cameron 2016g)

In stark contrast to the British positions, Romanian leaders sought to argue that migration of the poor who claimed welfare benefits was in fact only a marginal issue. In a joint press conference with the German Chancellor Angela Merkel, Romania's incumbent President Klaus Iohannis considered that the main problem his country faced was a brain drain from among young citizens. He stated that free movement of educated people from Romania to Germany was a significant challenge for Romania but a net win for Germany. He also emphasized that the number of educated Romanian migrants in Germany was much higher than that of poor migrants. He acknowledged that there was a problem related to poor people moving around, but downplayed its scope. He also insisted that something should be done to prevent those who were economically beneficial to Romania (educated people) from leaving:

> The problem of poor migrants is a problem, which, unfortunately, has too many times been confused with the problem of the free movement of workers in Europe. The free movement of workers is a great achievement, enormously important for all of us in Europe. Unfortunately, with regard to Romania, one first sees the migration of the poor, which is not numerically significant, and one very often ignores an important phenomenon, which is problematic for Romania and is a net gain for Germany, namely the question of the migration of the qualified and highly qualified workers who leave Romania for Germany. (Iohannis 2015c)[34]

The discussion above has created an overview of the ways in which politicians articulated the potential burdens and disadvantages of free movement in their respective countries. Although seemingly objective on the surface, economic arguments also related to the questions of outsiders and insiders: non-beneficial outsiders should not be allowed to enter.

6.5 'A Europe that delivers': Mobility justified with material benefits

Free movement policies approached from the utility perspective are intimately linked to the ideal of a 'Europe that delivers'. In this context, the prospect that some people receive benefits from integration, while others do not (Vaciago 2015: 128–32), may incur criticism towards the principle of free movement, and indeed it has. The analyses above drew a fairly negative picture of the views towards free movement, in many respects undermining the status of free movement as a self-evident Europe-wide right. There were utterances that demanded a common immigration policy in the EU and utterances that discussed free movement in terms of benefits and costs related to work and welfare. Functionality was utilized as a justification for demanding more integration, national economies were seen to benefit from workers' movement and the movement of people deemed as unbeneficial was not to be tolerated.

National interests tended to determine the understanding of the benefits of free movement. The most beneficial scenario for the countries was to have the possibility to recruit EU workers and simultaneously to provide the individualistic option of free movement for the citizens of one's own country. Politicians from across the continent also repeatedly pondered negative issues such as welfare tourists and irregular migrants – seen as potential threats to local welfare systems. The national utilitarian perspective thus favours the free movement of the advantaged, whereas for the poor, the argumentation required a value- and agreement-based justification, as we saw in Chapter 4.

Calls for a common European immigration policy have been increasing over the past fifteen years (Wallace, Pollack and Young 2010) – several politicians from the largest member states have demanded a common policy. Despite this, such a policy has not been agreed upon; some of the analysed countries have also been sceptical about it. Did these politicians not believe in the prospect of solving immigration problems at the European level; did they not recognize these problems in the first place? In light of the above analysis, one can wonder whether narrow utilitarian interest after all undermines the demands for a common immigration policy. Moreover, deciding who is allowed in and who is not is a core sovereign right of individual states. Many states are thus not willing to relinquish this right, in spite of the fact that common policies could justify the restriction of the overall entry and naturalization conditions (cf. Bauböck 2009: 24).

There were marked differences between the utilitarian free movement attitudes in different countries, as is visible in Table 6.1. Politicians in Italy, Spain and France openly called for common policies in the field of immigration. The focus of the commissioners and German politicians rested on the cost–benefit calculation of free movement as an instrumental principle, such as impacts on the workforce. It should be noted that the positive utterances on worker movement observed in Germany were not only related to highly qualified workers, but low-skilled (and low-paid) workers were also considered crucial to the economy. The national level and European level seemed to be complementary in free movement issues in Romania, while in the UK,

Table 6.1 Utilitarian discourses observed in the analysis

	Integration in the focus	Mobility in the focus
More universalization	France, Italy, Spain	
More movement		Germany, Commission
Concern over movement		UK, Romania

these levels appeared to be contradictory, at least in the sense that welfare abuse was not addressed in the current framework of the Union. Of course, the situations were different; while a country cannot prevent its citizens from leaving, it has the authority to determine who may enter the country, making immigration and emigration morally asymmetrical (Walzer 1983: 40).

In order to depict a 'Europe that delivers' in the free movement context, the EU represents a union of private *hospitals*, whereby the member states embody profit-seeking hospital units. The union (or perhaps even cartel) seeks to define what the overall rules are and what kind of income a patient needs to have in order to be treated in one of its hospitals. The hospitals seek to guarantee that people have a better life in future, but they only try to find (and keep) the patients that can pay well and would prefer to unload the non-paying poor on public healthcare paid by others. At the individual level, the right to free movement resembles a right granted to each patient to choose which doctor in which country they want to visit (money follows the patient). This analogy obviously provides a stark picture of what the EU, together with its member states, seeks with free movement. One can indeed wonder how good an overall 'healthcare' system such an institution has.

Overall, utilitarian discourse was common (see also Chapter 9), but it was hardly in tune with the universal ideal of R. M. Hare, that is, with the idea that all relevant actors' concerns should be taken into the equation in an equal manner. Even the seemingly EU-oriented countries in Section 6.2, sought to further their own national interests through a common approach to immigration. The European Union represented an institution that delivers, but its primary function is to deliver something to each member state. Indeed, with state-centred political institutions, promoting European interests may not pay off in elections. This fact may predispose some European politicians to emphasize national interest instead of the European-wide benefits of free movement.

7

Solidarity dimension: Solidarity as the ultimate aim

The difference between the two sentiment-based categories of utterances based on community and those based on solidarity is analytically clear. The community dimension focuses on a pre-existing *duty* to uphold free movement, whereas solidarity utterances deal with the *outcomes* that the principle of free movement may actively produce or challenge. The community dimension is thus based on a primordial sense of a European community, but the focus of the analysis here is on the patterns of *constructing* unity; the task of politicians and other elites is to construct a European sense of 'us' – or simply Europeanness. For example, when solidarity is employed in justifying European Union enlargement, what is important is that the 'Other' becomes part of 'us' (Fierke and Wiener 2001: 137).

7.1 Solidarity-based reasoning as a theoretical ideal: Wider sense of 'us'

The solidarity dimension is inspired by Richard Rorty's ideas about enlarging solidarity in any human society. For the purposes of my analysis, the crucial premise in Rorty's writings is that solidarity can be deliberately widened through interaction; it refers to the sense of 'us', that is, unity or common identity created among different groups of people. This idea relates to what I term 'a Europe of solidarity', where the purpose is to deepen and widen solidarity, above all, through free movement.

Rorty's pragmatist, sentiment-based yet instrumental view of ethics provides an intriguing counterbalance to the previous three dimensions: agreement, community and utility. This type of solidarity does not require any profound or primordial sense of sameness, but rather a recognition of the similarity of people's ultimate hopes and desires, of human dignity. The purpose here is to make people previously thought of as 'them' become part of 'us' (Rorty 1989).[1] In practice, the solidary identification denotes a process whereby identities are learned and emotional ties are created in order to achieve durable solidarity (cf. Eder 2009: 431). The key issues include internalization and exposure to proper influences and symbolic contents that carry the sense of identity (cf. Recchi 2013: 186–91). Values may also play a part in the construction of solidarity, but they are instrumental rather than intrinsic in nature.

Rorty argues that an *ethnocentric consensus* can only occur in a single society that shares the same culture, history and language. In contrast, a sense of solidarity is the key to achieving what Rorty calls a *pluralist consensus* (Rorty 1989: 198). According to Rorty, solidarity is part of the moral identity that people often happen to have, and such solidarity enlarges the sense of 'us'. There is no universal obligation for solidarity, but people typically just want to help others, for example, if they see a starving child (Rorty 2000b: 61).

In Rorty's terms, supranational rights such as human rights are a matter of solidarity and aid, not any rational deliberation. In other words, Rorty does not share the Kantian sense of a moral obligation based on knowledge and communication; rather, he argues instead that human rights rely more on a sentiment of widening solidarity (Rorty 1999: 77). Human rights are based on the sense of solidarity and require solidarity to be fully realized. The pursuit of a universal solidarity does not mean that smaller cultures and communities should be dismantled but that solidarity should be felt towards people who are not considered 'us' (Rorty 2000a: 262–77). Rorty arguably believes in the human good in the sense that he sees widening solidarity as the instrument that potentially results in a deeper respect for universal human rights (Rorty 1999). The European Union is what Rorty himself cites as an example of such an instrument; its purpose is to redescribe the 'familiar in unfamiliar terms', which 'is being attempted by those passionate advocates of European unity who hope that their grandchildren will think of themselves as European first and French or German second' (Rorty 2000a: 87–8).

I have wanted to keep the solidarity and community categories separate in order to better understand the differences between the value-based (community) and instrumental (solidarity) approaches in the free movement context. This is an important division in moral philosophy and reveals something about moral thinking in general: whether our actions should be based on something that has been determined before or whether we should focus on optimizing future results. To some extent, these two perspectives are also intertwined as the norms we determine beforehand are also related to what is expected to occur when the norms are actually applied. We can, nevertheless, observe a difference in whether the community naturally includes norms as communal duties or whether norms are constructively created to increase the sense of solidarity in the wider society.

How does free movement, then, relate *theoretically* to the Rortyan solidarity ideal? From the negative perspective, it can be argued that free movement and pluralism threaten shared national solidarity and identity, which is, according to Rorty, 'an absolutely essential component of citizenship, of any attempt to take our country and its problems seriously' (Rorty 2000a: 253). Solidarity can also result in the disappearance of national identities, if general identification and wider solidarity are emphasized instead of particular identities (cf. Young 2000). Indeed, as noted by Aradau, Huysmans and Squire, 'the assumption that mobility can function as an integrative force that knits people together into a territorially bound and culturally defined collective conscious [*sic*] ignores the destabilising and decentring role that mobility can have' (2010: 949). Utterances suggesting these types of destabilizing effects can also be observed in the analysed material.

Solidarity, from the positive perspective, however, is regarded as a deliberate aim that the political elites try to advance. Indeed, some measures that Rorty identified as potentially producing solidarity as an outcome include political discussion and even poetry; with them, desired sentiments can be aroused in the public (Rorty 1989: 53). Political utterances can thus portray a picture of the right to free movement as essentially a question of European solidarity. The solidarity created by free movement, however, tends to lead to the exclusion of others, providing EU citizens with exclusive entry into this VIP area (see also Olsen 2012).[2]

Does mobility, then, increase the sense of solidarity? The assumption of transactionalist European integration theory is that mobility advances the sense of European identity (Deutsch et al. 1957). However, studies have not been able to fully confirm that the exercise of mobility actually strengthens a sense of European solidarity and identity (e.g. Kuhn 2012, Recchi 2013: 211) and there are several reasons for this. One such reason is that pro-European people are more likely to utilize that right in the first place than those for whom 'Europe' is a distant category. The exercise of free movement is mainly driven by affective ties and the search for a better quality of life. On the individual level, free movement may, however, serve as a sort of legitimating instrument for the entire process of European integration and European citizenship (Recchi 2008, Strumia 2013: 225–9); it is, indeed, something that EU citizens also value very highly about the European Union.[3] Further, the notion that residing in another EU country should strengthen the feeling of Union citizenship was officially pronounced in preamble 17 of the 38/2004/EC Directive on Free Movement. The preamble provides that 'Enjoyment of permanent residence by Union citizens who have chosen to settle long term in the host Member State would strengthen the feeling of Union citizenship and is a key element in promoting social cohesion, which is one of the fundamental objectives of the Union.'

The sense of solidarity may also increase in a process, whereby national elites 'teach' attitudes to the wider public. In this regard, free movement could serve as a symbol of European solidarity, socializing citizens with the feeling of sameness. The idea of a solidaristic European identity as a constructed phenomenon is supported by the fact that political elites have tried to promote the concept of 'European identity' time and again over the course of integration history. Examples of these attempts include, for example, the Commission's campaigns concerning the common currency, 'European Years' and banal tools such as flag, anthem and Europe Day (Recchi 2015: 124).

As we observe in the ensuing analyses, many of the analysed solidarity utterances relied on a sentiment of solidarity (supposedly) created with free movement. The different *topoi* that were found in the analysis included, for example, usefulness/advantage and uselessness/disadvantage. The keywords included free movement as creating European unity, enlarged free movement, 'thanks to free movement' and decreased solidarity. The keywords and *topoi* were partly similar in the utility and solidarity dimensions, but there was a difference in whether the desired goal was concrete or more related to an enlarged sense of 'us'. The solidarity utterances also relied on a means–goal premise, but the goal was based on enlarging the sense of 'us' rather than on furthering material welfare.

Free movement connected to deeper Europeanness, burden-sharing in immigration and negative transactionalism constitute the themes of this chapter. While the first approach focuses on a more restricted scope of European solidarity, similar to the construction of a national identity (Rorty 2000a: 253), the second approach is closest to the Rortyan solidarity ideal of enlarging unity (Rorty 1999). The third approach, in turn, could be termed 'negative transactionalism'; mobility decreases rather than increases the sense of solidarity (cf. Deutsch et al. 1957).

7.2 Goal of deeper Europeanness

The most common view reflected an awareness of the importance of solidarity and promoted deeper European unification. Not only was a borderless Europe related to the idea that mobility concretely increases European unity (the so-called transactionalist view, see, e.g. Deutsch et al. 1957), but an open Europe also functioned as a symbol of European solidarity. Free movement appeared as a force that could bring Europeans closer together and increase their mutual solidarity. The main *topos* found in this section is that of usefulness, often *pro bono nobis* (to the advantage of us) (Wodak 2001: 74).

EU commissioners argued that free movement could build deeper Europeanness. For example, Commission President Barroso referred to border controls as obstacles to European unity (Barroso 2007). In 2011, at the 'Youth on the Move – Make it Happen' event Mr Barroso also talked about Europe as a 'home country'. He insisted that people could de facto utilize free movement and thus regard Europe as their home. He connected European solidarity to the devaluing of national identity while simultaneously reinforcing a European one, effectively constructing Europe as an 'imagined community' (Anderson 1983).[4] In this case, the *topos* of advantage was connected to the benefit to young workers. He apparently meant the Commission when he spoke about 'us' who should ensure the possibility for free movement:

> Whether it is to study or to work, Europe should be your home country. We wish to breathe new life into the systems that make these opportunities possible, because we know that the promise of free movement depends on many things, including affordability and making sure that the diplomas of young people and their skills are also recognized all over Europe. (Barroso 2011b)

In their solidarity discourses, the commissioners also emphasized the importance of cultural diversity, which can be understood as solidarity felt towards other countries. In 2009, in addition to economic benefits, Employment Commissioner Vladimir Špidla referred to the 'rich diversity' created by free movement.[5] He relied on the *topos* of advantage for the benefit of 'us', utilizing free movement in an instrumental manner: 'Free movement of workers, people and services are core values of the European Union. It is what allows British, Czech or Swedish citizens to travel, live and work where they wish in the Union. This openness has contributed to economic growth and to the rich diversity of our communities' (Špidla 2009).

Free movement as a means to enhance deeper Europeanness appeared less often in national discourses. In Germany, for example, Chancellor Merkel did not discuss free movement in the context of solidarity (at least not in the research material), but the interior ministers in her governments twice explicitly referred to free movement as a factor that builds European unification.[6] In 2007, during a German debate concerning the consequences of the emigration of qualified people from Germany, Interior Minister Wolfgang Schäuble lent his support for the movement of *workers*, citing it as a 'wanted process for unification'. He simultaneously implied, however, that (high-qualified) Germans abroad should be taken better care of. This position appears somewhat contradictory: If free movement increases the sense of unity, why is it so important to look after the interests of Germans abroad and make them return? In this vein, Mr Schäuble employed the *topos* of advantage to the benefit of 'us' as both Germans and Europeans:

> The free movement of workers is one of the fundamental freedoms of the European Union: this is also visible in the statistics. The movement of workers is a necessary and – I would also say – wanted process for unification. We should thus not be too afraid that qualified people go to work abroad. We should have better contact with them, so that they return one day. Perhaps we should also think about taking better care of Germans abroad. The closer the contact is with Germans abroad, the more we all benefit from the experience they gain abroad, and the sooner we can smooth the way back for them. (Schäuble 2007)[7]

A few years later, in 2012, at the German–Dutch Integration Conference, the interior minister of Merkel's second government, Hans-Peter Friedrich, stated that free movement was the 'greatest success story in the European unification process'. He argued that there must be a more profound acceptance of free movement in order to continue the successful writing of the common European history and that there should be a welcome culture towards other EU citizens. Although he talked about free movement in general, the fact that he connected it to economic benefit and demographic necessity suggests that he really meant the free movement of workers. Making use of the *topos* of advantage, he described free movement as also producing cultural value:

> The development of the free movement of all Union citizens is perhaps the greatest success story of the European unification process. The influx of Union citizens has economic and cultural value and in many places, also a demographic necessity. That is why we should not leave it to chance, whether and how well the integration of immigrants succeeds within Europe. We must improve the social acceptance for immigration also within Europe and create a real welcome culture. Because when we also have different pasts, it is a question of together writing forward our history successfully. (Friedrich 2012b)[8]

Chancellor Merkel only made two utterances that were classified as solidarity-based, both made in the political context of increasing asylum-seekers and the upcoming

Brexit referendum. The first of the two speeches was held on 7 October 2015 in the European Parliament, in which Merkel praised the importance of free movement as a connecting factor, especially between Western and Eastern Europe:

> The old member states had, for example, fears and scepticism of almost doubling the number of European Union member states. Many people viewed the freedom of movement for millions of new EU citizens as a threat to their own jobs. New decision-making structures had to be developed. European support funds had to be redistributed in favour of the new member states. Today we recognize that this effort has paid off for us all. It has not brought us less prosperity, but more prosperity. It has not brought us less freedom, but more freedom. It has not brought us less diversity, but more diversity. In brief, it has brought us more Europe, because we Europeans have learned in the course of our history to make the most of our diversity. The quality that has enabled us to do this, that has enabled freedom and responsibility, is tolerance. It is a valuable asset. (Merkel 2015e)[9]

Merkel thus equalled Europe with freedom and diversity and praised the tolerance of European people. In another utterance, she talked about Schengen as a factor for the 'growing together' (*Zusammenwachsen*) of Europe, but justified the existence of the temporary internal border controls that Germany had also put in place in its border to Austria. The utterance was made in a press conference on 7 January 2016 with the Romanian Prime Minister Cioloş, and Merkel also praised the progress Romania had made in meeting the requirements for joining. She made use of the *topos* of advantage while responding to a journalist's question about the temporary border controls and Romanian Schengen membership:

> Firstly, I think that the Schengen project is very topical and that there are significant grounds for doing everything in order for us to be able to continue actually enjoying free movement within the Schengen borders. That is why we also need to urgently control the issue of migration and also to regulate the issues of migration, in order to turn illegal migration into legal migration. The temporary border controls that you mentioned, are indeed part of the Schengen system, but of course also include risks that we, when we do not actually solve the problems, then Schengen can either work like we would want it to. I think that Schengen is both something that European citizens appreciate a lot, and also a factor for European unification and economic growth. That is why I think we need to put all effort to maintain Schengen and of course also to give the countries that are not yet part of the Schengen the possibility to become part of the Schengen system. (Merkel 2016f)[10]

In a similar vein to the utterance of minister Schäuble above, a worry for qualified people leaving abroad was present in Romanian utterances. For example, on the European Day reception in 2008, President Băsescu highlighted the importance of free movement as one essential part in the construction of the European project; free movement appeared as a result of integration, which brings forth more integration.

Employing the *topos* of advantage, President Băsescu assured his listeners that 'you' could benefit from free movement and from other opportunities:

> You had the chance to be raised and educated in European values. The opportunities you can benefit from are enormous and I am not only referring to the freedom to move within the Union or to study anywhere in the area. I am referring to the extraordinary chance to effectively participate in the construction of the European future. (Băsescu 2008b)[11]

This was not the only occasion when President Băsescu referred to the desired principle of free movement. In 2010, while speaking to the Romanian Parliament, he recalled that entrance to the Schengen Area and gaining free movement was the wish of 'us all'. In this utterance, entry into the European borderless area was something to pursue that symbolized the Romanian people's need to be a full-fledged European state. While in the previous utterance, Mr Băsescu set himself apart from the (young) beneficiaries, here he relied on the *topos* of advantage to the benefit of 'us' as Romanians: 'We wanted free movement. We can have it completely one day by finally acceding the European area without borders' (Băsescu 2010d).[12]

Free movement as a principle that builds deeper Europeanness also appeared in the French discourses. One example is from 2005, when UMP President Jacques Chirac discussed free movement in the Schengen Area as one of the Union's projects through which the pioneer states may deepen their integration.[13] He compared free movement in the Schengen Area to the Eurozone, in which certain member states go forward with their integration while others opt out. In this manner, he presented free movement, that is, the lack of borders, as a factor deepening integration between already close states.[14] The utterance below also implies that there are different peoples and cultures in Europe, but that the entity called 'France' will pursue a single approach to European policies:

> In the same spirit, if France challenges the idea of a directorate – because the Union needs everyone and has to respect everyone – I think that it is necessary to let states that want to act together, complementing common policies, do that. These pioneer groups, which I have proposals since 2000, must be able to form among all countries that have the will and the means, and to stay open for all those that are ready to join them. That is what we did with the single currency, free movement of persons in the Schengen area or some defence initiatives. ... I.e. by gathering its powers, while respecting the diversity of its nations, of its peoples and of its cultures. Such is the framework to which France, with its partners, will contribute in every way. (Chirac 2005d)[15]

A more recent solidarity utterance could be found from French President Hollande, who referred to free movement as stemming from a certain idea of Europe. In his speech made in the inauguration of the Gotthard Tunnel on 1 June 2016, Hollande describes the sense of Europeanness as something that can be 'instilled' and constructed, for example, through free movement. In line with the *topos* of usefulness, President

Hollande thus presents the construction of tunnels as similar to the construction of a European identity:

> Those who had the idea of the tunnel under English Channel, like those who had the idea, for more than twenty years ago, of the tunnel of Gotthard, had in mind a certain idea of Europe. A Europe that is not only made of norms, procedures and institutions. A Europe that is embodied in the plans, in the ambitions, in the will to progress. A Europe that invests in innovation, in mobility, in sustainable development. A Europe that ensures, and it is very important, the free movement of people and goods. It is this spirit, it is these dynamics that we still need to instil into the countries that are members of the European Union, into those that are not members but are in Europe. We are in the same group, we are in the same space. We have the same desires, the same hopes. (Hollande 2016e)[16]

The solidarity utterances revealed that integration can also take place step by step between certain countries. One example is the energy interconnections being built between Spain, Portugal and France. In March 2015, these countries, the European Commission and the European Investment Bank signed a so-called Madrid Declaration on energy interconnection. The aim is to integrate the energy market of these three countries, and the Madrid Declaration has been later complemented with the Lisbon Declaration in July 2018. It was particularly the host of the Madrid Declaration, Mariano Rajoy, who presented the project as an important step in dismantling borders and advancing European integration, in line with the *topos* of usefulness *pro bono nobis*:

> Three great nations, three of the oldest nations in Europe: Spain, France and Portugal, together with the EU institutions represented by the European Commission and the European Investment Bank, are taking a very important step forward to transcending boundaries. This is a sign of the times and of our common project of European integration: to unite, integrate and connect. We have done away with the artificial borders between us and we now want to do away with the natural borders. Technology allows us to do that; but the most important aspect is political determination, the only attribute capable of overcoming technical and bureaucratic obstacles. And today we have expressed the maximum level of political determination in setting this project in motion, together with the mechanisms and resources necessary to achieve this. (Rajoy 2015e, official translation)[17]

This section has illustrated how free movement appeared as an instrument conducive towards deeper Europeanness. Leaders in the Commission, the Franco-German axis, as well as the Romanian and Spanish presidents all seemed to be convinced of the integrating force created by the free movement regime. The utterances were inclusive in the sense that they did not exclusively concern the movement of certain people, although the commissioners' and German politicians' discourses, in particular, related to the free movement of high-qualified workers. In addition to these utterances on deepening European internal unification through free movement, free movement was also connected to stated solidarity towards migrants, as we can observe in the following section.

7.3 Goal of burden-sharing in immigration

The view of Spanish and Italian politicians seemed to come closest to the ideal of Rorty concerning larger solidarity in which solidarity does not only concern Europeans and in which free movement should also cover people coming from the other side of the Mediterranean. The main *topos* found in this section was that of a subtype of the *topos* of advantage: *pro bono eorum*, to the advantage of them (Wodak 2001). At least at the superficial level, there was thus a sense of enlarged solidarity towards non-Europeans. In practice, however, the calls related more to solidarity between states – in the sense that different EU states should help each other out in migration issues – than to wider solidarity with non-Europeans.

In particular, the Italian discourses did not seem to genuinely rely on Rortyan pursuits for enlarged solidarity but on calls for European burden-sharing in migration. For instance, Italian minister of the interior, Roberto Maroni (Northern League), declared in 2011 that refugees should be able to move freely in the Schengen Area. He emphasized solidarity between the European countries, which should materialize in the granting of free movement to refugees. This is unsurprising, given that Italy is one of the most popular destinations (or transit countries) for African refugees. Mr Maroni appeared to be willing to let anyone leave Italy while simultaneously restricting the entry of others, such as the Roma (see Section 4.2). He justified free movement for refugees based on a principle of solidarity, which he deemed a fundamental principle of the European social system. Minister Maroni relied on the *topos* of advantage; he could think of no objections for enlarging the scope of free movement:

> There has been a small but significant step forward thanks to the initiative of the Mediterranean countries guided by Italy as well as Cyprus, Greece and Malta, countries which requested the implementation of a principle of burden- sharing 18 months ago, with the consequence that the Stockholm Programme, for the first time, discusses the Mediterranean from the point of view of security – which has never happened before – undocumented immigration, the risk of terrorism, and the principle of burden sharing is implemented, albeit on a voluntary basis .... I believe this is a justified request, which takes place during difficult times, times of crises and emergencies, and implements a principle of solidarity, which is one of the fundamental principles of the European social system. I do not honestly see any objections why the free movement of persons, of citizens and of goods should not apply in the case of refugees, so that they could not move freely even in the Schengen area. (Maroni 2011a)[18]

Italian politicians have also had their quarrels with other EU countries concerning the free movement of third-country nationals. In 2011, France prevented Tunisian migrants holding a humanitarian residence permit from entering the country from

Italy. This action then sparked a debate on European solidarity in immigration matters (Garelli and Tazzioli 2013: 1007) and encouraged Italian politicians to promote the free movement of refugees by appealing to Directive 2001/55/EC (see also the utterance of Cancellieri 2012).[19] This attitude endured: in 2014, Minister of the Interior Angelino Alfano claimed that Europe should grant free movement to North African migrants. According to him, they should not be forced to stay in Italy but should be allowed to exploit their right to free movement, if granted a residence permit in Italy. In an interview given to *La Sicilia*, published on the website of the Ministry, Minister Alfano demonstrated his solidarity towards the immigrants and criticized 'Europe' for forcing them to stay in Italy. He employed the *topos* of advantage to argue that the immigrants should have the permission to move around Europe:

> Also in this, Europe must intervene quickly, because the movement of such immigrants in the European Union countries, who have the grounds for making an application for a political asylum, must be made fluent, possible. Also, because more and more often we do not face 'work-based' immigration of people who look for any type of work, but professional people arrive, such as Syrians, who flee from life-threatening situations. And Europe forces them to be stuck in Italy because they land here. With regard to this, our pressure will be more and more persistent. Also, because I think about the immigrants and free movement, which should be guaranteed, I repeat, to whoever has the grounds, while the others should be sent home, but I also think about Sicilians. They are showing, as always, their grand hearts, their capacity to be solidary but who request, and rightly so, that they too are not put in a condition, where they feel besieged by immigrants who do not want to be here. (Alfano 2014a)[20]

Also later, after the utterances above, there have been signs of dispute concerning migrants coming from North Africa. The disputes have taken place especially between the French and Italian publics (see, e.g. Casella Colombeau 2015), as France has not wanted asylum-seekers to be granted the right to free movement. There were even Italian proposals to give all asylum-seekers a temporary humanitarian residence permit so that they could travel anywhere as other EU countries did not appear willing to help them with the issue (see, e.g. Traynor 2015, Manconi 2017). Also in April 2016, Prime Minister Renzi sent a letter to Jean-Claude Juncker and Donald Tusk, in which Italy criticized the reintroduction of internal borders in certain countries and called for more cooperation with third countries. In line with the *topos* of advantage, Renzi called for solidarity between the member states, though not wanting to enlarge free movement to third countries:

> The management of migratory flows towards the European Union has entered a critical phase, in which the solidarity of Member States is put to the test on a daily basis. Despite recent initiatives by the Commission and the Council, the closure of borders by some Member States, sometimes not adequately motivated, coupled with the widespread refusal to sharing the burden of this huge challenge, threaten the foundations of the Union itself. The Commission's proposals, strongly

supported by Italy, to set up a European Border and Coast Guard, together with the 'Back to Schengen' Communication and the Dublin System reform proposals can yield concrete results only if the management of migratory flows moves from an emergency stage to a more strategic and organized one. From this perspective it is clear that the external dimension of migration policies is fundamental for the survival of Schengen and the principle of free movement. The management of migratory flows is no longer sustainable without a targeted and enhanced cooperation with third countries, both of origin and transit. Much has already been done but we need to do more and to act rapidly if we want to prevent a deteriorating systemic crisis. (Renzi 2016, official translation)[21]

The Spanish discourse also touched upon third-country migrants, although there was only one Spanish utterance classified in the group of burden-sharing. Nonetheless, in 2014, Premier Rajoy's utterance reflected the Rortyan idea that solidarity should expand when one interacts with someone previously thought of as 'them'. Mr Rajoy called for more dialogue with the neighbours of Europe and for more solidary management of the Union's external borders. Of course, the discourse of 'helping them at home' is also connected to the European interests in bringing down the number of immigrants. Prime Minister Rajoy made use of the *topos* of advantage related to 'them':

Secondly, we need a European Union without internal borders, able to control the borders of the Union in an integrated and solidary manner. That is, a real European immigration policy, more efficient and more solidary with the countries we confront at the external border, with more European measures and with an external dimension that is complemented with a dialogue with the countries of origin and of transit, and more development cooperation in order to contribute to the construction of an area of prosperity shared with our neighbours. It does not mean making Europe a fortress. Today, it is necessary to tackle the problem at its roots: emigration has to be an option and not an obligation in order to survive. (Rajoy 2014a)[22]

German minister of the interior, Thomas de Maizière, presented another recent solidarity utterance related to free movement in 2016. Whereas Prime Minister Renzi criticized the introduction of internal border controls, de Maizière justified the German decision to reinstate temporary border controls. He also called for solidarity between the member states to take care of the refugees, most of which were received by Germany:

At the moment, only a few EU member states receive the vast majority of the refugees who come to Europe, above all Germany. Other member states watch and disregard that it is the EU that must address worldwide migration and that we must react together and with a spirit of solidarity. What happens, when we do not act together at the European level, has been visible during the last weeks and months, when – temporary – border controls had to be reintroduced in different border sections in the Schengen area. Also Germany had to prolong the border control measures introduced in mid-September 2015, in the face of the large number of people. However, no people will by no means be turned back. In the end, this would be contrary to a common European approach. Borderless movement of people within the European Union and the complete free movement of refugees within Europe cannot be permanently reconciled with the great achievement of the open internal market. (de Maizière 2016)[23]

The points of emphasis thus varied significantly between the utterances discussed above. The Spanish utterance utilized free movement as a justification for larger solidarity in immigration matters, the German utterance called for more solidarity in order to retain free movement, while the Italian utterances demanded solidarity from other states towards Italy. Although the Italian politicians insisted that free movement cover asylum-seekers and refugees in Italy, the claims appeared to relate to European burden-sharing rather than to actual solidarity felt towards the migrants – of course, acts of burden-sharing within Europe can indeed also be conducive to the efforts of constructing solidarity. Overall, it does indeed seem that politicians in all countries utilized free movement as a justification for sharing the burden concerning refugees. Italian ministers even argued that providing concrete free movement for refugees would be a sign of European solidarity, whereas the German minister of the interior called for joint responsibility in refugee policy in order to maintain the free movement of EU citizens and the internal market.

7.4 Goal to prevent negative transactionalism

Negative transactionalism, as intended here, refers to a view according to which the exercise of free movement decreases rather than increases solidarity between groups of people. It is the opposite of transactionalism, which basically maintains that mobility increases the sense of Europeanness (Deutsch et al. 1957, Recchi 2013, Kuhn 2015). The utterances in this section thus bring to light the view that mobility can have destabilizing effects (Aradau, Huysmans and Squire 2010: 949). The most common *topoi* here related to uselessness/disadvantage (Wodak 2001: 74).

In Romania, the predominant view of solidarity was that free movement should build deeper Europeanness, as we saw in Section 7.2. However, certain problems related to the removal of borders were also discussed in the vein of negative transactionalism. In 2008, President Băsescu paid attention to the potential problems of free movement with respect to the Roma. He utilized the *topos* of disadvantage, arguing that free movement has revealed difficulties related to socially disadvantaged groups. It is noteworthy that he wanted a European strategy to address the 'problems of social integration', rather than just merely national measures:

The application of the free movement of European citizens has also demonstrated some specific difficulties with which certain socially disadvantaged groups are confronted. I am referring especially to the ethnic Roma, a minority transnationally spread in different proportions in every Union country. The European dimension of the social integration problems of the Roma requires, alongside systematic national policies of inclusion, also a European strategy to concentrate relevant policies at the EU level – strategies that will enjoy all our support. (Băsescu 2008a)[24]

The problems related to free movement did not make Romanian politicians question the principle of free movement, but politicians in other countries assumed a more critical approach towards the free movement regime. In 2008, French President Nicolas Sarkozy elaborated the demand that other states should be able to influence each other's decisions. He opposed the idea of paperless people from outside the European Union having the right to free movement and referred to the will of the people of the Union in arguing that this should not occur. Mr Sarkozy maintained that there was a need to ask for other states' opinion in regularization matters.[25] Relying on the *topos* of disadvantage, President Sarkozy argued that Europeans do not want states to decide alone on the provision of the right to free movement of paperless people:

> We create the Schengen Area, i.e. anyone who is hosted by us is hosted by others or anyone who is hosted by others is hosted by us. At the same time, we witness massive regularizations of undocumented migrants without our opinion being asked. Who can believe that this is the Europe that Europeans want? It is not the Europe that Europeans want. (Sarkozy 2008a)[26]

President Sarkozy was not the only politician to question the desirability of the contemporary practices. In Britain, Prime Minister David Cameron was even more critical and argued that the scale of free movement decreased the sense of European solidarity. During Mr Cameron's term in office, there was an intense discussion about the 'European question' of whether the UK should leave the EU (Oliver 2015), which was apparent in PM Cameron's utterances. In his November 2014 speech, one of the four British utterances classified as solidarity-based, Prime Minister Cameron first described Britain as a pluralist and open country, and subsequently argued that free movement threatened European solidarity. It should be noted that Premier Cameron did not consider movement as a threat to national solidarity but to European solidarity; European solidarity thus existed and appeared worth preserving – but it was precarious. Although he described the UK as a perfect example of people from different backgrounds building a common home, the same appeared virtually impossible to take place Europe-wide. Free movement did not seem to create solidarity but hamper it, in line with the *topos* of disadvantage:

> I am extremely proud that together we have built a successful, multi-racial democracy. A country where in one or two generations people can come with nothing and rise as high as their talent allows. A country whose success has been founded not on building separate futures, but rather coming together to build a common home. ... Across the European Union, issues of migration are causing real concern and raising real questions. Can movements on the scale we have seen in recent years always be in the best interests of the EU and wider European solidarity? (Cameron 2014b)

The other three utterances of Prime Minister Cameron that were classified as solidarity-based took place in 2015–16. In retrospect, arguing in favour of remaining in the European Union but claiming that free movement is a problem causing mass migration may not have been the most effective alternative. In March 2015, Cameron stated that 'We've clamped down on benefit tourism at home and we've kicked off a debate across Europe about what more must be done to ensure that freedom of movement is not an unqualified right, and that when new countries join the EU this does not trigger mass migration across our continent' (Cameron 2015g). In May 2015, he continued with the same line arguing that 'I don't think it was the intention of free movement that the movement would be on this scale' (Cameron 2015f). Finally, after the referendum resulting in the decision to leave the European Union, Prime Minister Cameron stated in his final press conference after the European Council that the concern over free movement caused people to vote in favour of leaving the EU:

> Yes, I did talk about what I think happened in the referendum. I think people recognised the strength of the economic case for staying, but there was a very great concern about the movement of people and immigration, and I think that's coupled with a concern about the issues of sovereignty and the ability to control these things. And I think, you know, we need to think about that, Europe needs to think about that, and I think that is going to be one of the major tasks for the next Prime Minister. (Cameron 2016a)

The utterances above clearly bear traits of the idea of negative transactionalism: people from different countries should not necessarily move around, at least in great numbers, in order to preserve mutual solidarity between states. In addition to Prime Minister Cameron, only one French and one Romanian leader uttered similar comments, but these did not represent the main discursive lines in these countries. Negative transactionalism thus seems to provide an antithesis to what the other approaches maintained and deny the solidarizing function of mobility. In these solidarity utterances, it was not the economic burden that was presented as the problem but the scale of movement, which in turn created concern among the Brits.

7.5 Europe of solidarity: Mobility justified as enhancing solidarity

The European free movement discourses in the analysis did not contain a significant number of references to the ideals of solidarity, neither intracontinentally nor regarding outsiders. Several interesting findings nevertheless came to the fore. There was no consensus that free movement would increase solidarity between people and across states, although there was a widespread aspiration to strengthen the sense of European solidarity. Possibly the most salient point of reference was the principle of free movement as a *symbol* promoting European unification. In a few utterances, solidarity was linked to the free movement of workers. To sum up all the approaches, free movement proved to be an instrument that was used to promote deeper

Europeanness and burden-sharing in immigration policy but that can also potentially lead to less solidarity.

Most solidarity utterances displayed a positive understanding of the relationship between free movement and *European* solidarity. However, national interests were also often emphasized in the utterances. For example, some politicians wanted help in coping with migration problems in their home countries, while others were concerned about the way in which their citizens were treated abroad. It is noteworthy that free movement as an opportunity to leave one's country, more or less permanently, rarely came to the fore in a positive light. This may also be due to the sense of national pride: Why would anyone want to leave 'our' country if there was nothing wrong with it?

We observed that Italian, German and Spanish politicians were the ones who discussed 'outsiders' in the context of free movement, while politicians in other countries were more concerned about EU 'insiders'. In the French and British views, overly open movement policies were also depicted as potential threats to European solidarity. Commissioners, as well as German and Romanian politicians, argued that the European Union has been (and will remain?) united, partly because of its free movement policy. The analysed countries can be seen to form different groups with varying emphases of solidarity and EU-centredness, as visible in Table 7.1. The table sums up some of the primary findings: The solidarity dimension materialized in calls for more European solidarity, widening solidarity and concern about solidarity.

The solidarity utterances did not seem to reflect the view that exercising mobility would increase the sense of European identity in a transactionalist vein (Deutsch et al. 1957, Kuhn 2015). Nevertheless, free movement seemed to constitute a crucial aspect of European integration in a symbolic manner. The temporary migration of 'Eurostars' – those who eventually return to their home countries – was deemed to enhance the sense of solidarity from the national perspective in particular (Favell 2008). From the individuals' perspective, the aspect of the free movement principle that creates the most solidarity seemed to be the *possibility* of leaving, leaving for other European countries, however symbolic that may remain for many people. In spite of this, the aim of European people considering themselves Europeans first, and national citizens second, appears as a fairly distant aspiration, even in Euro-enthusiastic political speeches.

The solidary-based approach could be depicted with the analogy of the European Union as a state primary *school*. In this school, teacher-politicians seek to deliberately socialize the pupil-citizens into a European sense of solidarity. From this perspective, European unification is not based on, say, genes or historical duties, rather unification

Table 7.1 Solidarity utterances regarding free movement

	Extra-European solidarity	European solidarity
Deeper solidarity		Commission, Romania, Germany
Burden-sharing solidarity	Spain, Italy	
Concern about solidarity		France, UK

comes about by teaching the pupils more or less the same things and viewpoints about the continent and its political affairs. Free movement represents one of the subjects in the curriculum of the school. The teachers, however, tend to have differing views on what to teach to the children: how much and what sort of mobility is optimal for a sense of solidarity.

On the basis of the analysis, the European Union cannot be argued to constitute a Rortyan 'Europe of solidarity' in the free movement context. There was no general consensus that mobility would increase the sense of Europeanness. In contrast, a few politicians contended that free movement may decrease the sense of solidarity among EU citizens and between states. Moreover, with respect to the movement of third-country nationals, there were repeated calls for burden-sharing but often in vain.

In the next chapter, I provide a short historical overview of the migration policies of the analysed countries before moving on to looking the country-specific free movement discourses.

8

Setting the scene: Migration policy histories of the analysed countries

This chapter briefly summarizes the migration policy histories in the analysed countries, aiming to set the scene for the country-specific aspects examined in the following chapter. The migration histories, and thus the migration policies, of the countries demonstrate considerable variety, reflected even in today's discourses.

8.1 The history of migration policies in Germany: From Gastarbeiter to immigrants

Throughout its history, Germany has imported labour from other countries. Already before the First World War, Germany had become the second-largest labour importing country after the United States, the number of foreign workers reaching up to 1.2 million before the war. Most of these migrants were Polish and despite attempts in the 1920s to increase the arrival of ethnic German workers from abroad to balance the number of Poles, it was Polish workers who outnumbered all other nationalities especially in farming (Oltmer 2016: 153–4).

The Second World War changed the entire migration image in Germany. Germany was divided into East and West and not all people fleeing the country could or wanted to return to Germany. Nevertheless, West Germany continued to import workers from other countries. The largest group were Yugoslavs, only outnumbered in the 1970s by Turks (Molnar 2016: 194). Most migrants in the post-war years, however, were refugees and expellees, also coming from East Germany, Poland, Czechoslovakia and Hungary (Münz and Ulrich 1999: 22).

The labour recruitment programme from the 1950s to the 1970s was based on the premise that the workers would return home after their services were no longer needed. Another major guest worker agreement was with Italy in 1955, and by the early 1970s, there were already two million foreigners in Germany (Chin 2010: 80). Calculated together, citizens of the 'old' EU member states, such as Italians and Spaniards, constituted the largest group of migrants until the 1970s (Münz and Ulrich 1999: 21). Germany has also been the main target of European East–West migration, and according to Fassmann and Munz, between 1950 and 1992 ca. 68 per cent of

East–West migrants moved to Germany, mostly ethnic Germans or labour migrants and their dependents (Fassmann and Münz 1994). It is to be noted that before the 1980s, migration did not really appear as a political issue, partly because guest workers were thought to return home afterwards and partly because politicians with openly anti-immigrant attitudes were largely condemned in the country with the Holocaust legacy (Schmidtke 2015: 382).

Germany issued an *Anwerbestopp* in 1973 in order to halt recruitment and make the guest workers return home, but the policy did not have the desired effect. The share of Turks was rising, while that of EEC workers was decreasing due to the ease of coming and going; they did not have to fear that they could not come back if they returned home (Chin 2010: 86). It was, however, only in the late 1970s that it was acknowledged that most of the guest workers do not intend to return to their home countries. In the 1980s, immigration also became a politicized issue when the parties started to make immigration a part of their political campaigning; for example, the CDU blamed the SPD of creating an immigration problem (Chin 2010: 90–3). However, it was only in the 1990s that immigration started to move towards the centre of party politics (Schmidtke 2015).

In addition to labour migration, the post-war migration policy of Germany was characterized by the so-called *Aussiedler* (resettler) migration, in which ethnic Germans from the Eastern Europe were provided the right to migrate to Germany (Panagiotidis 2016: 210). Most of these migrants, who received German citizenship almost automatically, came from Poland (62 per cent), and 15 per cent or 206,000 came from Romania (Münz and Ulrich 1999: 24). This was not a case of temporary labour but permanent settlement and citizenship, which was granted to those who were considered to represent the German *Volkstum*. The criteria, however, were fluctuating, varying from German language skills, ethnic endogamy and political convictions (Panagiotidis 2016: 220).

Germany only issued its first immigration law in 2005 in the post-9/11 climate, which caused fierce debates between the centre-left and the centre-right parties. In the end, the migration debate became to be characterized by the rational debate linked to labour market and by the more sentiment-related discourse related to national interests and identity (Schmidtke 2015: 384–5). These two strands are also visible in the contemporary free movement debates, though with the rational labour market rhetoric prevailing.

These policies illustrate the approach towards the nation and outsiders, in which even after the Nazi period, the idea of a unified people and temporary migration prevailed. As discussed in more detail in the following chapter, the idea of guest workers and circular migration still prevail in the contemporary German mobility discourses, even with regard to the mobility of EU citizens. The idea is to gain benefits by importing labour from other countries, while simultaneously providing the possibility for Germans to move temporarily in other EU countries to gather experience. Even though we can observe a sense of community and solidarity towards other EU citizens in the German discourses, the prevailing idea seems to be to receive benefits from labour originating from other EU countries.

8.2 The history of French immigration policies: Republican assimilation

Unlike Germany, France has historically welcomed people from all over the world and quickly granted them citizenship and apparent equality vis-à-vis all other French citizens. France has been a popular target of people throughout centuries, and already in 1926, there were almost three times as many foreigners in Paris as there were in the entire Germany (Rosenberg 2018: 31). Workers from Europe and beyond have come to France, which has needed foreign labour such as miners, steel workers and fruit pickers; in the 1930s, many of the immigrants, such as Italians, entered irregularly as France tried to restrict immigration due to depression (Cross 1983: 187–8). Repatriation policies similar to those utilized with contemporary Roma migrants were also utilized in the 1930s, as migrants from Eastern European countries were transported to the frontiers of their home countries. However, this policy only lasted a year from May 1935 on, but the number of recorded repatriations in 1935 was an all-time high: 67,215 (Cross 1983: 200).

One issue related to the history of free movement not yet touched upon in this book is the debate on overseas territories and the right to free movement of people from the overseas territories. In the negotiations of the Treaty of Rome in the 1960s, the free movement of Algerian workers was one of the most contentious issues to be settled. While Italians did not want Algerian workers to compete with Italians in the labour markets of the more Northern member states, the French did not want to differentiate between French citizens in France and Algeria. In the end, it was decided that the issue of the Algerian free movement was to be settled within two years of the treaty's entry into force. As stated in Article 227(2) of the Treaty of Rome (1957), 'The conditions under which the other provisions of this Treaty are to apply shall be determined, within two years of the entry into force of this Treaty, by decisions of the Council, acting unanimously on a proposal from the Commission.' Eventually, however, the issue was completed only in 1968 when Algeria had already become independent (in 1962) and was thus excluded from the EEC (Hansen and Jonsson 2017: 230–3).

Before 1962, Algerians in France were not immigrants since they had French citizenship, and the immigrants in the post-war years mostly consisted of South European workers from Italy, Spain and Portugal (Geddes 2003: 53). The number of non-European immigrants, however, grew increasingly, and the French politicians aimed at assimilating the migrants as well as they could. In a similar vein as in Germany, immigration became a politicized issue in the 1980s, with *Front National* gaining more popularity against the ruling Socialist party. Before that time, immigration was mainly discussed in terms of the migrant worker's right, but the right and the far right took ownership of the immigration debate by focusing on security and terrorism (Noiriel 2018: 133). A Socialist government took the office in 1981 and wanted to break from the right-wing immigration policy. For example, they declared an amnesty for those undocumented immigrants who could justify their presence in France (Schain 2008: 52). As discussed elsewhere in this book, the contemporary French leaders have been eager to criticize Spain and Italy for regularizing immigrants, but the French government made recourse to similar policies in the 1980s, regularizing up to 123,000 during a single winter (Geddes 2003: 56).

Unlike other European countries, France has considered itself as an immigration country already from the nineteenth century, but the dividing lines related to ethnicity and nationality only became generally discovered in the 1980s. The 1980s also saw a major diversification in immigration, as migrants from the Iberian Peninsula and from France's colonial empire began to increase, foreign population constituting 6.8 per cent (3.6 million people) of the population (Noiriel 2018: 134–6).

The French idea of integration has often been considered a republican one, centred on common rules and the idea of '*l'assimilation nationale*' (Noiriel 1988: 341–56). This means that the French state does not acknowledge minorities but considers that all people become French as they acquire citizenship (Geddes 2003: 66). As Geddes summarizes, the republican ideas of the French immigration policy rest on four premises: 'universalism as enshrined in the Rights of Man of 1789, unitarism in *la République une et indivisible*, the separation of church and state (*laïcité*), assimilation with an onus on foreigners to become French and on French institutions to facilitate this process' (Geddes 2003: 57). According to Odmalm, this means that 'everyone can and should become French but at the price of giving up one's cultural baggage' (Odmalm 2005: 25). This aim to undermine the role of religion and culture is still apparent in today's policies.

In light of the French free movement discourses, the idea of republican traditions and allegedly neutral legal principles seems to be present also in the EU mobility context. The French policies for controlling mobility appear to rest on drafting laws, which everyone should obey in order for the policies to be successful. The terms for acquiring French citizenship have been rather lax when compared to other European countries, but France has also had denaturalization policies in place in case dual citizens, for example, commit a serious crime (Weil 2017).

It seems that the French mobility policies rest on the principle that a seemingly objective legislation treats everyone in the same manner. Despite this apparent neutrality, the immigration policies have been considered racist at least to some extent due to the practical consequences for different nationalities (Weil 1995). Nevertheless, it is preferable to aim at equality, though it may not materialize, rather than to exercise openly discriminatory policies.

8.3 Migration policy history in Italy: A late country of immigration

Italy has been more of a sending rather than a receiving country throughout its history. We are all aware of the millions of Italians who left for the United States, but some have also been forced to leave Italy. For example, it has been estimated that in the 1920s and 1930s, approximately 800,000 Italians fled from fascism. The difference with Italian and other refugees was, however, that an Italian refugee was not stateless, but unofficially defined as 'an Italian living abroad, who cannot return to his country without personal danger, because of his political activity against fascism'. Even though Italian refugees pleaded for the League of Nation's protection, they were left without international legal protection (Sallinen 2013: 272–3).

After the Second World War, Italy was mainly a country of emigration, providing labour force for the countries to the North, especially after the creation of the ECSC. It was only in the mid-1970s that the Italian migration balance became positive, that is, there were more people coming to Italy than leaving the country. However, as argued by Colombo and Sciortino, this does not mean that Italy did not receive immigrants before. In addition to labour migrants and refugees, Italy has always attracted people due to its nature and history, a group of immigrants mainly consisting of affluent people (Colombo and Sciortino 2004: 49–51).

In the early phases of European integration, Italians utilized the free movement of workers in order to leave to work in large numbers in, for example, Belgian mines and Germany (Gabaccia 2012: 214). The migration into Italy in the 1970s was still very small; there were only ca. 121,000 foreigners, or 0.2 per cent of the population in 1971. Furthermore, this number included students, businessmen, diplomats, researchers and artists who were only temporarily in Italy (Gabaccia 2003: 253–4). Most immigrants came from Europe and the United States, but as Italians returned from former colonies, they also brought service personnel with them, for example, from Tunisia and Eritrea (Colombo and Sciortino 2004: 52–5).

The Italian industrialization process simultaneously created an underground job market in Italy for irregular immigrants. The Italian state has also recently made use of regularization amnesties, criticized by other EU countries, the first of which took place already in 1986. This was also the year when the first law regulating foreign labour was passed. The first amnesty regularized 119,000 migrants while the second in 1990 regularized 235,000 (Mingione and Quassoli 2000: 45–50). The regularization campaign in 2002 was the largest, however, regularizing 646,000 migrants out of whom 240,000 were Romanians (Einaudi 2007: 306, Gattinara 2016: 59). This contributed to the doubling of the number of foreigners in Italy, from 1.3 million in 2001 to 2.6 million in 2006, also due to the fact that the number of arrivals increased during the 14-month period between the regularization proposal and the deadline for submitting the regularization request (Einaudi 2007: 306–19). The campaign consisted of two parts, one for domestic help and the other for other professions (Einaudi 2007: 367). The latest regularization campaign in 2009 only concerned domestic and care workers, which more than 2.5 million Italian families employed at the time (Massetti 2015: 482–8).

Immigration to Italy since the 1980s has demonstrated that many Italians faced foreigners with the same hostility Italians had faced during the past decades, even though the numbers were small. The around 70,000 Africans and Asians aroused heated public debate, while female migrants from the Philippines mainly working as home aid were more warmly welcomed. Furthermore, Italians faced migration across the sea already in the 1980s, when Albanian refugees were received by soldiers and gathered in a stadium to wait for the authorities' decision (Gabaccia 2003: 254–6). While immigration seemed to constitute a labour market issue in the 1980s, in the 1990s it became increasingly an issue of responsibility and the fighting of irregular migration, turning into a more securitized issue towards the late 1990s (Magnani 2012). The securitization of migration was related, inter alia, to the rise of the Northern

League and to other actors blaming immigrants for the rise in criminality (Tsoukala 2005: 174–8).

In addition to labour migration, refugees, students and entrepreneurs are migrant categories that have increased in recent years. For example, asylum requests have ranged from less than 1,000 a year to more than 100,000 in 2016 and 2017 (Commissione Nazionale per il Diritto di Asilo 2019). The number of foreigners in total has increased in the twenty-first century, foreigners constituting ca. 5 per cent of the population in 2005 and 8.5 per cent of the population in 2018. This is very much in line with the projections presented by Einaudi in his book in 2007; by 2020, Italian foreign population would come close to the French and British numbers, rising up to 5.1 million or 8.7 per cent of the population (Einaudi 2007: 398). The current number of foreigners in Italy is even a bit higher than in France, though not reaching the numbers of the UK and Germany, totalling ca. 6.3 million and 9.7 respectively, according to Eurostat (2019).

I have illustrated in this book that migration discourses in Italy have had diverse patterns also in the twenty-first century. While the focus was more on intra-European migrants in the first decade of the new millennium, the second decade witnessed a shift towards concern over third-country migrants crossing the Mediterranean. In the discourses analysed in this study, the majority seems to have a humanitarian approach, but critical opinions became more vocal after the so-called migration crisis in autumn 2015. In the years to follow, the politicians further restricted the entry of rescue ships in Italian ports and curbed legislation on providing humanitarian assistance. It still seems that the past experiences of Italian emigration do not play out in the contemporary Italian politics (cf. Gabaccia 2003). Furthermore, it appears that in the Italian case, immigration and EU policies are tightly attached. People who are critical of immigration blame the EU for not helping Italy out with migration, encouraging people to become more EU sceptical at the same time. While the populist governments a decade ago were worried about EU citizens (particularly from Romania) constituting a security threat, currently the focus has shifted towards third-country nationals.

8.4 Migration policy in the UK: Restrictions to mobility towards the country

Britain has been a popular target for immigration from all over the world, and the country has paid much effort in drafting restrictive immigration laws and policies (Geddes 2003: 29–50). This is also one of the four particular characteristics identified by Anthony M. Messina in the British post-war migration history when compared to other countries. Furthermore, as a result of this curbing of labour migration, the British society has also been less penetrated by foreign workers than other large EU states. In addition, Britain has not experienced a major political anti-immigration movement (also due to the election system), and finally, it has been under fewer pressure of irregular migration, also thanks to being an island (Messina 2001: 259–60). Although Messina made his observations in the turn of the millennium, the situation has not changed much.

A good illustration of the differences to other European countries in curbing immigration is that Britain was exactly 100 years ahead of Germany in drafting its first immigration law, the Aliens Act of 1905 (Schain 2008: 121). The Aliens Restriction Acts of 1914 and 1919 followed it; a comprehensive Immigration Act substituted the latter only in 1971. As the titles suggest, these acts have usually aimed at restricting immigration. Sometimes 'migrants' have also been warmly welcome, however, although people from the Commonwealth have not always been categorized as such. Especially after the Second World War, Britain was in need of labour, which was the primary motive for recruiting workers from the Commonwealth. Irish workers and later workers from the Caribbean and other parts of the Commonwealth arrived in great numbers, which prompted the UK to introduce five immigration laws during the Cold War focused mainly on colonial issues. Immigration only became a politicized issue in the 1960s, which is still earlier than in other European countries. It was at that time that the increasing numbers of Commonwealth migrants proved conducive to making immigration a tool of political campaigning, though not resulting in a large-scale anti-immigration party such as the French *Front Nationale* (Messina 2001: 284).

In addition to Commonwealth migration, the UK received refugees from Eastern Europe in the post-war period. As genuine political refugees, some 200,000 people arrived after the Hungarian revolution in 1956. In addition, political refugees from Poland, Romania and Czechoslovakia also entered the UK. The number of Poles totalled more than 130,000, and in 1947, the Polish Resettlement Act was introduced to direct Poles to the areas of labour shortages in the country (Knox 1997). After this immediate post-war period, not many Eastern Europeans entered the UK before the Soviet Union collapsed in 1991. Since the 1980s, many workers started to enter the UK under a work-permit programme, and there were already more than 1.1 million foreign workers by the turn of the millennium (Schain 2008: 137).

Most immigration also after the Soviet collapse consisted of Commonwealth migrants, while migrants from Central and Eastern European became more numerous after the eight CEE countries joined the EU in 2004 and 2007 (Bloom and Tonkiss 2013: 1070). Britain still wanted to maintain border and migration control in its own hands: The UK decided not to participate in drafting the Schengen agreement in the 1980s and opposed the initiatives of the 1990s concerning the development of a supranational immigration policy (Ette and Gerdes 2007: 95–7, Heinikoski 2015c).

This book looks at migration from a political level, primarily not only from the perspective of leading politicians but also from the perspective of European legislation. However, one should not think that what is provided in legislation or stated by a single politician does represent the opinion of the 'society'. Analysis of phenomena on a high political level necessarily hides the views of the people that think differently. On a legislative level, the UK migration history seems more anti-immigration than the image of the contemporary society being proud of its diversity (Nava 2014). A case in point is the UK's refugee policy (Kelly 2003: 70). Only a total of approximately 12,000 refugees arrived in the UK as a result of the wars in Yugoslavia, which displaced approximately 3.7 million people. It has even been argued that it was mainly as a result of international pressure that the UK set refugee quotas for those from the former Yugoslavia in the first place (Guild 2000).

Even the current British migration policies display marked differences between those of other member states, for example, the fact that the anti-immigration UKIP party has not gained much prominence in the elections. With the system of two major parties, Tories and Labour parties have both been prudent with their migration policies, without strong anti- or pro-immigration stances (Schain 2008: 180). Another special characteristic is the British decision not to fully participate in European integration in justice and home affairs. As discussed elsewhere in this book, in the Maastricht Treaty negotiations, the UK received an 'opt-in' option in immigration issues in the EU, where it can decide on a case-by-case basis whether it wants to join measures related to JHA matters, such as Schengen (Ette and Gerdes 2007: 97). The choice was justified by Minister for Europe Joyce Quin in 1999 as follows: 'We will keep our border controls – we feel as an island that this makes sense – but we will make sure that our immigration systems do not hinder the movements of European peoples' (Quin 1999).

People from the EU have hardly been the main concern in the history of the British migration policy. It was only after the EU enlargement in 2004 that free movement became a politicized issue in the old member states. As argued by Dennison and Geddes, immigration and the EU became political concerns in the UK in the early 2000s, and the conflation of the EU and immigration without differentiating EU and non-EU immigrants was constitutive for the result of the referendum (Dennison and Geddes 2018). The Labour was more positive towards the economic benefit from EU workers, but the Conservative Party could capitalize in the 2010 elections on people's fear of increasing number of (Eastern) Europeans, coupled with the global recession. It was also at that time when the anti-immigration and Eurosceptical UKIP party started to gain popularity, which probably prompted the Tories to harden their rhetoric for the 2015 elections, with infamous results.

8.5 History of Spanish migration policy: Emigration and regularizations

In a similar vein to Italy, Spain has traditionally been a country of emigration, only turning to an immigration country in the 1980s. It has been estimated that in the 1960s and 1970s, up to three million Spaniards migrated to France, Germany, and other European countries (Arango and Martin 2010: 263). Since Spaniards started returning and the net immigration became positive in the 1980s, the main issues discussed with regard to immigration policies have been the number of irregular migrants, the solution to which has been the regularization of such migrants.

Until the turn of the millennium, most labour migrants were recruited from Morocco, but since then, the focus has been on East European workers (Arango and Martin 2010). Migration being mainly based on work rather than refugee or asylum, together with the small scale of extra-European migration to Spain has been cited as one reason why there has not been a major anti-immigration party, unlike in other major European countries (Arango 2013: 10). Another reason may be the consensual political culture established after Franco's dictatorship by the interparty Moncloa Accords (1977) and the democratic constitution in 1978 (Encarnación 2004). Not even after the

2008 financial crisis, which made a third of immigrant workforce unemployed, did an anti-immigration movement gain ground. This has been accounted by the economic contribution of migration, the young age of most migrants reducing the issues of long-term settlement, immigration not being perceived as a threat to the national identity and, again, the anti-populist political legacy after Franco's regime (Arango 2013: 9–12). The Spanish model thus provides a very different type of political situation with regard to migration.

Until the 1980s, the migratory flows were mostly oriented from Spain to Northern Europe and to the Americas. In the 1960s and 1970s, there were already some communities of retired Europeans as well as some immigrants from Morocco and Latin America, but the total number of foreigners in Spain hardly surpassed 200,000 in the early 1980s. By the mid-1990s, the figure had already surpassed half a million and totalled around 800,000 and 2 per cent of the population at the end of the 1990s, excluding irregular migrants and unregistered EU citizens (Arango 2000a: 253–6). In light of these small numbers, an extraordinary feature of Spanish politics is that Spain recognized already in 1991 that it was a country of immigration. The change has thus been rather rapid from the 1980s to today, and Spain also quickly brought the Spanish legislation into line with those of other EU countries (Geddes and Scholten 2016: 186). Despite the parliament drafting migration legislation since the 1980s, especially Spanish left-wing politicians have deliberately sought to prevent the politicization of migration, which has been relatively successful (Martín-Pérez and Moreno-Fuentes 2012: 647–9). Some debate took place in Spain regarding the migrant boats arriving to the Canary Islands, especially in the twenty-first century, but it was mainly discussed in the context of EU migration policy (Dudek and Pestano 2019).

Contrary to the other European countries, immigration legislation in Spain has been more proactive than reactive – first immigration legislation was stipulated in 1985 before significant immigration flows and one year before Spain became a member in the EC. The 1985 act was, however, criticized for increasing illegal immigration and for its weaknesses in border control. The following Immigration Act was provided in 2000 and has also been amended numerous times (Sánchez Alonso 2011). The Spanish state has even been quite liberal in its family reunification policies, for example, by not adding an economic requirement for reunification (Mato Díaz and Miyar Busto 2017).

As a reactive component of migration policy and similar to the Italian policy, Spain has made use of regularization campaigns since the first immigration act in 1985. Approximately 44,000 immigrants benefited from the first regularization campaign of 1985. Another was conducted in 1991, when 109,000 workers were regularized (Arango 2000a: 266–8). Regularization campaigns were again organized in 1996, 2000–1 and 2005 (Sánchez Alonso 2011, Marcu 2014). The regularization campaigns may contribute to the high number of irregular immigrants in Spain, but there are also other reasons, such as linking residence permits with work permits, which are often very short, and the complicated bureaucracy in obtaining a residence permit (Sánchez Alonso 2011).

One group of EU citizens numerous in Spain are Romanian citizens. Romanians have entered Spain in increasing numbers since the early 1990s and migrated mainly for work, primarily in the construction and domestic service sectors. Spain removed the visa requirement for Romanians in 2002 and agreed on workforce recruitment with Romania, which caused a steep rise in the number of Romanian migrants, culminating in the Romanian accession in the EU in 2007 (Marcu 2014: 138–40, Stângaciu 2016: 71). After the free entry of Romanians to the Spanish labour market in 2009, Romanians constituted the largest group of foreigners in Spain. As discussed elsewhere in this book, this resulted in the extraordinary decision by the Commission to allow Spain to again restrict the entry of Romanian workers.

As we have observed in this book, the Spanish immigration policies have been rather lax when compared to the other countries, reflecting a solidarity approach towards immigrants and emigrants. The similarities of the discourses of Italian and Spanish leaders can to some extent be accounted for by the similar migration histories of the country; little focus on immigrants and large shares of paperless workers, who were later regularized. However, in contrast to Italy and many other countries, Spain has not witnessed a large-scale anti-immigration movement in its national politics.

8.6 History of Romanian migration policy: Curtailing emigration

Romania did not attract many migrants before the prospect of joining the European Union. Indeed, during the communist period, migration was mainly internal from urban to rural areas and vice versa. In addition, emigration was significant already in the communist Romania, as approximately 230,000 people of German ethnicity and 200,000 Jews left Romania for Germany and Israel (Abraham 2015: 295). During the Communist era, it was neither easy to leave Romania temporarily. Romanians needed an exit visa, which was difficult to obtain, but it was possible to get one to travel to the West during the 1960s–70s (Boia 2001: 126).

After the fall of the Iron Curtain, many German, Hungarian and Jewish minorities as well as Romanians left for Hungary, Germany, Italy, Turkey and France. Towards the late 1990s, more Romanian citizens started leaving Romania, and among the popular destination countries were also Spain, the United States and Canada. After the 2002 visa waiver agreement with the EU, Italy became the most popular destination country before Spain and Israel (Abraham 2015: 295–8), remaining the main target for Romanians until today.

Roman and Voicu have categorized the post-Cold War migration history of Romania in five different phases (Roman and Voicu 2010). The first phase was from 1990 to 1993, when especially German and Hungarian minorities left Romania due to political turbulence and poverty. In 1994–6, it was mainly Romanians who moved West for seasonal or informal work. The years between 1996 and 2001 witnessed different types of migration: permanent migration to the United States and Canada, irregular migration to Europe for work, increase in human trafficking and since 1999 a labour force agreement with major European countries such as Germany, Spain, Portugal and Italy as well as immigration of ethnic Romanians from Moldova. The fourth phase, from 2002 to 2007, saw an increase of Romanian migrants to Spain and Italy due to the possibility to stay three months without a visa in the Schengen countries, thus enabling also informal work. The final period began in 2007, when Romania became an EU member state and Romanians could move more freely in the European Union, especially after the end of transitional restrictions (Roman and Voicu 2010: 56). The material included in this book mainly covers the last phase, during which Romanian politicians also became concerned about the brain drain to Western Europe.

Romania is a peculiar country in the sense that the numbers of permanent migrants abroad are relatively small, arguably less than 100,000, but the temporary migrants rise up to several millions, most of them in Spain and Italy (Heller 2013: 256–7). However, why have the Romanians migrated and why Italy and Spain are the most popular target countries of Romanian migrants? Joaquín Arango has argued that the political dimension primarily impacts migration flows: 'nothing shapes migratory flows and types more than admission policies' (Arango 2000b: 293). Even though admission policies may not explain why many Romanians leave Romania in the first place, they seem to have a large role in explaining where they head. As discussed earlier in this chapter, Italy and Spain are recent immigration countries and have traditionally been relatively permissive towards migration and naturalization policies, even regularizing irregular migrants from time to time. Matichescu et al. have found out that while the wage gap is the main reason to move to Western European countries, Romanians do not choose the countries with the highest wages but the countries with the most permissive migration policies, even towards irregular migration (Matichescu et al. 2015). Pânzaru and Reisz also paid attention to the cultural and linguistic factors in addition to legislative factors, which they argue play a significant role in the decision of many Romanians to head to Italy and Spain (Pânzaru and Reisz 2013: 105–6). Be that as it may, Romania clearly appears as a country of emigration in contrast to the other analysed countries.

That said, some significant groups of migrants into Romania should be mentioned, as outlined by Heller (2013). First, there are more than 200,000 Moldovan labour migrants, for many of whom Romania is a transit country on their way to Western Europe. Second, Romania has welcomed employees of foreign investors who have shifted parts of their enterprise in Romania partly due to low wages. Third, there are some keepers of small businesses from countries such as China, Turkey and Arabic countries, the number of which reaches several tens of thousands (Heller 2013: 264–5). Even though the numbers are low compared to other countries, immigration to Romania may increase in the coming years as the country becomes more prosperous.

The history of Romania in general and the migration history of the country are obviously very different from the other countries discussed above. During the communist period, it was difficult for Romanians to leave the country for either work or pleasure. Subsequently, after 1989 the country has seen an increasing emigration flow, currently ca. 2.7 million Romanians, close to 15 per cent of the population, officially residing in other EU countries (Eurostat 2019). As I have argued elsewhere in the book, the massive emigration of nationals seems to constitute a negative phenomenon not only for the national labour market but also for the national self-image. Although the Romanian state benefits from the huge remittances received from the emigrants, the outflow of especially highly qualified individuals appears something that all national leaders must lament. Migration, however, does not seem to constitute a very politicized issue in Romania, where the political debates mainly deal with emigration.

After this short historical overview, the following chapter presents national discourses country by country. The historical trajectories, as we observe, are still visible in today's political discourses in these countries.

9

Free movement discourses by country

The focus of the discourse analysis was on the four practical reasoning dimensions from an all-European perspective, but the policies and political views of the individual countries play a significant role in the analysis; it is important to look at that level in more detail, and not only qualitatively. Henceforth, the discussion turns into the macro-level of discourses; the individual *topoi*, instruments utilized in categorizing the utterances, receive little attention. As visible in Table 9.1, agreement and utility utterances were by far the most commonly utilized ones. Community utterances were equally common or slightly more common than solidarity utterances across the research material. Of course, attitudinal variation within the four categories is considerable, but it nonetheless provides an impression of the general patterns.

9.1 German emphasis on free movement as a commonly agreed beneficial principle

The German governments operated with(in) relatively coherent patterns of discourse during the selected period, emphasizing the economic consequences of free movement and common rules; almost half of the German utterances were agreement-based, and almost the other half utility-based. Only one leader, Chancellor Merkel, dominated the discourses, while the majority of her utterances belonged to the utility group (see the speaker-specific tables in the Appendix; in these tables, all the utterances have been classified by politician and type of reasoning). In addition, agreement-based utterances were common as all the analysed German politicians referred to those. As the CDU was in power for most of the analysed period, it is difficult to find any party-political differences in the discourses. During the early years of the analysed period – the mid-2000s – free movement was much less discussed than towards the end of the period, twelve years later.

Another noteworthy feature in the German discourses when compared to the other countries is that the so-called migration crisis or security concerns were *not* often articulated in terms of free movement. In practice, this meant that the German discussion primarily dealt with the free movement of workers and free movement was mainly discussed in terms of a desirable labour force. With their agreement-related free movement utterances, German politicians emphasized that EU rules must be

Table 9.1 Free movement utterances by country

	Agreement	Community	Utility	Solidarity	Total
Germany	27	3	24	3	59
France	28	13	14	4	59
Italy	24	9	5	4	42
UK	20	4	26	4	54
Spain	14	6	18	2	40
Romania	25	10	14	4	53
Commission	32	6	31	3	72
Total	**170**	**51**	**132**	**24**	**379**

followed although they can also be changed in a shared political process; they cannot be sacrosanct. Overall, the German politicians were seldom concerned about aspects of sovereignty with respect to free movement, which were salient topics first and foremost, in the British discourses.

Germany's internal situation also appears important in this regard; people have the right to move freely between the German *Länder*, but in cases of people burdening the local community, this right can thus be suspended (Maas 2013: 15). Article 11 of the German Basic Law states:

(1) All Germans shall have the right to move freely throughout the federal territory.

(2) This right may be restricted only by or pursuant to a law, and only in cases in which the absence of adequate means of support would result in a particular burden for the community, or in which such restriction is necessary to avert an imminent danger to the existence or the free democratic basic order of the Federation or of a Land, to combat the danger of an epidemic, to respond to a grave accident or natural disaster, to protect young persons from serious neglect, or to prevent crime. (Federal Law Gazette I: 1478, translated by Christian Tomuschat and David P. Currie)[1]

Moreover, free movement is also restricted for those people who have been granted a *Duldung*, a temporary suspension of deportation (Castañeda 2010: 245–61). The intra-German movement regulation thus resembles the situation of the right to free movement in the European Union, where becoming a burden on the host society and the absence of legal residence can be utilized to justify the restriction of mobility. The restrictions of free movement within the EU were discussed in terms of limited social security for EU citizens, perhaps because the existence of such restrictions is taken for granted in the country's own legal context.[2]

The utilitarian attitude to labour migration reflects the fact that the country has been a popular target for labour *Einwanderung* since the 1990s, particularly from Eastern Europe. German immigration history provides a possible explanation for this attitude. For decades, the German policy of immigration was characterized by the so-called

Gastarbeiter policy: immigrants, mostly Turkish workers, were assumed to return to their home countries at some point (see also Section 8.1). No real integration measures were therefore required (Ellermann 2015: 1235–53). The foundations of this policy were questioned towards the end of the twentieth century, but German politicians only came to acknowledge that Germany is a normal country of immigration in the beginning of the twenty-first century (Klekowski von Koppenfels and Höhne 2017).

In the material analysed here, German politicians made no explicit calls for a common European immigration policy regarding free movement issues – unlike in several other countries, particularly Spain. This may reflect the fact that free movement has been highly beneficial for Germany; no such security or economic problems regarding third-country nationals that would require a common European solution had emerged during that time.[3] Secondary literature also mentions some reasons for the German opposition to a common immigration policy. One important argument has been the fear that the German *Länder* could lose their capacity to control their area and have to carry the growing financial burdens of immigration. Moreover, the political elites have been afraid that the Europeanization of immigration policies might lead to a less restrictive approach (Prümm and Alscher 2007). After the 2015 migration crisis, however, German Foreign Minister Steinmeier, together with his French counterpart, promoted the idea of a common immigration policy in Europe (Steinmeier and Ayrault 2016).[4]

The focal point in the German agreement discourses on free movement consisted of demands that the common rules would be followed. In addition, free movement was seen as a principle that should be guaranteed by the EU, which the Union should ensure that nobody can abuse. The German discourses, in this respect, reflected the understanding of justice in terms of constitutional patriotism: under similar conditions, the same jointly negotiated rules apply to each and every one; free movement is an unquestionable right (cf. Pettit 1997).

Overall, German free movement discourses appeared rational and somewhat emotionally detached – solidarity and community utterances were the least utilized out of all countries. The most important issue for politicians seemed to be compliance with rules and maximizing the economic benefits from labour migration, an issue that clearly separates the German utterances from those made in the other analysed countries. The emphasis on rules became particularly evident during the pre-Brexit period, when German politicians reiterated the need to maintain free movement but enable restrictions on social security. Similarities to the historical migration approach can be found: Mobility rules are intended to maximize the supply of labour, but they need to be reconsidered if they no longer prove economically beneficial.

9.2 French focus on free movement rules

Similarly to the German ones, the French utterances placed significant emphasis on rules – both existing regulations and those that should be drafted – in order to tackle the abuse of free movement. However, the French politicians did not highlight that much the utility dimensions of free movement. What also makes France different from

Germany is the relative lack of political continuity, which is likely connected to the presidential nature of the political system. In the presidential system of France, the incumbent President's party-political affiliation is a major factor regarding political preferences, and the terms in office of the analysed politicians were generally short there (see the speaker-specific table in the Appendix). Nicolas Sarkozy (president 2007–12, interior minister 2002–7) is the only figure who spoke about free movement over a longer period of time – for seven years in two different positions – while the terms of the other politicians included here never surpassed three years.

The French emphasis on compliance with jointly agreed rules without a utilitarian emphasis is a possible reflection of the country's alleged (or imagined) republican tradition, that is, the state's raison d´être should be constructed upon the idea based on people's equal rights under the law (Parker and Catalán 2014: 379–95). The republican idea also guarantees fundamental constitutional rights for all individuals, while rejecting most group-specific or special rights (e.g. Walzer 1997: 37).[5] The constitutional *laïcité* of the French society can also be seen as an explanatory factor: *laïcité* is indeed a strong agreement that people are generally willing to adhere to. As discussed in Section 8.2, the ideas of similar rights, republicanism and *laïcité* have underpinned the French approach towards migration for decades, but these noble principles have not prevented, for example, the repatriation of Eastern European immigrants.

In the French free movement utterances, much attention was paid to migrants from outside Europe and to the relation that this migration had to free movement policies.[6] The discussants repeatedly emphasized the *problems* related to these migrants and some expressed a wish to find the solutions through a common European immigration policy. The French also brought up the problems stemming from the immigration policies of the other EU states. Representatives of both UMP and Socialist parties exploited these perceived problems to promote the drafting of a European immigration policy (see also Section 5.2). Throughout the years, France has indeed been concerned about security threats related to the Schengen Area. In 1995, France already refused to drop all the passport controls when the Schengen agreement came into operation, by appealing to potential threats concerning terrorism and drugs (Geddes 2000: 83).

Despite certain similarities, the French free movement discourses bring to light differences between political parties – or at least between their leading figures, the presidents. Mr Sarkozy presented himself as a firm supporter of free movement, but claimed, for example, that the Roma tended to abuse the right. The interior ministers during his presidency also explicitly discussed the problems of free movement, mainly connecting these to the mobility of the Roma. The general tone was not very different from the socialist interior ministers in this respect; they too focused on the view that free movement created threats to collective order. However, President Hollande (2012–17) discussed free movement as a question of European Treaties and thus ignored public order aspects in his utterances.

Both presidents supported the creation of a common immigration policy, but with slightly different tones. For President Sarkozy, promoting a common immigration policy was an instrumental undertaking; free movement was the main justification in his demands for a common immigration policy. A common immigration policy was one of the major projects of the UMP president, culminating in his initiative for the European Pact on Immigration and Asylum that was adopted during his presidential term in 2008. The Pact has indeed been considered an attempt to upload French policies at the European level (Parker and Toke 2013: 376) and to create a less open Europe. The Socialist leadership, in turn, only began to discuss a common European immigration policy after the migration crisis (Steinmeier and Ayrault 2016), and it was in August 2015 that the issue came up in Hollande's utterances analysed in this book. Whereas Sarkozy wanted a common immigration policy due to Southern member states allegedly mismanaging their borders, Hollande was more concerned over the equal responsibility for asylum-seekers.

There was also party-political variation in the few sentiment-based utterances. In his numerous community utterances, President Hollande presented free movement as an issue the European Union was based on, whereas President Sarkozy expressed a concern about countries failing to control their borders properly. The few solidarity utterances focused both on free movement's role in building deeper Europeanness and on negative transactionalism. President Chirac (2002–7) cited free movement twice as an instrument in European unification – put forward by certain pioneer states, and President Hollande praised physical infrastructure that facilitates people's movement and thus strengthens the European spirit. President Sarkozy, in turn, suggested that EU member states should not make immigration decisions without consulting others because the uncontrolled exercise of free movement could threaten European solidarity.

As discussed in Section 8.2, the polarized politicization of migration since the 1980s may also explain some of the stances: whereas the Socialist Party has wanted to break loose from the *Front Nationale*, Sarkozy's party perhaps wanted to attract the voters of *Front Nationale* with the utterances placing guilt for the number of irregular migrants on other EU member states. The Socialist politicians, in turn, have presented themselves as more pro-migration.

Unlike in Germany, the sovereignty related to migration seemed to be present in the French utterances. Although the rights related to free movement did not seem to constitute an issue for the French politicians, the ability to control one's borders appeared more important. This was reflected in the French decision not to open border controls in 1995 when the Schengen Agreement entered into force, citing security threats related to, for example, bomb attacks in Paris in 1995 (Siebold 2013: 132). It took another year for France to open its borders and France has also been eager to re-establish temporary border controls in connection with special events or after terrorist attacks, such as the ongoing border controls implemented after the November 2015 terrorist attacks. It seemed that UMP politicians were more inclined to connect free movement to border controls. Socialist politicians, in turn, predominantly discussed free movement from the perspective of the right to free movement, which explains few references to the so-called migration crisis in the material.

9.3 Italian discussion on the free movement of specific groups

In the Italian discourses, one may discern at least two specific periods: the Roma debate, beginning from Romania's EU accession in 2007, and the shift towards third-country migration after the 2011 Arab Spring. Quantitatively speaking, the Italian discourses differ from the other discourses in the sense that an absolute majority of the utterances were agreement-based. This owed, above all, to the utterances of the Interior Minister Roberto Maroni, representing the anti-immigration Northern League party (see speaker-specific table in the Appendix). Another significant difference when compared to the other countries was that the number of utility utterances was smaller than that of community ones (emphasizing the duty to guarantee free movement for future generations). This suggests that the Italian approach to free movement was value- rather than instrumental-based. The Italian value-based approach may be partly explained by the short history of immigration in the country, as it was only in the 1980s that the country started drafting immigration legislation (see Section 8.3). Hence, Italy does not have a similar history of labour immigration and related instrumental discourses on foreign people as other countries.

In the Italian material, in addition to Silvio Berlusconi's agreement utterances, only ministers of the interior relied on agreement utterances in the discussion of free movement issues, which may be related to the fact that the agreement dimension was mostly employed with respect to the public order aspects of free movement. However, the lack of such utterances in the discourses of other prime ministers is surprising. The only centre-left politician making use of an agreement type of articulation was Interior Minister Giuliano Amato (2006–8), who expressed worry about potential criminal behaviour among Romanian citizens.

Until 2011, before the number of African migrants arriving across the sea began to accelerate rapidly, the focus of the Italian free movement utterances was mainly on immigration from Romania. A Romanian Roma brutally killed an Italian woman in 2007, which further deteriorated the image of both the Roma and Romanians, often conflated in public debate (Cetin 2015: 384). In 2008, voters elected Silvio Berlusconi to lead a centre-right government, which then initiated several new legislative measures targeting the Roma in particular. More specifically, the cabinet's minister Maroni introduced the so-called 'Security Package' (*Pacchetto Sicurezza*), of which all aspects came into force by 2009. The 'Security Package' continued the line of the Bossi-Fini Act of 2002, which had restricted the arrival of third-country migrants and enabled the expulsion of people without the right to residence. The Maroni Act also stipulated that clandestine immigration is a crime; this was only decriminalized in spring 2014. In addition to referring to the Roma, this Berlusconi government (2008–11) presented illegal residence as a significant problem and, in conjunction with this, regularly spoke about security concerns and risks. The politicians were part of what Marzio Barbagli called a moral panic, in which the politicians, media and the population at large became concerned over the criminality of Romanians, without there being a rise in the number of criminality conducted by Romanians in Italy (Barbagli 2008: 154–6).

Despite the period of Romanian prominence in the Italian discourses, it should be noted that the Italian approach towards Romanian migrants has not always been security-related. In fact, according to one study, Romanian migrants were discussed as victims in the 1990s rather than criminals in Italian political debate (McMahon 2015: 79). A comparable, albeit dissimilar in nature, transformation may have occurred after Berlusconi's government left power, when Romanians no longer seemed to be the focus of the discourse on free movement. This points to the notion that dominant discursive perspectives can indeed change significantly over time.

After Mr Berlusconi's government, the discursive focus did indeed shift from Romanian citizens towards migration from third countries. The debate on extra-European immigration was reinforced, especially after the 2013 Lampedusa boat accident, where the surviving migrants had to be accused formally and publicly of the crime of illegal immigration because the Maroni Act was still in force. As we observed in the utterances, regarding the immigrants arriving across the sea, Italy also called for solidarity from the other member states to assist the country.

Utility-based discourse in Italy was almost non-existent, which is surprising when compared to the other countries. However, there were a few cost–benefit utterances made with regard to immigration.[7] Minister Maroni demanded a common immigration policy in the EU, as he considered it useful for tackling illegal migration and mass movements to Italy.[8] He was the only Italian politician who directly suggested the establishment of a common European immigration policy, while in the French and Spanish cases, as we learned, several politicians had explicitly from different parties expressed their support for such a policy. Taking into account the similar migration histories of Spain and Italy, it can be considered surprising that only one of the countries is completely in favour of a common migration policy. One explanation could be the politicization of migration in Italy, as we saw in Section 8.3, which may make politicians avoid migration-related topics that cause controversy.

An Italian peculiarity is that the debate on free movement and migration in general seems to be mainly in the hands of the minister of the interior, which obviously makes the debate more security-related. Unlike his colleagues in other countries, Italian Prime Minister Renzi (2014–16) barely had any utterances defending the right to free movement or the Schengen Area in the analysed material. It seems that he let the minister of the interior do the commenting on the topic.

9.4 The UK concerned about the control of free movement

The British discourses focused on the need to publicly control free movement. The UK clearly appeared as the most Eurosceptic country in this book; therefore, Brexit was not that great a surprise in light of its (pro-EU) leaders' attitudes towards free movement. Although a similar fear was shared across the political spectrum, there was a clear difference between the Conservative and Labour politicians; the latter were usually more positive towards free movement though mainly utilizing similar utterance types (see also the speaker-specific table in the Appendix). For example, in 2004, Labour-led Britain, together with Ireland and Sweden, placed no transitional restrictions on the countries that joined the Union (requiring only that new arrivals had to register for the Worker Registration Scheme). However, the same Labour-led government decided that workers from Bulgaria and Romania, which joined the EU in 2007, were to be subject to restrictions until 2014.[9] After the Conservatives came to power in 2010 (in a coalition with the Liberal Democrats), the approach gradually became stricter towards free movement. Regardless of the increasingly restrictive views, the general patterns of reasoning did not significantly differ from other countries: the dominant types of utterances were utility- and agreement-related, while sentiment-based utterances played only a marginal role.

Already in the 1990s, it was evident that the UK politicians wanted to retain their immigration control in the EU and they decided not to participate in the Schengen Agreement and to maintain the UK's independent decision-making power regarding border issues (see Ette and Gerdes 2007: 93–115).[10] The politicians observed in this study made significant efforts to convince people that the UK could control migration; indeed, the UK was the only analysed country in which European cooperation was perceived as a threat to the British independence and *sovereignty* (cf. Lunn 1996: 84). This attitude may be, at least to an extent, historically determined. It springs from, in the words of P. W. Preston, 'a failure to understand that the British Empire and the cultural baggage of that apparatus is long gone and that the polity is deeply enmeshed in wider political and economic networks' (Preston 2014: 217).[11] The fear of losing sovereignty seemed truly pertinent in free movement debates. Overall, it appears that the European free movement regime was presented as a threat to the British society in many different manners, ranging from the threat of terrorism to threats to the welfare state (see also Robertson 1989: 314–39). This fear of uncontrolled flow of people seems to have characterized British migration policy in the history, even though the public attitudes have varied (see also Section 8.4). Free movement seemed to also constitute the major reason for people to vote for Brexit, at least in the words of David Cameron (2016a). However, there was also the Left-wing anti-EU constituency, or lexit, which was not visible in the discourses analysed in this book (Guinan and Hanna 2017).

The frequency of free movement utterances in Britain changed considerably over time. Before the 2010s, free movement was not widely discussed (at least according to the study's material);[12] however, it soon became politicized when the politicians that presented arguments about free movement the most, including Prime Minister David Cameron and Home Secretary Theresa May, assumed power (2010–16). Especially striking is the difference in the number of utterances between Home Secretary May and her predecessors, who did not pay much attention to free movement. Although May was not in the Brexit camp, her views may have inadvertently supported it.

Many of the utterances related to the question of whether it is fair and economically viable for EU citizens to claim benefits in Britain. Several British politicians explicitly condemned such action. Labour politicians, when they headed the government, also argued that the situation was fair in that EU movers contributed more taxes than they consumed in their use of UK social services. Prime Minister David Cameron was particularly vocal about his willingness to limit free movement, or at least the social benefits of EU citizens. He was willing to do so despite the fact that the economic effect of EU mobility has been positive for the UK, as evidenced in a number of economic studies: EU immigrants' employment rate is higher, they pay more taxes and take up fewer benefits than UK nationals (Springford 2013, Dustmann and Frattini 2014: F593–F643). The British utilitarian utterances were not only focused on the actual material costs and benefits, but a few politicians also implied that EU movers unfairly claimed benefits that they should not be entitled to.[13]

Although the sentiment-based dimensions were less visible in the material, there was a marked difference between Labour and Conservative approaches towards the idea of a European community. Whereas Labour Prime Minister Gordon Brown (2007–10) acknowledged a sense of duty towards the other EU member states, Conservative PM Cameron's community utterances can be characterized as aimed at ensuring that the UK obtains what it needs from the other EU states. In the solidarity utterances, negative transactionalism was particularly apparent: David Cameron simply argued that current free movement policies threatened solidarity among Europeans. It should be noted, however, that such concern implies that European solidarity exists and should be preserved. Overall, the negative attitudes towards free movement expressed by Prime Minister Cameron and Home Secretary May clearly stood out from the selected material. They were, however, both on the 'Bremain' side of the Brexit referendum. If the pro-EU politicians are that critical, it seems even less surprising that the Brits eventually voted to leave the Union.

9.5 Spain connects free movement to European integration

Of all the analysed countries, Spanish politicians seemed to have the most positive approach towards free movement as a European ideal across the party-political spectrum. Both the conservatives and socialists argued that a common immigration policy would be a necessary complement to free movement (see also speaker-specific table in the Appendix). Spain is also the only country analysed in this book that did not implement any conditions related to 'sufficient economic resources' for EU citizens, while transposing the Free Movement Directive. This means that those staying for more than three months in Spain do not have to prove that they do not constitute a burden on the national social security system (Parker and Catalán 2014: 385–6). Spain has also, for example, more liberal family reunification rules than most of the other member states (Staver 2013: 80).[14] This welcoming approach may relate to the country's history outlined in Section 8.5; it joined the European Community in 1986, and Spanish workers were themselves initially subject to transitional restrictions in the other EC countries for seven years (see also Viñas 2000: 77, Kochenov 2008: 48). Spain has witnessed significant emigration to other European Union countries since it joined the Union in the 1980s, which may also have an effect on its fairly positive approach towards migration (Johns 2013: 95).[15] As discussed in the previous chapter, the first migration legislation in Spain was only stipulated in 1985 and it was around the late 1980s that the net migration in Spain became positive. These similar migration traditions of Spain and Italy may also explain their fairly similar approaches to free movement, though the issue seems more politicized in Italy.

Despite its relatively open approach to migration, Spain established transitional restrictions for workers from all the countries that joined the Union in the twenty-first century. The restrictions against Bulgarian and Romanian workers were removed in 2009, but by appealing to a safeguard clause concerning labour market disturbances, the Commission gave Spain a permission to re-establish restrictions for Romanian workers during Prime Minister Zapatero's term.[16] When Spain appealed to serious disturbances in its labour market in order to re-establish transitional restrictions for Romanian workers in 2011, the concerns were mainly due to the economic crisis, which also more than doubled the unemployment rate of Romanian nationals (McMahon 2015: 60).

Free movement has not created significant political cleavages between the major parties or between Spain and the other member countries. Only the 2005 regularization amnesty of Spain, granting, inter alia, residence permits to more than half of the irregular Romanians resident in Spain – not EU citizens at the time – was not positively viewed in all member states (McMahon 2015: 58). In total, Spain regularized almost 800,000 migrants in 2005, which German and French politicians, in particular, criticized after Spain simultaneously asked for help in controlling its borders (Zapata-Barrero and Witte 2007: 89–90). This regularization amnesty was only continuation for the immigration policies relying on regularization since the 1980s (see Section 8.5). In a similar manner to their Italian colleagues, Spanish politicians insisted on national discretion in order that the implementation of EU rules would be carried out in the best possible way. Spain hosted a considerable number of undocumented migrants from outside the EU, the regularization of whom then affected the relations with the country's European partners.[17] Some of these regularized migrants were soon-to-be EU citizens, as many Romanians were also provided with residence permits (indeed, the accession of Romania and Bulgaria into the EU drastically diminished the irregularity of immigrants in Spain (González-Enríquez 2009: 152)). Spanish leaders appeared to have taken a very diplomatic approach to free movement issues; however, the regularization of irregular immigrants aroused critical utterances in the context of free movement discourse. Although the Spanish decision may be justified from the moral equality perspective, many of her European partners held a different opinion; they claimed that such amnesties only provided an incentive for illegal migration. However, despite some critical comments, no actions were taken by the other EU states against Spain during the most heated debate in 2005. Only in the European Pact on Immigration and Asylum in 2008 did member states commit themselves to not conducting massive regularizations of irregular migrants (see also Vogt 2009). Spain further announced that it would not employ more regularization programmes in the future (Finotelli and Arango 2011: 495–515). Perhaps due to the sensitivity of the matter, the material analysed in this study did not include utterances on the regularization amnesties made by Spanish or German politicians, although a few comments were made in the media (e.g. Le Monde 2005).

Overall, the Spanish approach can be described as diplomatic. The politicians did not express particularly ardent opinions regarding free movement, necessary reforms of policies or the mobility of certain groups of people. Furthermore, the approach of the Spanish state towards a generally controversial group, Romanian migrants, has been found to be more positive than that of Italy, another common destination for Romanian migrants (McMahon 2015). Many of these Romanians who move to Spain belong to the Roma minority, and it has been argued that they receive better treatment in Spain than in other European countries as Spain has also had successful Roma integration programmes (Dietz 2003, Gehring 2013b: 149). The utterances of Spanish politicians analysed in the book did not criticize the free movement of the Roma or Romanians, but stated that the EU rules apply equally to their free movement.

It also became clear in the utterances that Spain was willing to pass more power to the European Union in immigration matters (see also Geddes 2000: 89, 117). A common immigration policy was seen as a guarantor that the principle of free movement remained beneficial or at least eased the negative consequences related to it. Although Prime Minister Zapatero and Prime Minister Rajoy represented opposite political ideas, they both supported the principle of free movement and common immigration policy with similar kinds of utterances. Indeed, differences between competing political parties were far more visible in other countries. This could also be interpreted as an illustration of the firm, positive approach to free movement in Spain; a common immigration policy was an idea supported for the sake of the country's interest.

Further, in agreement terms, the Spanish approach towards free movement appeared reliant on the EU and the country's leaders demanded that the Commission decide whether national measures undertaken by the EU member states were in accordance with EU law and that EU legislation would be fully realized. Prime Minister Zapatero, in particular, was committed to the EU as the highest judge for determining which actions were right. His successor, Conservative Prime Minister Rajoy, did not question free movement either, but discussed it more often in the context of the other three fundamental freedoms.

Although sentiment-based utterances were not common, the strong reliance on the EU stood out in the Spanish discourses, in particular before the Brexit referendum when Prime Minister Rajoy emphasized the duty to uphold free movement. All in all, the majority of the utterances focused on a common European immigration policy that utilized free movement as an instrument with which to argue its necessity.

9.6 Romania focuses on the need to receive equal rights

The Romanian discourses insisted that Romanian citizens receive equal rights to free movement, which seems to have been one of the major incentives for Romania to become an EU member in the first place. The Romanian politicians thus urged the other EU member states to respect the European Union Treaties. Citizenship-level discrimination was seen as inappropriate and Romanian leaders maintained that the citizens of all the member states should have the treaty-based right to free movement. This insistence was related to the end of the transitional restrictions on Romanian workers – until the abolition of these restrictions in all countries in 2014. After this, the need to belong to the Schengen Area has dominated the agenda. Even in 2020, it seems unlikely that member states will unanimously accept Romania into the area, despite the fact that already in his 2017 State of the Union Speech Commission President Jean-Claude Juncker argued that this should occur *immediately* (Juncker 2017).

Reflecting the rights-based discourses emphasizing the equal right to free movement of all EU citizens, Romanian utterances were particularly reliant on value-based agreement duties (see also the speaker-specific table in the Appendix). It is noteworthy that value-based community utterances were much more significant than in other countries. Community utterances were often specifically related to the need to guarantee free movement for Moldovans as well. The overall prevalence of value-based utterances implies that free movement was seen as a fundamental right rather than as an explicit instrument for achieving material benefits.[18] Other scholars have also come to a similar conclusion. For example, in the case of the French expulsions in 2010, researchers found that Romanian press coverage focused primarily on free movement as an integral part of European integration (Balch, Balabanova and Trandafoiu 2014).

A couple of specific characteristics of the Romanian context should be mentioned. First, among European Union member states, Romania has possibly the most pro-European population. In a Eurobarometer 2018 survey, Romanians had the most 'positive image of the EU', with 60 per cent deeming it positive.[19] Second, a characteristic feature of Romanian migration patterns, also visible in the analysed discourses, is the significant number of Romanians residing in other EU member states. Italy hosts the largest number of Romanian citizens, and until 2015, Romanians also represented the most numerous foreign citizens in Italian prisons. However, one has to keep in mind that more than one million Romanians officially reside in Italy (Bird et al. 2016).

Romanian utterances thus differ from those in the other countries and Romanian politicians have primarily approached the issue from an emigration perspective. This is not surprising if we look at the migration history of Romania; the country has mainly attracted ethnic Romanians from Moldova, while migration policies have aimed at limiting the number of people leaving Romania (see Section 8.6).

The mobile Romanians included both 'qualified' and 'poor' migrants, as the Romanian politicians referred to them.[20] With respect to the former, the politicians seemed to fear that qualified Romanians would leave for other EU countries. Although Romanian leaders reiterated the need to encourage educated people to stay in Romania, people leaving Romania may also benefit the state (e.g. through remittances, less burden on social welfare). This may be particularly true if there is no shortage of labour force in the state-funded institutions in Romania. Romanian utterances, however, seemed to imply that free movement could be more beneficial for Romania if a smaller number of qualified Romanians left the country.

On the other hand, Romanian politicians sought to downplay the movement of 'poor migrants', a euphemism for the Roma, which politicians in other countries often associate with Eastern European migrants. In the UK, for example, a study found that Eastern European migrants sometimes suffer from the negative 'othering' associated with the Roma, 'surrounding perceived economic worth and contribution' (Tonkiss 2013a: 151). A particular issue in this respect was, as the Romanian politicians repeatedly indicated with references to injustice, that Roma problems allegedly blocked

Romanian accession to the Schengen Area. While the Romanian 'brain drain' indeed appeared to be a national problem, Roma integration was viewed as something that the EU should solve.

As discussed in Section 8.6, political debates mainly concern the emigration of Romanians and migration does not constitute a very politicized issue in Romania. There is no large anti-immigrant movement in Romania, but free movement is approached positively across the political spectrum and in the society at large. This is also visible in the discourses that emphasize the equal right to free movement and how beneficial the principle is for the individuals who move and for the receiving society.

Overall, Romanian leaders mainly approached free movement from the Romanian perspective of participating in European integration rather than from an all-European perspective. The politicians hardly ever referred to free movement as a community-type European duty but focused more on the mobility of ethnic Romanians in Moldova and those residing in the other EU states. With regard to the solidary results of free movement, however, they did refer to free movement as a way to increase the general sense of Europeanness across the continent.

9.7 European Commission emphasizes EU Treaties

The most apparent issue in the Commission's free movement discourses was the unequivocal support for free movement, reflected through an emphasis on free movement rules and economic benefits. By and large, the pattern of utterances of the European commissioners was similar to that of the national discourses: the reason-based agreement and utility utterances were almost equally common and the most often employed. One diverging issue from the selected countries was the fact that the commissioners less often created a linkage between free movement and threats. This is, of course, unsurprising; the Commission is bound to present European principles in a positive light. The commissioners did raise a few threat-related concerns, focused on the control of the external borders.[21] Free movement as a contractual duty with beneficial consequences characterized their dominant depiction of the principle. From the sentiment-based perspective, the commissioners praised the role of free movement both as a historical duty and as a mechanism for deepening the sense of Europeanness.

A recent study has similarly noted that the Commission seemed to mainly present free movement as an individual right (Roos and Westerveen 2019: 7), reflecting, in their view, a liberal cosmopolitan approach. The researchers, however, argued that the discourse became more conditional in the 2010s, emphasizing, for example, security-related and economic arguments for restricting free movement. This book did not specifically examine the conditionality of the discourses, but it is true that certain commissioners did consider economic and security-related arguments valid for some restrictions. We need to recall that also the EU law allows restrictions to individuals' free movement when public security so requires or when EU citizens constitute a burden for the social security system of the host country. The debates on restrictions to free movement became more vivid in the member states after the end of the transitional restrictions of the citizens from the new member states in 2011, and the Commission obviously had to react to the national concerns.

The commissioner who discussed free movement most often was José Manuel Barroso. Barroso was the Commission president for almost the entire period of analysis, from November 2004 to November 2014 (see also speaker-specific table in the Appendix). The analysis revealed that the commissioners in Barroso's later Commission discussed free movement much more often than those in the first one did. This also reflects the number of controversial issues during the latter period, including French measures against Roma mobility as well as the British insistence on restricting the free movement and social security of EU movers. It is also noteworthy that the utterances of the last twenty months of the analysed period – one-seventh of the total duration – accounted for almost a quarter of all utterances. This is mainly due to the migration crisis and the upcoming Brexit referendum, which the commissioners needed to address.

After Mr Barroso, the commissioners that referred to free movement most regularly included Employment Commissioner Špidla (2004–10) and Migration Commissioner Dimitris Avramopoulos (2014–19), which implies that free movement appeared as a workers' right in the eyes of the Commission before the 2010s and was more contrasted to the migration from third countries since 2015. Right behind them came the utterances of Justice Commissioner Reding, in turn, which employed the most outspoken – and controversial – argumentation in her utterances, comparing, for instance, the Roma expulsions in France to the events of the Second World War. The portfolios of these commissioners aptly illustrate the keywords related to free movement in the Commission's discourses: labour, migration and justice.

What is also noteworthy is that the Commission apparently sought to depoliticize free movement by presenting it both as a fundamental right and as an economic benefit rather than as an object of political bargaining. Depoliticization has not only been apparent in free movement issues. In a similar vein, Max Haller has noted that the campaign for the euro was depoliticized and only presented as a venture providing positive consequences for all (Haller 2008: 257–9). Contrary to this, Liesbet Hooghe has found the EU Commission to be culturally and politically diverse and its actions guided by individual backgrounds, identities and values – and this diversity necessarily means political conflicts (e.g. Hooghe 2001). This is *not* the conclusion one can easily draw from the utterances on the right to free movement, as all commissioners who handled the issue showed considerable similarity in their rights-emphasizing approaches towards free movement.

The Commission justified free movement with benefits it brought to the EU countries and their citizens, but the utterances usually focused on the movement of workers instead of all people. The fact that the Commission paid so much attention to economic benefits regarding free movement gives the impression that utilitarian rationales also matter, instead of free movement only constituting a self-evident fundamental right. The same is true for national policies: if the society discusses migrants from the point of view of the economic contribution that they produce or do not produce, they appear as surplus producers or, alternatively, as an economic strain, instead of as fellow human beings.

In the Commission's utterances, national concerns obviously did not play an explicit role. Indeed, the Commission appeared as a promoter of the overall European community; free movement was a crucial historical value of European integration and a fundamental pillar of the EU. The commissioners believed free movement to constitute a duty to be upheld as part of the European community. Sentiment-related utterances were, however, much less common than reason-based ones. This may also reflect the role of the Commission as both responsible for monitoring compliance with free movement and as an actor trying to justify European policies.

9.8 Concluding remarks on the country-specific patterns of discourse

As we have seen above, the number of utterances in each of the four dimensions was roughly similar across the countries – and across the political dividing lines. We have also observed that each country had its specific points of emphasis content-wise, and it was also possible to find some party-related specificities. Right-wing parties proved, in general, more critical towards existing free movement policies than more left-leaning parties.

The two sentiment-related types of reasoning were scarcely used in any of the countries. The French, Italian and Romanian documents, however, included sentiment-related, particularly community-based, attitudes regarding free movement. This may be connected to the finding that in all three countries, agreement utterances were utilized much more often than utility utterances. In the countries, free movement thus appeared more as a value-based issue rather than as an instrumental one. There was no need to articulate its material benefits, but politicians sought to guarantee that the principle itself remained respected. In other countries, the division between value-based and instrumental utterances was more balanced.

An interesting finding of the study was that overall societal development hardly changed the nature of discourses, but whatever changes there were, they could primarily be attributed to party differences. It was, however, clear that towards the end of the analysed period, the references to free movement became more numerous.

A few other aspects of the analysis are worth noting. First, *no* utterance demanded that free movement be abolished in its entirety. Second, it was unsurprising that some politicians often tended to criticize the alleged problems of free movement, but there were also cases when other politicians justified the right against this criticism. In general, the value-based reasoning was predominantly Europe-centred, while the instrumental utterances included more nation-centred views. This was expected in the sense that creating conditions for free movement is ultimately a *European duty* that results in positive and/or negative *consequences to the state*.

In Table 9.2, I have summarized the results in terms of the important dimensions that informed the analysis above, that is, the distinction between 'more nation' and 'more Europe'. In France, Italy and the UK, there was divergence between the discursive strategies across the political spectrum, while in Germany, Romania and Spain, no major domestic differences appeared in the discussion. The table is, of

Table 9.2 Different groups of utterances on free movement

	EU-led policies	Status quo on free movement policy	More power to member states
Fundamental right	Commission	Romania	Italian
	France	Italy: PD	*Forza Italia* & LN
Instrument	Spain	UK Labour	UK
		Germany	Conservative

course, a simplification. However, it nonetheless shows the tendencies that arose from the material. Variations also exist within the different groups (i.e. cells) in the table. For example, the status quo category includes politicians who did not express strong views either for a common immigration policy or for increasing national decision-making power in free movement issues. In the case of the other two categories, politicians called for either more EU-led policies or national discretion.[22]

The trajectories varied, partly due to the internal dividing lines of the countries. In Italy, Prime Minister Berlusconi's governments were the ones that employed the most restrictive rhetoric towards Romanians, whereas the centre-left politicians paid more attention to the movement of third-country nationals. The British discourses also reveal a clear division between the main parties, where the Conservative Party became very critical towards free movement, while Labour politicians were relatively satisfied with the existing free movement policy. The commissioners argued for EU rules and the European-wide material benefits of free movement, while the French politicians focused on EU rules and called for more of them. German discussion emphasized abuse of rules and the material benefits achieved both in the national and European contexts. The Spanish discourses focused on the optimization of free movement benefits through a common immigration policy. Finally, the Romanian discourses were centred on the national context, primarily by promoting the rights of all EU citizens.

In order to sum up the discourses, it is possible to draw a matrix with a tentative generalization on the emphases of different actors. In Figure 9.1, we can observe that the UK politicians focused on the consequences of free movement caused by the 'destitute', that is, people unfairly claiming welfare benefits in the country. French and Spanish politicians also paid attention to the destitute (such as the Roma), but their discourses were more reliant on EU-wide policies. The Italians and Romanians focused on the fates of the destitute in relation to the EU rules. The Commission, in turn, discussed both the destitute and qualified workers, and justified the movement of both groups with value-based and instrumental utterances, respectively.[23] German politicians placed the most emphasis on (also not-so-qualified) workers' movement and used their mobility as an instrumental justification for free movement. All this suggests that workers' movement can be easily justified with instrumental utterances, while the mobility of the destitute is a much more complex question involving issues of various actors' responsibility.

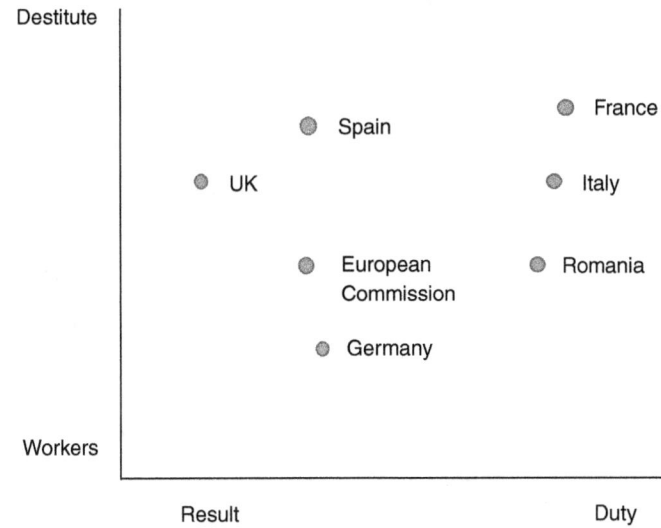

Figure 9.1 Matrix on the discursive emphases.

10

Free movement discourses as practical reasoning

Now, it is time to look at the results from a larger perspective. Although all of the selected countries displayed a range of different discourses, one general – and not too surprising – pattern of reasoning became clear: people who constitute a burden on the host country should leave, while those who potentially provide gains should stay.

10.1 Who should stay and who should go?

Given the findings of the preceding chapters, provided that we can generalize them, there is a crucial question to be asked: In the opinion of European politicians, who should and who should not exercise the right to free movement? There was, as we have seen, much variation in the discourses, but some common tendencies were also apparent.

Even in the case of the superficially equal right to free movement within the EU, we can observe hierarchies regarding the people who move, which makes it important to examine the groups in more detail. In Table 10.1, I present the most wanted and unwanted mobile groups and the types of reasoning that usually backed up the discourses related to these groups. The approaches towards those who leave and those who enter proved relatively different. Therefore, I have divided the table into groups of people who were encouraged/discouraged to leave/from leaving and those encouraged/discouraged to enter/from entering the country. Politicians discussed European mobility as a two-way matter in all of the analysed countries. This not only concerns those who enter but also those who leave; the principle of free movement appears, in a sense, reciprocal. In general, the destitute (such as the Roma or Moldovans) were mainly addressed in a value-based tone, while utilitarian arguments mainly justified (skilled) workers' mobility. Unexpectedly, the free movement of people genuinely contributing to societal development is connected to benefits, while the mobility of the underprivileged is a question of the duty of equal treatment.

One issue that did not come up in the approaches towards different types of mobile people is gender. The politicians discussed migration in very vague terms without paying attention to the gender patterns of free movement or the gender implications of the social benefits. Previous research has shown that the social benefits related to

Table 10.1 Most encouraged and discouraged free movers

Leaving		Entering	
+ High-skilled workers should be able to leave and return (utility)	– High-skilled workers should not leave permanently (utility)	+ Low- and high-skilled workers should come (utility)	– Criminals should not come (agreement)
+ EU youth should have the possibility (community)	– National citizens should not leave permanently (community and solidarity)	+ EU students should come (utility)	– Welfare tourists should not come (utility and agreement)
+ resident refugees should be able to leave (solidarity)	– Welfare tourists should not leave (utility)	+ Unemployed people should come to work (community)	– Irregular migrants should not come (utility)

free movement do have gendered effects (e.g. Shutes and Walker 2018), but this came rarely up even when discussing social security. German Interior Minister de Maizière mentioned the abuse of child benefits in two of his utterances (2015a, 2015b), but referred to EU citizens in general, rather than mothers, as claiming these benefits. It seems that politicians made an effort not to bring up the issue of gender, not even in autumn 2015, when the press was talking about the male-dominated numbers of asylum-seekers. In contrast, many politicians explicitly discussed 'women and men' seeking asylum, perhaps in an effort to counteract the image of male dominance among the asylum-seekers.

Even though gender did not seem to constitute an issue in the free movement discourses, the utterances included several other categorizations, the most common of which are visible in Table 10.1. Gender and ethnic characteristics did not come up as significant categories in the discourses, but education and citizenship seemed to be more neutral issues with which people could be categorized as more and less desirable leavers and comers. As one could expect, criminality and irregular migration were considered negatively.

The most obvious issue in the discourses was that practically all of the analysed leaders supported the free movement of workers, as it was perceived to be economically beneficial for their countries. This is historically understandable: the original aim of the principle of free movement was to encourage labour mobility. However, the politicians utilized different discursive patterns with which they encouraged or discouraged workers' movement, depending on whether they considered labour mobility a win–win or a zero-sum situation. In the former group, the leavers and comers corresponded well; those encouraged to leave were seen as welcome guests in other countries. In an optimal win–win (see e.g. Schäuble 2009) situation, (the movers), the host countries and the countries of origin benefit from the movement, whereas in a zero-sum situation, one's gain is another one's loss, for example, an individual's gain may, in the end, lead to damage to the host country (cf. British discourses, in particular). In the zero-sum vein, the Romanian politicians displayed the most apprehensive positions regarding workers' movement; they were worried about the potential for a brain drain of its high-skilled labour force and thus argued that these valuable workers should not leave in such large numbers, since it is costly for the Romanian state but beneficial for the target country. Overall, the discourses appeared, however, contradictory in the sense that while workers seemed to be most strongly encouraged to utilize their right to movement, recruiting workers from third countries was more or less actively discouraged.

Workers' mobility has also been analysed in scholarly literature. Free movement can, in theory, be seen as a type of employment insurance correcting labour market imbalance in Europe, as a productivity enhancer improving the balance between supply and demand or as an innovation trigger allowing talented people to move freely (Recchi 2015: 43–7). While all these theories are certainly highly relevant, there is some empirical evidence that the corrective function of free movement vis-à-vis the labour market has been weaker than often thought, even during the financial crisis (Recchi and Salamonska 2014). Instead, it has been claimed that the main function of free movement is that of a legitimacy tool that makes people appreciate the European Union (Recchi 2015: 43–7). The discourses scrutinized in this study illustrate how the mobility of workers is believed to justify the current nature of free movement policies and thereby the entire process of integration, in line with the legitimacy thesis. The only documented patterns of reasoning that attached negative sentiments to workers' movement were the aforementioned Romanian fears of brain drain and the British fear of other Europeans taking British people's jobs.

Another positively approached group, albeit a less cited one, were young people. The young were discussed as circular migrants who study or work for some time in another country without incurring excessive costs to that country and potentially contributing to brain gain in the host nation. It should be noted that the group often consisted of university students or highly educated (young) workers. In this context, it did not appear difficult to affirm both leavers and comers, although one needed to utilize different types of reasoning. The possibility to leave appeared as a community-type duty to cultivate the sense of freedom for the younger generation. In contrast, politicians discussed incoming students with some sorts of utilitarian benefits in mind. The question of youth movement seemed the only one in which the possibility of free movement appeared as a self-evident right that should be expanded rather than restricted (see, e.g. Section 5.3). Further, no politicians expressed negative viewpoints with respect to the willingness of young people to learn the habits and customs of other European states.

The question of national citizens leaving and (possibly) returning proved more complicated in the analysed material. There were Romanian and German politicians who openly hoped that those who left would eventually return. The discourses were somewhat contradictory in both cases. In the Romanian utterances, the complete right to free movement had to self-evidently encompass all Romanians, but *the* place to be for them all was eventually in Romania (see Section 5.4). In Germany, politicians considered free movement an essential part of the European unification process but hoped that qualified Germans would one day return; circular migration was seen as optimal (see Section 7.2). In both Germany and Romania, circularity has also more generally been characteristic of the migration systems of these countries. Romanians have left in great numbers since the 1990s but the vast majority of them are temporary migrants (Heller 2013), while the idea of circular migration – in the opposite direction, though – is characteristic of the previous German *Gastarbeiter* policy (Klekowski von Koppenfels and Höhne 2017) and apparently the most desirable situation of current free movement regime.

The attitudes towards third-country nationals in general varied a great deal in the material. Politicians sometimes depicted those who try to (illegally) enter the Union as criminals. There were also less negative approaches towards the movement of third-country nationals: Italian politicians, in particular, wanted to extend the right to free movement to legally residing people who were granted international protection (see Section 7.3), thereby relying on European solidarity in terms of burden-sharing. None of the politicians explicitly welcomed refugees in the material (though Chancellor Merkel made such comments elsewhere in autumn 2015), and providing refugees the right to leave and enter thus proved asymmetrical. Instead of expressing concern for the human security of people fleeing for their lives, many politicians condemned the border-crossers' search for a safe place as illegal. This relates to the overall exclusive attitude towards immigrants from third countries: they have been seen as a burden or a security threat (see also Kmak 2015). This attitude has also occasionally, and in some countries, led to the criminalization of irregular migration. Between 2009 and 2014, as a result of the Security Package, Italy even punished immigrants for the crime of 'illegal entry' (see also di Martino et al. 2013).

In the free movement discourses, the most alienated people were 'criminals', irrespective of their backgrounds, that is, they may have been both third-country nationals and EU citizens. The aim of limiting criminal movement was purposefully used to legitimize border controls, other surveillance measures and police cooperation. Italian politicians sometimes saw Romanians in toto as criminals, but most leaders argued that criminality mainly stemmed from outside the Union; hence, the external borders should have controls that are more effective. It is noteworthy here that in the context of the European free movement discourses up until mid-2016, 'terrorists' did not appear to be a major concern.

There seemed to be a concern that some EU citizens move to another EU country just to claim benefits. Only British and German politicians, however, explicitly addressed the abuse of their national social security by EU citizens (see Sections 4.4 and 6.4). This proved to be, as we know, one of the central points of criticism in the pro-Brexit campaign in the UK. In the analysed material, British politicians justified the ban on 'welfare tourists' mainly through utility and agreement utterances. The UK and Germany have been popular destinations for EU movers; however, there is no evidence that EU mobility has been economically costly for member countries, quite the contrary in fact. Such discourses may also be directed at domestic citizens who voice concern about the large numbers of EU movers. By acknowledging this concern, politicians admit that social security for the sake of the original population is something to be preserved. This further strengthens the patterns of welfare chauvinism (Huysmans 2000a: 751–77), which has been an effective tool for attracting voters in recent elections across the European continent (Kriesi et al. 2012: 19).

Overall, the hierarchies and asymmetries attached to the groups of movers reveal how intricate and multidimensional the question of free movement is. As Delanty, Jones and Wodak (2008: 75) have pointed out, mobility means different issues for different groups. For some, mobility means the accumulation of cultural capital while others come to face discrimination and exclusion. Those who leave a country are often thought to gain in terms of diversified cultural understanding, which they bring with them when they return, while those who enter a county are often seen as potential criminals or welfare tourists. In Western Europe at least, these hierarchies also seem to relate to the differentiation between the old and new member states: people from the new member states are treated more negatively, which may simply reflect the fact that the number of migrants from these countries is larger. Notwithstanding, the restrictions and discrimination that third-country nationals come to encounter are typically greater than what EU citizens experience. The differentiation between these migrant groups persists and it is also discursively encouraged: the label 'immigrant' is no longer attached to mobile EU citizens (see also Hansen 2008).

10.2 European political discourses: A few weak signals

This book has pointed to several crucial issues regarding people's political attitudes towards fellow Europeans and non-Europeans and, by extension, the future of the European Union. The study has provided an analysis of the discourses in the most powerful EU member states and in the European Commission. Looking at the overall picture, the analysis revealed a few weak signals – understood as possible, still primarily underlying, future trends (Holopainen and Toivonen 2012: 199) – concerning European politics, which deserve further attention.

First, there seems to be a strong sense of trust in the European Union as the most appropriate decision-making level both in general and, above all, with respect to a variety of free movement issues. Some politicians promoted the establishment of a common European immigration policy, while others considered that there should be clearer European rules, specifically in the field of free movement. The politicians appealed to the Union and its rules in their national debates, that is, they sought to justify their policy proposals by way of the EU's viewpoints, through the Union's approval or disapproval.

To a keen observer of EU affairs, it seems that this trust in the European Union as an appropriate arena has further strengthened with the intensification of the British criticism of free movement policies and the referendum that resulted in the decision to leave the Union. A new willingness to deepen integration has emerged, for example, in the field of defence. In the post-referendum debate, many politicians across the continent insisted that Britain remain part of the free movement regime in order to guarantee the country's access to the Internal Market. They saw free movement as a *concession* that one must make in order to receive certain benefits. However, this is *not* the general impression conveyed by this study. In contrast, free movement appeared as a positive issue per se; it is beneficial, it is a fundamental right and it is a core value of the European Union. It indeed seems that the right to free movement holds a secure position in the mental landscape of European political elites.

Another positive and closely related weak signal suggests that European politicians are prepared to defend European principles when those tenets are contested. Free movement discourses, in fact, fairly strongly support this thesis. When David Cameron's government began to criticize the right to free movement and the social benefits attached to it, leaders of other countries promptly announced that this right is a principle that should not be questioned. The limits of free movement are sometimes stretched, such as in the French Roma expulsion case in the summer of 2010, but it does seem inviolable in principle – the French were immediately criticized. Indeed, even though migration rhetoric is often tough and restrictive measures have been introduced, the general respect for the principle of free movement has not really ever been threatened (see, e.g. Czaika and De Haas 2013, Thielemann and Schade 2016). Many politicians seem to understand free movement as a central symbol of European integration.

A worrying (and currently strengthening?) weak signal relates to how strongly national, or even nationalistic, self-images determine the understandings of mobility. The politicians did not seem to consider that those leaving their own country might cause a problem in the country to which they moved. This outlook seems to reflect a positively loaded image of the own nation: the country's citizens are considered valuable wherever they reside, whereas those coming from elsewhere are seen as too costly. Even if most national politicians generally acknowledge that migrants are beneficial for the host country, it still seems to be easier for them to blame outsiders than insiders for using the state's money.

There is the obvious risk that this national pride of belonging leads to the unjustified exclusion of some people. However, would it, in fact, be any better to construct a European version of national pride? Not necessarily. For example, the removal of the label 'migrant' from EU citizens – as referred to above – only shifts the exclusion problem to another level; 'migrants' from outside Europe have been branded as the costly movers. On the other hand, hierarchies related to people's mobility seem to persist, even at the subnational level. Further, different types of prejudices are attached to people on the basis of which cities, towns or rural regions they come from or on which level of education, for example, they possess. Mechanisms of exclusion caused by the pride of belonging thus exist at all levels; being aware of these mechanisms may relativize the national focus.

The main challenge for free movement, and even for the entire process of European integration, seems to stem from outside the European Union. Offering special rights to EU citizens seems to work fine until this practice is questioned as discriminatory towards 'outsiders'. This was visible in the material throughout the analysed period, but the so-called migration crisis (2015) clearly accentuated it. Indeed, many of the free movement disagreements between EU countries have sprung from some wish to allow free movement to people who are not EU citizens. Before 2015, the best-known is perhaps the 2011 dispute between Italy and France over the mobility of migrants who hold temporary residence permits that Italy granted under Directive 2001/55/EC (Carrera et al. 2011). In summer 2017, an Italian senator proposed that Italy should appeal to the same Directive in order to grant EU visas for the large number of migrants that had entered the county from across the sea;[1] however, other EU members strongly opposed this.

Overall, I observed both positive and negative weak signals in terms of European integration. The leading politicians seem to accept the Union as the appropriate arena for creating rules that the member states can follow and even defend; in this respect, the blessings of free movement are often nationally cherished. However, the hierarchies between different nationalities at both intra- and extra-European levels seem to persist. The trend of moving towards welfare chauvinism at the European level may not, in the end, be much better than the existing emphasis on the national sphere.

This brings us to the next theme: that of the contradictions and illogicalities prevailing in contemporary European free movement debates.

10.3 Practical reasoning: Contradictions in the free movement discourses

The utterances of the leading politicians are obviously carefully drafted and thought over, but the analysis revealed a number of internal *contradictions*, inconsistencies in the argumentation, which deserve to be mentioned. These contradictions primarily were visible, above all, at the national level, from which I found more or less explicit contradictions in all the selected countries. The discourses were often incoherent, and the same politician could sometimes employ different types of utterances carelessly. A contradiction does not indicate that the presented arguments would be logically incoherent or even untrue per se, but the argument stands in opposition to some other arguments or external phenomena. In many cases, we can talk of 'institutional' contradictions that spring from different understandings of the role of institutions, the EU in particular.

Understanding the nature of contradictions is important because discourses do not always comply with the logical ideal of practical reasoning (Walton 2007: 36). It is obvious, as Thomas Gil put it, that 'sometimes we have reasons to act in ways that contradict each other' (Gil 2012: 98). Ideally, however, all these contradictions should, at some stage, be revealed and can thereby be critically examined (by the speaker and by the listener). Does the existence of contradictions mean that the politicians have not critically examined their reasons for action? Perhaps not. They may also consciously express contradictory utterances due to underlying reasons that make it, in some sense, reasonable to contradict oneself. Outsiders can, of course, only guess what those underlying reasons are.

One particular economic contradiction related to the discussion on the costs and benefits of free movement in general. Both commissioners and German politicians saw free movement both as an economic benefit and as a fundamental right. However, one could assume that the status of a fundamental right makes utilitarian calculation unnecessary; if free movement were an acknowledged fundamental right, why would it have to be legitimized with economic utterances? The fact that the status of a fundamental right does not seem to suffice implies that free movement is not as self-evident a principle as many European leaders tend to claim.

In the Italian discourses, it became apparent that the inability of the Commission to address violations of people's rights provided a justification for the politicians to continue their policies and claim that the Commission legitimized the ensuing measures. More generally, it seems that when the Commission did *not* intervene in Italy's free movement policy implementation, it represented the entire European Union for the country's politicians. However, when there was a disagreement, the European Union was expected to convince the Commission of the right opinion. The politicians thus seemed to consider that the Commission should always side with Italy. They appeared to employ the belief that all actions supported by the European Union are issues that the public ought not to question. In a similar vein, the Spanish leaders supported a common immigration policy, allegedly because it was seen to enable the amendment of national immigration policies (Zapata-Barrero and Witte 2007). This is a phenomenon that has also been observed in previous scholarly works: appealing to the European Union can be utilized, for example, as a justification for taking or not being able to take certain actions, such as in scapegoating and credit claiming (e.g. Eder and Trenz 2003: 122).

Another institutional contradiction related to the relationship between the EU and national levels. Many political leaders promoted deeper integration while simultaneously trying to justify state-specific immigration measures. Particularly in Spain, politicians argued for a common immigration policy while implementing the much-criticized national regularizations of irregular immigrants. For French UMP politicians, in turn, a common immigration policy appeared contradictorily as a measure with which France could intervene in the actions taken by other states. These politicians did not seem to be happy with the Commission or other states meddling in their affairs, but meddling in other states' businesses seemed justified via the common immigration policy. A common immigration policy should restrict migrants' access to other countries, but in free movement issues, UMP politicians reserved the right to make independent decisions. This attitude may of course reflect the strong position of France in the European Union.

The British discussion on social security can also be seen to include a contradiction. British politicians saw it as unjust that non-British EU citizens can receive more benefits than they pay taxes. In this way of reasoning, there should, in other words, be guarantees that these EU citizens pay more than they get, whereas this requirement would not apply to the UK citizens themselves. Why is this so? The implication is, in other words, that people living outside their home countries always need to benefit the host society. The EU Treaties do state that EU citizens should not burden other states, but does this mean that they should somehow prove to be some type of 'win' for the host country? To avoid this question, the optimal solution may be to become aware of the multiple ways in which an outsider can be beneficial in her/his new environment; would it not be equally unfair that EU citizens pay more taxes than they receive benefits?

The final noteworthy contradiction played a particularly significant role in the Romanian discourses. While the politicians insisted that Romanian citizens have the complete right to free movement, they simultaneously declared that Romanians should not leave in such large numbers; the right to free movement was seen to belong to a 'proper' European Union member state. According to Romanian politicians, people should not be forced to stay in Romania; rather, they should choose to stay there. A positive aspect of emigration, remittances, was also completely ignored in the analysed discourses, although the remittances sent to Romania made up approximately $5.2 billion in 2018 (World Bank Group 2019: 17), more than 2 per cent of the country's GDP. The silence about remittances may also be related to the view that Romanian politicians do not want to be seen as being dependent on remittances, although they may actually constitute a significant reason to not address the problem of brain drain.

In terms of practical reasoning, the discussions above suggest that reasoning may not always be as rational as it first appears. Even if the politicians appealed to 'reason-based' premises of agreement and utility, their discourses were not consistent when observed in their institutional context. It, in fact, seemed that reason-based utterance types were selected due to their seemingly neutral and objective basis, while the actual reason for action may have been a sentiment-based one. For example, it is easy to hide behind the Commission's back when problems arise (agreement), and European mobility is easier to oppose if it is arguably costly for the host state (utility); in both cases, the speaker may simply fear that her/his local community will become too multicultural. Indeed, taking into account the potential underlying reasons, the argument that all practical reasoning is ultimately based on desires (Searle 2010: 131) does not sound too far-fetched. This study is obviously unable to reveal the real motivations of the politicians, but it has showed that these can indeed be important.

10.4 'L'Europa è mobile', or the existence of 'European' discourses

In the beginning of this study, I considered whether European free movement discourses could be called 'mobile' in a capricious sense. The findings of the preceding chapters indicate that the characterization was indeed appropriate. My intention was to draw a general picture of the EU discourses, but national and party-political differences remained unavoidably present. The analysis of the roles of the four types of practical reasoning has revealed a more nuanced picture of political discourses than the traditional division into instrumental and value-based reasoning could have provided (e.g. Walton 2007: 30–7). Values and instrumental interests have different characteristics, and this study has offered one perspective on how these traditional divisions can be made sense of in a more sophisticated manner.

The extent to which the national and European (epitomized by the Commission) views overlapped varied a great deal. Utterances in the largest member state, Germany, appeared to be closest to those of the commissioners: German emphasis was on the economic value of workers' movement and on a principled commitment to European rules. This possibly reflects the nature of the current European Union, where the Germans are safely at the helm as the most powerful EU member state. It is more difficult to say which of the countries moved the furthest away from the Commission's viewpoints, although the British were certainly the most negative Europeans here.

The study has illustrated that all four approaches can be utilized in justifying free movement and that public support for European policy measures could become higher if all decisions gathered their legitimacy from all these four dimensions. The analysis of the dimensions revealed that there is no one single tension dividing the EU countries on the issue of free movement. Several different tensions inform the political discourses, including: collective order vs. citizens' rights, community-based integration vs. utilitarian materialism, well-defined community vs. multicultural diversity, insiders vs. outsiders (intra-EU/extra-EU), states vs. citizens and sending country vs. receiving country. The tensions are unavoidable, but better awareness of them can alleviate their potentially problematic implications. I cannot propose clear recipes for solving the ever-present difficulties regularly attached to free movement, but perhaps the analyses above provide some hints as to what kinds of negative consequences different types of reasoning can lead to. The most important and obvious of such consequences is possibly the strong sentiment-based attachment to the national community that seeks to restrict free movement and, eventually, to even get rid of the European Union. We need to remember, as discussed in Chapter 8 and beyond, that the historical trajectories of EU countries are different and reflected even in today's political discourses. The history of actual free movement in Europe spans hardly a decade in some EU countries and we cannot assume that the approaches assimilate in countries with different migration traditions.

In spite of the more or less clear overlap between the national and European views, it still remains a moot question whether or to what extent we can talk of a properly functioning European public sphere (cf. Risse 2010, 2014, Drewski 2015). Based on the results of this study, I would argue that national and local viewpoints continue to matter to a significant extent; the leaders tend to emphasize national interest and peculiarities. This certainly does not prevent, however, the development of common European views in many a policy field, and the selected politicians strongly acknowledged the importance of European rules and values.

Be that as it may, on the basis of the free movement debates analysed in this study, European integration is far from doomed. In the empirical material, there were no utterances mentioning the dreaded F-word – federalism – that politicians often exploit to paint a worst-case scenario for European politics. Although European integration, to some extent, resembles a bicycle that needs to move forward in order not to fall over, federalism does not appear to be a desired destination. In the foreseeable future, European integration will not move forward without the consent of the member states. In order to survive, however, what is understood as 'Europeanness' has to be or become sufficiently inclusive in order to encompass the (remaining) twenty-seven 'nationhoods'. Although free movement policies are sometimes questioned in the fear of flows of people both from outside and within the European Union, free movement may ultimately be the issue creating that sense of inclusion. As German Interior Minister Schäuble (2007) put it: 'free movement is a necessary and wanted process for unification'. Free movement is well past its sixtieth anniversary and practically unaffected by numerous challenges, including the 'migration crisis' and one lost member state.

Appendix

Material selection and speaker-specific tables

Germany

I collected the German documents from the website of the *Bundesregierung*, selecting from the list of *Bulletins*, which consist of political speeches, addresses and interviews. It was possible to search using different free movement-related keywords found from the speeches of specific politicians.[1] After I located all of the documents mentioning free movement, I reviewed each of them to determine whether the speaker presented a stance on the right to free movement in the European Union.

The German politician that was most vocal during the analysed period was Angela Merkel, representing the Christian Democratic Party (*Christlich Demokratische Union Deutschlands*, CDU). She has been the chancellor of Germany since 2005, that is, almost throughout the entire period of analysis. I also analysed the utterances of her predecessor, former Chancellor Gerhard Schröder of the Social Democratic Party (*Sozialdemokratische Partei Deutschlands*, SPD). During Mr Schröder's term, Otto Schily, also from the SPD, was the interior minister. All the interior ministers in Ms Merkel's cabinet have come from the CDU, apart from Hans-Peter Friedrich, who is a member of the Christian Social Union (*Cristisch-Soziale Union in Bayern*, CSU), a sister party of the CDU. During the analysed period, there were three interior ministers in Chancellor Merkel's governments: Wolfgang Schäuble was the first interior minister, followed by Thomas de Maizière, who is currently serving in his non-sequential, second term as interior minister since 2013, while Hans-Pieter Friedrich was the third.

Table A.1 German free movement utterances, N=59

Speaker	Term	Agreement	Community	Utility	Solidarity	Analysed N
Chancellor Schröder (SPD)	2004–5	1	0	0	0	1
Chancellor Merkel (CDU)	2005–16	16	1	22	2	41
IM Schily (SPD)	2004–5	1	0	0	0	1
IM Schäuble (CDU)	2005–9	2	0	1	1	4
IM de Maiziere (CDU)	2009–11 2013–16	5	1	0	1	7
IM Friedrich (CSU)	2011–13	2	1	1	1	5
Sum		27	3	24	5	59

The quantitative results of the German utterances can be found in Table A.1, which outlines the division between different utterance types from among different politicians.

France

I collected the empirical documents concerning French politicians from the official websites of the French president and the Ministry of the Interior as well as from the official website *Vie Publique*, which archives political documents. It was possible to use keywords and locate the documents of different politicians during the period.[2] The documents that I found included both political speeches and statements as well as media interviews.

I analysed the utterances of the presidents and the interior ministers. I chose presidents instead of prime ministers as the president represents France at European summits and wields more power than the prime minister in EU politics. In the beginning of the timeline examined, November 2004, Jacques Chirac, representing the centre-right Union for a popular movement (*Union pour un movement populaire*, UMP), was the president of France, a post he held until 2007. He was succeeded by Nicolas Sarkozy, who also represented the UMP and was the president during most of the period examined, until 2012 when François Hollande from the Socialist Party (*Parti socialiste*, PS) took office after his presidential election victory.

All the analysed interior ministers were from the same party as the president, thus no major contradictions between them were expected. Analysing the utterances of the French ministers of the interior also allowed for a comparison between Nicolas Sarkozy's utterances during his time as the interior minister in 2005–7 and as his statements as the president of the Republic from 2007 to 2012. Dominique de Villepin was the interior minister before Mr Sarkozy took office in 2005, and after Mr Sarkozy's term as IM, François Baroin, Michèle Alliot-Marie, Brice Hortefeux and Claude Guéant have since held the post. During Hollande's term, Manuel Valls and Bernard Cazeneuve have held the post. While Interior Minister Sarkozy focused on

Table A.2 French free movement utterances, N=59

Speaker	Term	Agreement	Community	Utility	Solidarity	Analysed N
President Chirac (UMP)	2004–7	1	0	2	2	5
President Sarkozy (UMP)	2007–12	4	1	3	1	9
President Hollande (PS)	2012–16	9	11	3	1	24
IM Sarkozy (UMP)	2005–7	0	0	3	0	3
IM de Villepin (UMP)	2004–5	1	0	1	0	2
IM Alliot-Marie (UMP)	2007–9	1	0	0	0	1
IM Hortefeux (UMP)	2009–11	2	0	0	0	2
IM Guéant (UMP)	2011–12	0	0	1	0	1
IM Valls (PS)	2012–14	4	0	1	0	5
IM Cazeneuve (PS)	2014–16	6	1	0	0	7
Sum		**28**	**13**	**14**	**4**	**59**

his presidential campaign during spring 2007, François Baroin from the same UMP temporarily held the post for two months, but due to this short period and a shortage of utterances, he is omitted from the analysis.

The results concerning the French case are summarized in Table A.2, illustrating the division between different types of utterances among specific politicians.

Italy

I collected the Italian documents from the website of the Italian prime minister and its *siti archeologici*, that is, the previous versions of the site found on the website. I reviewed, at the level of titles, all the speeches, interviews and international activities on the site and collected those utterances that I deemed relevant for the analysis.[3] I also went through the titles of all the speeches and interviews found on the website of the Ministry of the Interior, as well as in the historical archive of speeches and interviews of the Ministry of the Interior. I opened documents that appeared to be relevant in the free movement context (dealing with the EU, state visits, immigration, etc.) and determined whether there were any utterances related to free movement.

In Italy, the governments tend not to be very long-lived and political institutions suffer from a lack of legitimacy and the inability to make and implement decisions (Guarnieri 2011: 119). Indeed, the period from November 2004 to 2016 witnessed five different prime ministers. Three premiers were centre-leftist, representing the Democratic Party (*Partito Democratico*, PD): Romano Prodi, Enrico Letta and Matteo Renzi, whereas there was only one centre-right prime minister from the *Forza Italia* (FI) party (Silvio Berlusconi). Mario Monti could be classified a centrist politician; he was appointed to lead a technocrat government in 2011 after Berlusconi's departure, and in the following elections he was the main candidate of a centrist coalition 'With Monti for Italy' (*Con Monti per l'Italia*).

Table A.3 Italian free movement utterances, N=42

Speaker	Term	Agreement	Community	Utility	Solidarity	Analysed N
PM Berlusconi (FI)	2001–6 008–11	4	0	0	0	4
PM Prodi (PD)	2006–8	0	3	0	0	3
PM Monti (tech.)	2011–13	0	1	1	0	2
PM Letta (PD)	2013–14	0	0	2	0	2
PM Renzi (PD)	2014–16	0	1	1	1	3
IM Pisanu (FI)	2004–6	1	1	0	0	2
IM Amato (PD)	2006–8	4	0	0	0	4
IM Maroni (LN)	2008–11	11	0	1	1	13
IM Cancellieri (tech.)	2011–13	0	0	0	1	1
IM Alfano (NC)	2013–16	4	3	0	1	8
Sum		24	9	5	4	42

The utterances of the ministers of the interior were numerous regarding free movement and only few of the ministers were from the same party as the prime minister. In the case of Mr Monti's government, the minister of the interior (Annamaria Cancellieri) was also not party-politically affiliated, and the interior minister in Silvio Berlusconi's first government during the analysed period was *Forza Italia* representative Giuseppe Pisanu. In contrast, the interior minister in Berlusconi's 2008–11 government was the Northern League (*Lega Nord*, LN) minister, Roberto Maroni. Giuliano Amato was the Democratic interior minister in PM Prodi's government, and Angelino Alfano was the final interior minister during the observed period, representing the centre-right party, 'New centre-right' (*Nuovo Centrodestra*, NC) in Enrico Letta's and Matteo Renzi's governments. The results can be found in Table A.3.

The UK

I collected the British documents from the official websites of the government as well as from the websites of the major parties. More specifically, I found the documents at the government announcement site as well as from the UK Government Web Archive, which includes previous versions of the sites of the Office of the Prime Minister and of the Home Office. In addition, speeches of the home secretary were found on the website of the UK Parliament, where the home secretary delivered, for example, post-Council statements. I went through, at the level of titles, all the speeches and statements of the governments of the period in order to find relevant utterances. Among the titles, I opened and specifically studied those documents that dealt with the EU, state visits, immigration, and so on.[4] Since the speeches on the government website should not contain party-political material, I also included speeches made by the prime ministers at their party conferences. The prime ministers usually addressed all major policy areas in such speeches, including issues related to free movement.

During the analysed period, Labour's Tony Blair was the prime minister until 2007, when Gordon Brown took his place as the leader of the party and the government. In

Table A.4 British free movement utterances, N=54

Speaker	Term	Agreement	Community	Utility	Solidarity	Analysed N
PM Blair (Labour)	2004–7	0	0	2	0	2
PM Brown (Labour)	2007–10	1	1	1	0	3
PM Cameron (Conser.)	2010–16	3	3	17	4	27
HS Clarke (Labour)	2004–6	2	0	0	0	2
HS Reid (Labour)	2006–7	0	0	1	0	1
HS Smith (Labour)	2007–9	2	0	0	0	2
HS Johnson (Labour)	2009–10	0	0	0	0	0
HS May (Conser.)	2010–15	12	0	5	0	17
Sum		**20**	**4**	**26**	**4**	**54**

2010, the Conservatives won the elections and formed a coalition government with the Liberal Democrats, with David Cameron serving as prime minister.

The home secretaries during the covered period have always been members of the same party as the prime minister, and therefore no major political divergences are expected. The home secretaries included Charles Clarke, John Reid, Jacqui Smith, Alan Johnson and Theresa May. It should be noted that Alan Johnson served as the interior minister for less than a year, and the official material from his period did not contain any free movement utterances as defined in this study.

The UK provides an illustrative example of a country in which prime ministers employ diversified justifications; the state allows for a comparison between Labour and Conservative politicians' discourses in the analysed period. The diverse approaches observed between the representatives of the two parties are summarized in Table A.4.

Spain

In the Spanish case, I collected the utterances of prime ministers from the website of the prime minister, which archives speeches and interviews. When tracing the relevant items, I went through all the documents at the title level, as no search functions were possible in the database.[5] In addition, I found interviews and speeches of the minister of the interior on the Ministry's website, as well as in the archive of the Spanish Parliament, where the interior ministers addressed free movement. In other countries, such addresses were often present on the interior minister's website. In this case too, I looked more closely into documents dealing with the EU, immigration and state visits.

During the analysed period, Spain has had two prime ministers, one from each dominant Spanish party. A representative of the Spanish Socialist Workers' Party (*Partido Socialista Obrero Español*, PSOE), José Luis Rodríguez Zapatero, was the first prime minister during the period analysed, serving two terms from 2004 to 2011. Mariano Rajoy has been in office ever since and represents the conservative People's Party (*Partido Popular*, PP). At the national level, these parties are the dominant ones; however, at the regional level, there is more variation, particularly in the Basque and Catalonia regions (McMahon 2015: 88).

All the ministers of the interior in Spain have also been from the same party as the prime minister, and few political differences between them can be expected. The first interior minister was José Antonio Alonso Suárez, the second Alfredo Pérez Rubalcaba and the last IM during the analysed period was Jorge Fernández Díaz.

The summarized results concerning the Spanish case can be found from the table below, which illustrates the division of different types of utterances among different politicians. Although both major Spanish parties were well represented in the material, it should be noted that no significant differences in their free movement approaches were observed. This implies that free movement was not considered a highly politicized

158   *The History and Politics of Free Movement*

Table A.5 Spanish free movement utterances, N=40

Speaker	Term	Agreement	Community	Utility	Solidarity	Analysed N
PM Zapatero (PSOE)	2004–11	5	0	3	0	8
PM Rajoy (PP)	2011–15	6	6	11	2	25
IM Alonso (PSOE)	2004–6	1	0	0	0	1
IM Rubalcaba (PSOE)	2006–11	1	0	2	0	3
IM Díaz (PP)	2011–15	1	0	2	0	3
Sum		14	6	18	2	40

issue in Spain. As is visible in Table A.5, the Spanish discourses were strongly reliant on agreement-based utterances and utility utterances, the latter of which were particularly in favour of a common immigration policy. Solidarity utterances in Spain, in turn, had the fewest number of occurences out of the analysed countries.

Romania

With regard to Romanian utterances, I collected the documents from the official website of the president of Romania, from the website of the prime minister and from the Romanian government archives. Because Romania has a semi-presidential political system, the utterances I included in the analysis consist of those expressed by both the Romanian presidents and prime ministers from November 2004 to the end of June 2016. Officially, the president of Romania should represent Romania in the European Council. However, Prime Minister Victor Ponta, who was in office from May 2012 until his resignation in November 2015, questioned this practice. Although the Romanian Constitutional Court decided in June 2012 that the president should represent the country, Prime Minister Ponta participated in the Council meetings anyway. The situation spurred a constitutional crisis involving protests, after which the president and prime minister signed an agreement of cohabitation at the end of the year. Because I included the documents of both presidents and prime ministers in the analysed material, I omitted interior ministers in order not to expand the number of Romanian documents. As it was not possible to use any digital search functions in the Romanian databases, I manually went through all the documents at the title level and looked more closely into documents I deemed relevant to the EU context.[6]

The Romanian prime minister at the end of 2004 was Călin Popescu-Tăriceanu, who was appointed by then President Traian Băsescu, who served two terms until 2014. Mr Băsescu represented the Democratic Party (*Partidul Democrat*, PD), while Mr Popescu-Tăriceanu represented the National Liberal Party (*Partidul Național Liberal*, PNL), which together constituted a centre-right electoral alliance called Justice and Truth Alliance (*Alianța Dreptate și Adevăr*). In 2008, Emil Boc, who represented the Democratic Liberal Party (*Partidul Democrat-Liberal*, PDL), which was created by the merger of Băsescu's Democratic Party (PD) and the Liberal Democratic Party (*Partidul Liberal Democrat*, PLD), was appointed prime minister. Following Mr Boc,

Table A.6 Romanian free movement utterances, N=53

Speaker	Term	Agreement	Community	Utility	Solidarity	Analysed N
PM Popescu-Tăriceanu (PNL)	2004–8	3	1	0	0	4
President Băsescu (PDL)	2004–14	10	6	7	4	27
PM Boc (PDL)	2008–12	1	1	1	0	3
PM Ponta (PSD)	2012–15	6	1	1	0	8
President Iohannis (PNL)	2014–16	2	1	3	0	6
PM Cioloș (ind.)	2015–16	3	0	2	0	5
Sum		25	10	14	4	53

Mihai Răzvan Ungureanu held the post of prime minister for a few months, but I omit his term due to its short duration. Prime Minister Victor Ponta was Emil Boc's successor and represented the Social Democratic Party (*Partidul Social Democrat*, PSD), serving as the opposition leader until he was appointed the prime minister. After Ponta, independent Prime Minister Dacian Cioloș served in office until 2017.

After the presidential elections of 2014, Klaus Iohannis became the new president. He represented the Christian Liberal Alliance consisting of the National Liberal Party (PNL) and the Liberal Democratic Party (PLD), which later merged into the PNL. The Romanian party system appears rather confusing, but PSD (PM Ponta), PDL (President Băsescu and PM Boc) and PNL (PM Popescu-Tăriceanu and President Iohannis) have dominated the political system since the collapse of communism, although the names of the parties have changed over the years. During the post-communist era, PSD, the successor of the communist party, has been the largest party. PDL has been the second-largest party and PNL has been the third largest. PSD and PNL also formed a winning alliance in the 2012 parliamentary elections (Gherghina and Volintiru 2015: 11), and the PSD won the elections in late 2016. Although the largest party has usually been the PSD, the second largest party dominated the period analysed in this book, primarily through the ten-year presidency of Mr Băsescu and the four-year prime ministership of Mr Boc. The summarized results of the analysed utterances can be found in Table A.6.

European Commission

The period determined for Commission utterances begins from the start of the first Barroso Commission on 22 November 2004 until the end of June 2016. I included the speeches and statements of the following commissioners, all of them vocal about free movement issues: President José Manuel Barroso (2004–14); President Jean-Claude Juncker (2014–16); Commissioners for Justice, Freedom and Security Franco Frattini (2004–8) and Jacques Barrot (2008–10); Commissioner for Employment, Social Affairs and Equal Opportunities Vladimir Špidla (2004–10); Commissioner for Employment, Social Affairs and Inclusion Lázló Andor (2010–14); Commissioners for Justice, Fundamental Rights and Citizenship Viviane Reding (2010–14) and Martine Reicherts (2014); Commissioner for Home Affairs Cecilia Malmström (2010–14);

Table A.7 Commissioners' free movement utterances, N=72

Speaker	Term	Agreement	Community	Utility	Solidarity	Analysed N
President Barroso	2004–14	8	0	10	2	20
Justice Com. Frattini	2004–8	2	0	3	0	5
Justice Com. Barrot	2008–10	1	0	1	0	2
Employment Com. Špidla	2004–10	1	0	2	1	4
Employment Com. Andor	2010–14	4	0	5	0	9
Justice Com. Reding	2010–14	4	2	2	0	8
Justice Com. Reichters	2014	1	0	0	0	1
Home Affairs Com. Malmström	2010–14	3	2	1	0	6
President Juncker	2014–16	2	0	1	0	3
Justice Com. Jourová	2014–16	0	0	1	0	1
Employment Com. Thyssen	2014–16	1	1	2	0	4
Migration Com. Avramopoulous	2014–16	5	1	3	0	9
Sum		**32**	**6**	**31**	**3**	**72**

Commissioner for Justice, Consumers and Gender Equality Věra Jourová (2014–16); Commissioner for Employment, Social Affairs, Skills and Labour Mobility Marianne Thyssen (2014–16); and Commissioner for Migration, Home Affairs and Citizenship Dimitris Avramopoulos (2014–16).

In the latter Commission, two new positions were established, one for Justice, Fundamental Rights and Citizenship and one for Home Affairs. Cecilia Malmström served as the latter, while Viviane Reding held the former post until July 2014, when Martine Reichters took over for the few remaining months. In the later Commission, László Andor served as the commissioner for Employment, Social Affairs and Inclusion, which only includes one word (citizenship instead of inclusion) that is different from the position held by his predecessor, Vladimir Špidla. The Juncker Commission also established a commissioner for Migration (Avramopoulos), but otherwise the titles of the Juncker Commission were similar to the former ones, with some changes in vocabulary.

The commissioners' documents were by far the easiest to collect, due to the European Commission Press Release Database, which enabled searching by time and topic the speeches of different commissioners.[7]

As visible in Table A.7, the most vocal commissioner on free movement was President Barroso, who served two terms as the head of Commission. The second most vocal were Employment Commissioner Andor during Barroso's later Commission (2010–14) and Migration Commissioner Avramopoulos during the Juncker Commission (2014–16).

Notes

1 Introduction

1 For the sake of the brevity of the text, when I speak of the 'analysed countries', I often also include the European Commission.
2 Regularization refers to providing irregular migrants with a residence permit in the country.
3 It should be noted that the implementation of the transfers has not been realized even in 2020.
4 Other characterizations of the EU's external actorness include, inter alia, a responsible Europe, though with a question mark (Mayer and Vogt 2006).
5 Adrian Hyde-Price has, however, voiced some criticism concerning the concept of ethical power as, according to him, the EU pursues its own interests; normative emphasis can turn the Union into a weak actor; and aspiring ethicality may have undesired consequences (Hyde-Price 2008). Hyde-Price takes a realist perspective on the issue with an emphasis on instrumental power and excludes the viewpoint that ethical thinking can involve pursuing interests.
6 I utilize the original language versions of these documents, all available on the internet. Thanks to my extensive language studies, including an MA degree in Translation Studies, and my secondary occupation as a translator-entrepreneur since 2012, I was able to analyse the original language versions.

2 The context: The history of free movement in Europe

1 In their op-ed in the *Financial Times* on 31 August 2014, Karl Lamers and Wolfgang Schäuble discussed 'freedom of establishment – the right of people and companies to carry out business wherever they want' (Lamers and Schäuble 2014).
2 However, the approach to free movement in the non-EU countries has not always been uncomplicated (e.g. Ambühl and Zurcher 2015).
3 Another interesting aspect of the treaty is that French Algeria was excluded from the treaty and Algerian coal and mine workers thus did not have the right to work in the ECSC countries (see also Hansen and Jonsson 2017: 120–8).
4 It has also been claimed that the construction of the 'Fortress Europe' already began with the Council Regulation 1612/68/EC, which determined free movement as the right of only the citizens of member states (Ugur 1995: 977, Huysmans 2006: 66).
5 The Charter of Fundamental Rights originates from 2000, but it only legally came into force with the Lisbon Treaty that was adopted in 2009. This is where I argue that free movement also became acknowledged as a moral norm as it is accepted in the supranational list of fundamental rights, which are moral in character (see also Alexy 2006: 18–22).

6 Although discrimination should never occur among EU nationals inside the European Union in terms of the right to move and acquire real estate, the EU, however, authorizes certain discriminatory practices. For example, for Finns it might be easier to settle in another EU country than in the Åland Islands, which are part of the Finnish state. This is because only people who have been residents for five years and are fluent in Swedish may buy real estate on the Islands. The EU has permitted this as it related to the autonomous status of the said Islands. Further, Denmark itself also has residence-related conditions for buying a second home. These are relevant exceptions that relate to the free movement of capital in the European Union, but that might also hinder the free movement of people.
7 Transitional arrangements mean that a country may restrict the access of workers from the new member states but may not restrict the freedom to travel. Typically, transitional measures include the requirement of a work permit and such arrangements may last a maximum of seven years.
8 In 2004, only Sweden, the UK and Ireland did not impose transitional restrictions for new member states of the EU. For Bulgarians and Romanians, among the 'old' member states, only Sweden and Finland provided free access. However, for Croatia, which joined the Union in 2013, most of the countries (14 out of 27) provided free access from the very beginning, and all countries except Austria removed the transitional restrictions before July 2018. Austria is able to continue the restrictions until 30 June 2020.
9 Since December 2007, the Schengen Area has also covered 9 out of 10 countries that joined the Union in 2004 (Cyprus being the exception), while Bulgaria and Romania have not yet received membership in the convention due to the lack of unanimity among other Schengen countries. Croatia, which joined the Union in 2013, started its evaluation and monitoring mechanism to join the Schengen Acquis in July 2015, and the Commission announced in October 2019 that Croatia has met the conditions for joining the Schengen Area.
10 The Tampere (1999–2004), Hague (2004–9) and Stockholm (2009–14) programmes have complemented the provision on the AFSJ.
11 A three-pillar structure consisted of the community pillar with supranational decision-making as well as common foreign and security policy pillar and police and judicial cooperation in criminal matters, which were intergovernmental in nature.
12 Third-country national (TCN) is the clinical term employed to refer to anyone who is not an EU citizen residing in their country of citizenship (first-country national) or in another EU member state (second-country national). EU citizens were almost never referred to with such a numeric characterization, whereas the acronym TCN is commonly employed for non-European Union citizens (see also Wodak and Boukala 2015).
13 It should be noted that the concept of Fortress Europe has also been criticized for its oversimplification of the complex issues of borders and migration (Bigo 2005, Rigo 2011, Tallis 2015). Indeed, Fortress Europe does not mean that people are not able to physically enter the Union, but that third-country nationals appear as a threat and their settlement rights in different EU countries are restricted.
14 All EU countries are currently part of the Dublin system, although three countries have the possibility of not participating in issues related to immigration. The UK and Ireland participate in the Dublin arrangements, but they negotiated an opt-in option in the Amsterdam Treaty, under which they may participate in measures related to

the Area of Freedom, Security and Justice on a case-by-case basis. Denmark, in turn, participates in both the Schengen Agreement and the Dublin system, but already opted out of Justice and Home Affairs in the Maastricht Treaty (1992). Denmark held a referendum on 3 December 2015 on changing its opt-out status to an opt-in one, which would have enabled the country to participate more easily in the cooperation on Justice and Home Affairs. However, the referendum resulted in their maintaining the opt-out policy.
15 Among the countries discussed in this book, regularization campaigns in the twenty-first century have been mainly conducted in Spain and Italy (Finotelli and Arango 2011).

3 Conceptual framework and methodology

1 The pioneers of critical discourse analysis, Isabela and Norman Fairclough, in contrast, argue that practical reasoning is always based on goals of different kinds; even values represent 'ethical goals' (Fairclough and Fairclough 2011: 247).
2 Guiding reasons, as understood here, affect what one should do, related to, for example, certain moral principles or desires (Raz 1978: 4).
3 I employ the term 'dimension' while referring to the four perspectives as part of the framework for analysis. 'Attitude', 'approach' and 'outlook' are the terms employed elsewhere.
4 While Helene Sjursen refers to the EU as a rights-based, post-national Union that is based on universal rights, this book only focuses on the right to free movement, which is far from universal.
5 Often, when I refer to 'politicians' or 'countries' whose discourse is analysed in this study, it also includes the European Commission and commissioners.
6 There are almost three million Romanian citizens residing in other European countries, out of which ca. 1.2 million live in Italy, 674000 in Spain, 587000 in Germany, 416000 in the UK and 118000 in France. This means that 15 per cent of the country's citizens live in other member states, and they account for over two-thirds of other EU citizens in Italy (Eurostat 2019).
7 In addition to the sample selection being justifiable due to its representatives, one of the incentives to select these particular countries was that I was able to analyse the material in the original languages of these countries.
8 The former are usually responsible for free movement matters, and the ministers of the interior of the five largest states represent their state in the G6 group (which currently also includes Poland) that often discusses free movement matters. In Italy and Spain, I have included prime ministers and ministers of the interior, and in France, presidents and ministers of the interior. In Germany, the politicians include the federal chancellors and the ministers of the interior, and in the UK, I analyse utterances of the prime ministers and the home secretaries. From Romania, I analyse the discourses of the presidents and the prime ministers, both active in EU affairs.
9 An issue to be noted in the material is the small number of women in these positions; only Chancellor Merkel, Home Secretary May, and European Commissioners Reding and Malmström played a somewhat larger role in the discourses.

4 Agreement dimension: Emphasis on common duties

1 Habermas's 'Europatriotism' has also been criticized for being non-reflexive (e.g. Lacroix 2009), that is, having too optimistic and Eurocentric of an approach to European integration.
2 As discussed before, free movement is stipulated in the European Charter of Fundamental Rights, and constitutional patriotism has also been discussed with regard to the Charter. According to John Erik Fossum, constitutional patriotism in the context of the Charter would mean commitment to personal autonomy, citizens as the authority of the law and the incorporation of the Charter in the constitution (Fossum 2003: 231–2). He concludes that the Charter does not carry features related to public autonomy or democracy, although the spirit is that of constitutional patriotism (Fossum 2003: 254). In addition, the status of the Charter was ambiguous in 2003, while currently it is part of the Union legislation, thus enforcing constitutional patriotism and the rights-based character of the Union.
3 Mr Sarkozy was also found to utilize 'securitizing' discourse during his terms as the interior minister, but such utterances related to migration from third countries (Bourbeau 2011). However, as the president of the Republic, he was concerned about illegal activities in France undertaken by immigrants.
4 That was also the case in the 2011 ban on covering/concealing one's face in public spaces with, for example, niqab of burqa, which was also justified with public order arguments (Fredette 2015: 585–610).
5

> Parallèlement, je souhaite que nous engagions une importante réforme pour améliorer la lutte contre l'immigration irrégulière. Chaque année, une dizaine de milliers de migrants en situation irrégulière, dont des Roms, repartent volontairement avec une aide de l'Etat. Et l'année suivante, après avoir quitté le territoire avec une aide de l'Etat, ils reviennent en toute illégalité pour demander une autre aide de l'Etat pour repartir. Cela s'appelle « un abus du droit à la libre circulation ».

6

> Ma alla fine tutte le menzogne sono state smascherate: la Commissione Europea ha riconosciuto come "non discriminatorie", anzi "pienamente in linea con il diritto comunitario" le norme che abbiamo varato, comprese quelle sulle impronte digitali dei bambini rom finalizzate al solo scopo di sottrarli allo sfruttamento e a genitori che preferiscono mandarli a rubare invece che a scuola.

7 The procedure was launched because the Italian implementation of the free movement directive involved the possibility to repatriate EU citizens, which was especially targeted at Roma camps (McMahon 2015: 84).
8 In contrast, Spain did not establish any of these economic conditions for EU citizens, although it did take advantage of the situation and launched transitional restrictions for new member states.
9

> Pero tengamos la prudencia, que es, en mi caso, sentido de la responsabilidad, de que la Comisión Europea, que es quien tiene la responsabilidad de velar

por Directivas europeas, porque lo que está en cuestión es si se vulneran o no directivas europeas, se pronuncie. Y, desde luego, yo estaré detrás de lo que diga la Comisión Europea. Si se ha actuado mal, lo criticaré y, si no, lógicamente no lo criticaré.

10 Wir hatten dann noch eine Diskussion, die sich angeschlossen hat, über die Frage der Roma und die Diskussion, die es zwischen Frankreich und der Europäischen Kommission gab. Diesbezüglich sind wir zu vier übereinstimmenden Punkten gekommen, die, glaube ich, auch wichtig sind, um dieses Thema einer Klärung zuzuführen, nämlich erstens, dass es das Recht und auch die Pflicht der Kommission ist, zu überprüfen, ob das Gemeinschaftsrecht von den Mitgliedstaaten eingehalten wird. Zweitens haben wir alle gemeinsam die Erklärung, die der Kommissionspräsident gestern im Namen der gesamten Kommission abgegeben hat, zustimmend zur Kenntnis genommen. Drittens haben wir noch einmal festgehalten, dass es wichtig ist, dass es um Respekt zwischen Kommission und Rat geht, weil das die Grundlage für eine gedeihliche Zusammenarbeit ist. Viertens haben wir gesagt, dass wir uns in der Sache mit den Fragen der Roma beim Oktoberrat noch einmal beschäftigen werden.

11 Generally speaking, the Agreement is more related to security questions, which are also visible in the discussion on 'Schengenland', where external borders are 'potentially highly permeable lines that require active defence' (Crowley 2003: 38).

12 'Sunt unele state care încearcă să pună problemele de liberă circulație a minorității rome în sarcina accesului nostru în spațiu Schengen, lucru care mi se pare incorect și nu este în conformitate cu Tratatul.'

13 In plus, cei mai mulți români care au vrut să meargă în Germania sunt deja acolo: sunt cu precădere tineri bine pregătiți care muncesc din greu și plătesc impozite. Folosesc societatea in care trăiesc acum. Pentru România, plecarea lor reprezintă o pierdere; lucrăm în acest sens pentru a-i putea ține pe acești oameni aici. ... Soluția pe termen lung constă în integrarea romilor aici in România. În acest sens avem nevoie de sprijin financiar si de o strategie pentru zece, cincisprezece ani. Este legitim dacă Germania dorește să combată abuzurile asupra sistemului social prin noi legi. Noi înțelegem și sprijinim acest lucru. Tot ceea ce cerem este sa nu existe o discriminare a românilor fata de cetățenii altor state europene.

14 He joined Berlusconi's government the following year, relinquishing his commissioner post.

15 This is reflected in the image of a rights-based EU (Sjursen 2002: 500).

16 Les Roumains sont des citoyens de l'Union. Ils ne peuvent en aucun cas être traités moins favorablement que les autres citoyens de l'Union. Et la Commission s'assurera que leurs droits sont respectés. ... Les règles sur la libre circulation ne sont pas faites pour profiter aux criminels. La directive permet l'exclusion des personnes dont le comportement représente une menace réelle, actuelle et suffisamment grave pour l'intérêt fondamental de la société. La lutte contre la criminalité doit se faire dans le plein respect de l'État de droit.

>   Une décision d'exclusion peut uniquement être décidée au cas par cas et les garanties de procédure et les conditions de fond doivent être respectées. En cas d'exclusion immédiate, l'urgence doit être dûment justifiée. L'exclusion des citoyens de l'Union est une mesure extrême. Il s'agit d'une limitation à une liberté fondamentale du traité.

17 European commissioners repeatedly weighed the right to free movement against people's security concerns and the need for external border controls. On another occasion, Commissioner Malmström argued that secure external borders 'will safeguard the integrity of our cherished area of internal free movement' (Malmström 2012a).

18

>   El Consejo Europeo ha reafirmado, con el pleno respaldo de España, por supuesto, la necesidad de preservar el derecho fundamental de la libre circulación de las personas a través de todo el territorio de la Unión Europea y, en concreto, del Espacio Schengen. En ningún caso, el mecanismo excepcional de salvaguarda, que hoy hemos aprobado y que ha de desarrollar la Comisión, podrá ser utilizado para restringir de forma arbitraria esta libertad, ya que su objetivo es limitado para garantizar la eficacia en el control de las fronteras exteriores en situaciones excepcionales de movimientos descontrolados de personas.

19

>   Am subliniat necesitatea menținerii unui echilibru între libertățile fundamentale, precum păstrarea principiului liberei circulații a persoanelor în Uniune, legislația în vigoare și responsabilitatea pe care o avem de a asigura securitatea cetățenilor noștri. Am susținut că acțiunile noastre nu trebuie să creeze noi bariere, măsurile pe care le vom decide trebuie aplicate coerent în interiorul frontierelor Uniunii Europene, fără diferențe de tratament între statele membre Schengen și cele non-Schengen.

20 'Questa condizione [il semestre italiano di presidenza dell'Unione] ci responsabilizza ancora di più nel proporre soluzioni a livello dell'Unione … Il problema è che questi individui, i "foreign fighters", circolano liberamente per l'Europa, essendo cittadini dell'Unione.'

21 'É necessario dimostrare che una circolazione libera è anche una circolazione sicura: la sicurezza è un pezzo essenziale nella nostra libertà, lo sforzo è coniugare libertà e sicurezza nella circolazione. C'è il rischio di confondere le cose tra terrorismo e immigrazione, ma la gente ha paura.'

22 'La circolazione deve essere libera e deve essere anche sicura, e il modo per conciliare queste due cose è un rafforzamento dei controlli alla frontiera esterna, perché solo così possiamo salvare Schengen.'

23

>   La France et les Pays-Bas ont les mêmes principes: la libre circulation des personnes pour ce qui concerne l'espace Schengen et le droit d'asile pour accueillir celles et ceux qui fuient des régimes ou qui craignent pour leur vie. Nous avons aussi le devoir de protéger nos frontières extérieures et d'assurer la solidarité à l'égard des pays qui font face à des drames. C'est le cas de la

24 Turquie, du Liban mais aussi de la Jordanie et je n'oublie pas la Grèce en ces circonstances.

Auch wenn wir nach Italien blicken, stellt sich wieder die Frage: Ist eine europäische Lösung eine Lösung am Brenner? Ich würde sagen: Nein. Wir müssen also versuchen, eine Lösung an den Außengrenzen des Schengen-Raums zu bekommen und nicht an irgendeinem Ort innerhalb des Schengen-Raums, sonst ist es keine europäische Lösung. Meine These ist – und deshalb war es richtig, zu warten und trotzdem daran zu arbeiten, die Zahl der Flüchtlinge zu reduzieren –, dass eine gemeinsame Währung und ein gemeinsamer Binnenmarkt nur dann funktionieren können, wenn wir auch wirklich die Außengrenzen schützen und im Inneren Freizügigkeit lassen. Das ist in unserem tiefsten wirtschaftlichen Interesse; und darum ging und geht es. Gleichzeitig müssen wir die Fluchtursachen bekämpfen und legale Wege finden, wie Menschen zu uns kommen können – aber über von Staaten bestimmte, und nicht von Schleppern determinierte Wege.

25 Although the British Labour Government did not impose any transitional restrictions for the accessing countries in 2004, the same government launched transitional restrictions for Bulgaria and Romania in 2007. This might imply that there was apprehension about the migration of people from the Eastern European countries as well as less need for migrant labour. Prime Minister Brown appealed to EU-level legislation when he assured Britons that EU migrants would not come to the UK to claim benefits. This principle is provided in Article 7 of the Free Movement Directive, stating that people should 'have sufficient resources for themselves and their family members not to become a burden on the social assistance system of the host Member State' (see also Minderhoud 2013).

26 Este în interesul României ca imaginea țarii noastre și eforturile românilor cinstiți care muncesc din greu în Italia să nu fie afectată de câteva cazuri singulare. Românii au știut să se integreze, iar acum peste 1% din PIB-ul Italiei este asigurat de românii care lucrează în această țară ... Unul dintre principiile fundamentale ale Uniunii Europene este libera circulație a persoanelor, iar acest principiu trebuie respectat.

27 Cum a spus-o și domnul președinte, am constatat că avem puncte de vedere similare în ceea ce privește relația Regatul Unit-UE și mai ales pe aspectele privind drepturile sociale ale lucrătorilor, soluțiile pe care le vedem la solicitările Marii Britanii converg ... sau punctele de vedere pe soluțiile pe care le vedem converg, lucru care m-a asigurat foarte mult pentru că unele din interogațiile României este cum să facem să păstrăm regulile privind libera circulație a lucrătorilor și drepturile sociale conform a ceea ce prevede tratatul și am constatat că aici parlamentul are același punct de vedere, deci în măsura în care deciziile Consiliului European vor ajunge la parlament, înțeleg că parlamentul va susține punctul de vedere pe care îl are și România.

28 There seems to already be citizens of first and second class in Europe, second class being people who do not hold EU citizenship and are thus discriminated against with regard to the right to free movement (Talani 2012: 61–80).
29

> È questo l'oggetto del contendere con la Commissione europea, con cui abbiamo iniziato i colloqui un anno fa, posizione sostenuta e condivisa dalla Francia, e io spero che in questo caso l'unione possa fare la forza e si riesca a convincere la Commissione europea che è giusto stabilire regole, ma agli Stati membri devono essere dati gli strumenti per attuare effettivamente queste regole.

30 Prime Minister Berlusconi also made some questionable statements about the massive arrival of migrants to Lampedusa Island, reporting, inter alia, that he would empty the island of migrants within 48 hours (McMahon 2012: 7).
31 'La Unión Europea y sus instituciones deben hacer más, más rápido y más eficazmente para crear un verdadero mercado interior que garantice de manera efectiva la libre circulación de personas, servicios, capitales y mercancías.'
32 'Wir haben Probleme gehabt mit der Zuwanderung aus der EU in die Sozialsysteme – Stichwort: Armutsmigration-, und müssen dafür sorgen, dass Freizügigkeit heißt, sich seinen Arbeitsplatz in Europa frei wählen zu können, aber nicht die Wahl des Wohnorts danach zu treffen, wo das Kindergeld am höchsten ist.'
33

> Wir haben keine Zweifel daran, dass das Prinzip der Freizügigkeit nicht infrage gestellt werden sollte. Das gilt. Aber wir müssen uns auch mit dem Missbrauch beschäftigen. Wir haben hierbei sehr eng zusammengearbeitet. Wir verfolgen die Rechtsprechung sehr aufmerksam. Wir wollen denen, die in Kommunen und vor Ort betroffen sind, eben auch zeigen: Missbrauch muss bekämpft werden, damit Freizügigkeit als Prinzip auch durchgesetzt werden kann.

34 'Freien Zugang zum Binnenmarkt bekommt der, der die vier europäischen Grundfreiheiten akzeptiert: die der Menschen, der Güter, der Dienstleistungen, des Kapitals.'
35

> Si le Royaume-Uni veut accéder au marché intérieur, ce qui était le privilège d'être membre de l'Union européenne, ce qui était l'avantage majeur que le Royaume-Uni pouvait chercher dans l'Union européenne, si extérieur à l'Union il veut, comme la Norvège par exemple, être en droit d'accéder au marché intérieur européen, alors le Royaume-Uni devra respecter ce que l'on appelle les quatre libertés: la liberté de circulation des biens, la liberté de circulation des services, la liberté de circulation des capitaux, et la libre circulation des personnes, et il ne peut pas y avoir de dérogation. On ne peut pas prendre trois libertés, en écarter une quatrième, et notamment la liberté de circulation des personnes.

36

> Nous avons aussi besoin de renforcer ce qu'on appelle l'espace Schengen. Remettre en cause la libre circulation des personnes par le retour aux frontières intérieures serait une erreur tragique. Mais prétendre que Schengen, dans son fonctionnement actuel, permettra d'affronter les pressions à son périmètre serait

une autre erreur. Le contrôle effectif des frontières de l'Union passe par une assistance renforcée aux États- frontières, aux États concernés et par la mise en place d'un corps de garde-frontières, de garde-côtes européens, comme le Président de la Commission européenne en a fait la proposition.

37 As we learn in Chapter 6, the utilitarian discourse can also be concerned with threats to social security and social protection (see also Haller 2008: 299).
38 From the moral viewpoint, it is also difficult to justify only granting the right to free movement and residence to EU citizens, especially in the current situation with the number of refugees and immigrants greater than ever (Bauböck 2009, Tonkiss 2013a: 83–98).

5 Community dimension: Reproducing the community of the European Union

1 'liquidar uno de los principios más importantes de la Unión, que es la libre circulación de personas.'
2 'los pilares básicos de nuestro proyecto, incluido la libre circulación de trabajadores.'
3 'Por eso, yo quiero que el Reino Unido permanezca ahí; pero, claro, Europa se ha construido sobre la base de la libre circulación de personas, capitales, mercancías y servicios. Si el Reino Unido se fuera de Europa, los más perjudicados serían los ciudadanos británicos que no podrían circular libremente y que no podrían transferir capitales, ni mercancías, ni servicios.'
4 'Nous devons revenir au sens-même du projet européen, qui est un projet politique fondé sur des valeurs et sur la circulation des personnes, des connaissances, des idées, des œuvres, de la culture et de la création.'
5 'Je suis un dirigeant européen et je suis attaché au principe de l'Europe. La libre circulation fait partie des choix que nous avons voulus il y a maintenant plusieurs décennies en faisant l'Europe.'
6 'Nous en voyons d'autres en ce moment, demander l'application de la libre circulation pour leurs ressortissants et notamment pour travailler -c'était d'ailleurs les fondements de l'Union- et qui ferment leurs portes aujourd'hui, érigent des murs face aux réfugiés qui fuient la guerre ou la persécution.'
7 'Ca veut dire qu'à partir du moment où on a rétabli sa frontière intérieure, on peut aussi rétablir sa monnaie intérieure, puis sa loi intérieure et puis finalement, l'Europe se disloque.'
8
> Que c'est l'intérêt de l'Europe, que c'est l'intérêt du Royaume-Uni, que le référendum puisqu'il aura lieu puisse donner un « oui », mais ce n'est pas un « oui » qu'il faut conditionner, ce n'est pas un « oui » qu'il faut promouvoir, au détriment de l'Europe. Cela doit être un « oui » qui vienne renforcer les principes de l'Union européenne, notamment la libre circulation et les règles sociales.

9 'qui ont fondé l'Union européenne et notamment la libre circulation.'
10 'c'est précisément cet argument qui n'a pas pu convaincre et que les Britanniques ont rejeté à une majorité.'

11 Then again, it can be questioned whether the fixed and indispensable values were shared by all the countries that joined the Union later or whether they just learned those values in order to join the Union (cf. Checkel 2007).
12

> Heute ist die Europäische Union für alle Mitglieder und für jeden Einzelnen von uns von großer Bedeutung. Europa, das ist Stabilität und Frieden – für uns ist das auch schon selbstverständlich, aber man kann das gar nicht hoch genug schätzen. Europa, das ist Freizügigkeit und ein Rahmen, der nicht einengt, sondern schützt. Europa, das ist Vielfalt der Sprachen – ein Europa, das sich auch an den Unterschieden der einzelnen Mitglieder erfreut. Europa, das ist Zusammenleben und gegenseitiger Austausch, ohne dass man auf die eigene Heimat, auf eigene Traditionen, auf eigene Wurzeln verzichten muss. Außerdem ist Europa ein Bekenntnis zu den gemeinsamen Werten, die uns alle einen. Die politische Einigung Europas, davon bin ich überzeugt, wäre nicht denkbar gewesen, wenn das europäische Projekt nicht von Anfang an in bestimmten, unverzichtbar erklärten Werten gewurzelt hätte.

13 'Ich habe ein Interesse daran, dass die Schweiz so nah wie möglich an der EU bleibt, und ein Interesse habe ich auch an der vollen Durchsetzung der Freizügigkeit. Diese ist ein Kernelement der EU.'
14 'in fortezze in nome della sicurezza.'
15 'Il trattato è una conquista di libertà: se si ritiene che per vincere la paura bisogna diminuire la libertà, ci troveremo tra qualche anno con paure peggiori avendo compresso al libertà di circolazione.'
16 On another occasion, Premier Rajoy also presented an almost identical statement concerning free movement (Rajoy 2014g).
17 This is not surprising in light of Spanish economic problems and high youth unemployment, which Spanish politicians have been trying to solve (Díaz 2014).
18 'Europa debe ser un espacio de oportunidades para nuestros conciudadanos, especialmente para los jóvenes, protegiendo la libertad de los trabajadores para moverse libremente, residir y trabajar en cualquier país de la Unión Europea.'
19

> Il tema dell'Europa è dire ciascuno di noi a se stesso e poi agli altri e, permettetemi, poi ai nostri figli – noi che siamo la generazione Erasmus dobbiamo per i nostri figli avere qualcosa in più – se è possibile, o non è possibile immaginare che l'Europa nella quale mio nonno ha combattuto sparando contro qualcun altro in Francia possa essere per mio figlio il luogo nel quale non soltanto si vive la dimensione del confronto e del dialogo, ma si vive la dimensione di istituzioni in grado di rappresentare una speranza, già la speranza.

20 'Schengen, ça marche, parce que ça assure la libre circulation des étudiants européens au sein de l'espace intérieur.'
21 'Or, l'Europe, c'est la mobilité, c'est la libre circulation. C'est aussi la possibilité d'accéder plus largement aux procédures ERASMUS qui, pour beaucoup de jeunes pas simplement des étudiants puisque nous avons voulu l'élargir aux apprentis et même à ceux qui seront dans le premier emploi, pourront être une découverte et une expérience supplémentaire.'

22 An interesting cursory note is that Mr Pisanu has been considered rather moderate on immigration matters compared to his cabinet colleagues (Ruzza and Fella 2009: 136).
23 'Asseconderemo, com'è nostro dovere – dice infatti – la decisione della Francia di sospendere gli accordi di Schengen. E per parte nostra preferiamo rafforzare la sorveglianza lungo i confini con l'Austria e la Slovenia [...] Non possiamo limitare la libertà dei nostri cittadini per combattere i nemici della libertà. Se lo facessimo, concederemmo loro una vittoria.'
24 The interview was published in the French newspaper *L'Express* and reported on the website of Interior Minister Friedrich.
25 In Germany, nationalism has been a difficult question after the Second World War, and the pride of being German is arguably a controversial issue. Alternatively, European integration has served as a sort of substitute identity that has also psychologically rehabilitated Germany (Knischewski 1996: 130–4). Germany has witnessed conflicts over cultural issues as well, for example, concerning the right of teachers to wear a headscarf (Benhabib 2004).
26 Friedrich also referred to the multicultural discussion, which relates to the fact that Angela Merkel declared multiculturalism an utter failure at an event of the young members of her party in 2010. This declaration in turn spurred a lively discussion throughout Europe. Anthony M. Messina has noted that the problems related to multicultural policies in Europe may also deteriorate attitudes towards European integration (Messina 2014: 57), since the question is simply about different types of 'Others' being present. European politicians often argue that third-country immigrants should only integrate to the national culture and values, while it is simultaneously maintained that all the EU countries share the same values. It can be asked whether it would suffice for new immigrants to integrate to the EU values, then.
27

> Ich sehe Europa als großen Arbeitsmarkt für uns alle an. Auf diesem Arbeitsmarkt gibt es derzeit über 22 Millionen Arbeitslose. Es ist unsere Pflicht, zunächst diese Menschen in Arbeit zu bringen, bevor wir auch noch Arbeitskräfte von außerhalb Europas zum Beispiel nach Deutschland holen. ... Bis vor einigen Jahren gab es in Deutschland die irrige Vorstellung einer multikulturellen Gesellschaft. Viele Linke meinten, es sei möglich, dass verschiedene Kulturen nebeneinander leben könnten – also nicht Miteinander, sondern Nebeneinander. Doch das Nebeneinander führt zu Spannungen, die zu Lasten des gesellschaftlichen Zusammenhalts gehen. Deshalb spricht auch Bundeskanzlerin Angela Merkel heute vom Scheitern des Multi-Kulti-Gedankens. Wir brauchen ein Bekenntnis zu unserer kulturellen Identität. Diese Identität beinhaltet auch Toleranz, die wir im menschlichen Miteinander mit anderen Kulturen pflegen müssen. Diese Akzeptanz unserer Ideale und Werte ist Voraussetzung für eine erfolgreiche Integration.

28 The stricter tone may also relate to his desire to take votes from France's anti-European and anti-immigrant party, the National Front. Interestingly, from the beginning of European integration, France has had anti-European political forces from different political wings: in the post-war era they were right-wing activists inspired by the so-called Boulangist tradition and the French Communist Party, while the right-wing *Front National* has been influential since the 1980s (Jenkins and Copsey 1996).

29

> Si nous avons fait l'Europe, c'est pour être plus forts, pas pour être moins forts ! Et si nous avons fait l'Europe, c'est pour exercer notre souveraineté avec les autres, pas pour renoncer à l'exercice de notre souveraineté. J'ai demandé et j'ai prévenu: nous sommes d'accord pour gérer avec nos partenaires européens nos frontières mais à la condition qu'ils les gèrent vraiment. Nous ne pouvons pas accepter que la frontière entre la Grèce et la Turquie, sur 115 kilomètres, soit ouverte à tous les vents, régulée et contrôlée par personne.

30 The UK has also been characterized as a multinational state, 'created before the appearance of nationalist ideology' (Walzer 1994: 66, see also Tonkiss 2013a).

31 The UK is not able to set a quota for EU migrants, but neither are there obligations to allow third-country immigrants to enter, at least beyond the family reunification of EU citizens (see also Horsti and Pellander 2015).

32 The unification of Romania and Moldova was already on the political agenda after Moldova declared its independence in 1991; although Romania was the first to recognize its neighbour's independence, Romanian leaders hoped for an eventual unification similar to the unification of Germany. Still, the Romanian public did not share that objective, and it did not remain an important policy aim (Roper 2000: 126–7).

33 Despite the close ties between Romania and Moldova, Romanian leaders chose accession to the European Union over maintaining an open border with Moldova. It has been argued that Romania would not have even started controlling the border with Moldova 'without the external leverage of the EU' (Papadimitriou and Phinnemore 2008: 141). Although Moldova was often present in the Romanian discourses, Moldovan politicians have not been particularly eager to unify with Romania. Moldova only allowed dual citizenship in 2003, but banned the entry of dual citizenship holders into public office, which the European Court of Human Rights later judged as disproportionate (Roper 2005). As Romania joined the Union in 2007, Moldovans signed half a million Romanian citizenship applications in the hope of gaining the right to free movement in the European Union (Papadimitriou and Phinnemore 2008: 138). By 2013, already 500,000 Romanian passports had been granted to Moldovans (Panainte, Nedelciuc and Voicu 2013).

34

> Vom continua să acordăm sprijin persoanelor din Republica Moldova care se consideră români și simt românește, pentru a-și păstra identitatea. Nu putem accepta ca românii de peste Prut să fie izolați de restul Europei. Nu putem accepta ca, în special generația tânără, să nu aibă șansa de a circula liber și de a-și face studiile în țara noastră sau în restul țărilor europene.

35

> Reprezentanții asociațiilor de români din Italia au semnalat, de asemenea, unele disfuncționalități în ceea ce privește asigurarea serviciilor consulare de calitate și obținerea cardului european de sănătate, precum și aspecte legate drepturile cetățenilor români în ceea ce privește libertatea circulației muncii. Primul-ministru a precizat că aceste probleme vor fi analizate pentru a fi identificate soluțiile care se impun și a transmis românilor care trăiesc în străinătate că "mai devreme sau mai târziu locul fiecăruia dintre noi este acasă în România.

6 Utility dimension: Optimizing concrete benefits

1 Hare's theory, of course is not the only contemporary utilitarian philosophy. Authors such as Peter Singer and Henry Sidgwick can also be mentioned as influential utilitarian philosophers of the twentieth century.
2 As Parker and Toke put it,

> [t]hus, according to a functionalist logic that has been performatively enacted by European institutions, the free movement of coal and steel workers (Paris) was gradually extended to workers more generally (Rome) and the scope of rights accruing to such workers was extended over time through, inter alia, European Court of Justice (ECJ) activism and various regulations in the 1960s. Indeed, over time, 'workers' became 'persons' with ever more rights and, with the Maastricht Treaty they became European citizens able to claim rights associated with their movement from a European jurisdiction. (Parker and Toke 2013: 370)

3 In the liberal intergovernmentalist theory, free movement could be understood as an economic principle based on the interest formation of the states and the reform of free movement would be understandable if it no longer created economic benefits for the member states (Moravcsik 1998). Although the theory was supposed to be non-ideological, its approach is based on economic interests and is similarly ideological, as noted by Owen Parker (2013: 15). In addition, Andrew Moravcsik observed in the early 2000s that the EU tends to be overtly neoliberal in its policies, while its social dimension is less pronounced. For example, in immigration matters, evolving European norms tend to be stricter than the average national norm (Moravcsik 2002: 621).
4 'Comment imaginer qu'une Europe, dont la plupart des pays sont dans l'espace Schengen, qui pose comme postulat la libre-circulation des personnes et des biens, puisse continuer sans se doter de principes communs pour élaborer une politique d'immigration commune?'
5

> Nous devons aussi mettre en uvre un système unifié d'asile, parce que c'est la condition dans un espace de libre circulation comme Schengen, pour qu'il ne puisse pas y avoir de pays qui accueillent plus que d'autres en fonction de leur population. Nous devons aussi avoir une politique migratoire commune avec des règles communes et donc vérifier qu'il y a bien cette harmonization.

6

> Hemos impulsado una política en la Unión Europea. La inmigración ha de ser una política europea, dado que existe la libre circulación de personas en el territorio de las UE. Pero hemos de recordar una cosa: la mitad del crecimiento económico que hemos tenido en los últimos años es como consecuencia de la inmigración. Lo que cotizan a la Seguridad Social los inmigrantes equivale al pago de casi un millón de pensionistas españoles.

7

> Yo lo que he planteado y lo que voy a seguir planteando es que la inmigración requiere una política europea conjunta; requiere normas iguales en muchos

temas, es decir, atribución de los mismos derechos, de las mismas obligaciones y normas sobre repatriación iguales, pues, si estamos en un espacio donde hay libre circulación de personas, es absurdo que haya normas diferentes; y, sobre todo, requiere una acción decidida con fondos para ayudar a los países de donde vienen estas personas, porque es evidente que, si la gente en su país no puede llevar una vida digna, lo razonable y lo lógico es que intente llevarla en otro país.

8

Tuttavia, questo [politiche sull'immigrazione separate] contraddice il principio della libera circolazione nei Paesi, almeno di area Schengen, e quindi è opportuno che a partire da questo fenomeno – che, ripeto, non è solo, come ho sempre detto e ribadisco, di immigrazione clandestina, bensì di movimenti di massa che ancora non si sono manifestati nella loro complessità – l'Europa prenda l'occasione per trasformare un sistema di 27 politiche sull'immigrazione in un sistema europeo.

9 In the Maastricht Treaty negotiations in the early 1990s, the Commission was already in favour of putting immigration policies in the EC main pillar, a proposition made by German Chancellor Helmut Kohl. However, other states wanted it to remain in the intergovernmental third pillar (Moravcsik 1998: 452).
10 Public opinion also supported a common immigration policy in Spain and France. In the Standard Eurobarometer from spring 2019, 84 per cent of Spaniards supported the idea of a common immigration policy, which may also have been affected by the comments of the leading politicians. In France and Italy, the figure was 67 per cent (European Commission 2019: T90).
11 However, already in 2009, 61 per cent of A2 migrants (Bulgaria and Romania) and 49 per cent of A8 migrants (the 8 CEEs that joined in 2004) had stayed for over four years, and the figures were higher than the European average (Holland et al. 2011: 129). This implies that intra-European migration is not very short term in Germany.
12 'Sie schafft in der Sprache der Migrationsexperten eine "triple win"-Situation, von der die Aufnahme- und Herkunftsländer und auch die Migranten selbst profitieren. Sie sieht vor, dass Arbeitssuchende aus anderen Regionen dieser Welt durch befristete Zuwanderung unsere Arbeitsmärkte beleben und sich bei uns weiterqualifizieren.'
13

Freizügigkeit in Europa ist an sich überhaupt keine Drohung, sondern etwas, wovon auch viele Deutsche im Ausland selbstverständlich profitieren. Außerdem ist es doch längst nicht mehr so, dass Millionen Osteuropäer nur darauf warten, zu uns zu kommen. Gegen mögliches Lohndumping wurden in besonders betroffenen Branchen Mindestlöhne festgelegt, auch für die Zeitarbeit wird es eine Lohnuntergrenze geben. Manche Branchen, die händeringend Arbeitskräfte suchen, werden die neue Freizügigkeit sogar bald als Chance erkennen.

14 'Wir kennen das Prinzip der Freizügigkeit. Das heißt, dass jeder aus einem Mitgliedstaat der Europäischen Union, der in Deutschland eine Arbeit findet, hier arbeiten kann, ohne dass es besonderer Erlaubnisse oder Bestimmungen bedarf. Das ist natürlich für uns auch eine Möglichkeit, gut ausgebildete Fachkräfte zu bekommen, selbst wenn wir selbst einen demografischen Wandel erleben.'

15 However, it has not been convincingly demonstrated that free movement would increase, for example, productivity, but a stable workforce appears to be more important than worker mobility (Recchi 2013: 80).
16 Nevertheless, few infringement procedures have been launched by the Commission against states for violating the right to the free movement of persons, and mere public naming and shaming is not very effective (see e.g. Gehring 2013b).
17
> Ebbene andare avanti con il mercato unico dei servizi, è un fondamentale pilastro del mercato unico, ma che cosa vuol dire per i singoli paesi? Vuol dire fare le aperture, le liberalizzazioni a casa propria nei servizi, non solo rispettare gli aspetti di libero movimento, di libera prestazione, di libero stabilimento, e ciò su cui il Senato, a Roma ieri, ha votato definitivamente il pacchetto liberalizzazioni e concorrenza, riguarda in grandissima parte proprio i servizi, dai servizi di distribuzione del gas, ai servizi finanziari e bancari, alle libere professioni, e una vasta gamma di soluzioni economiche e di interessi che devono essere mossi per dare luogo ai mercati dei servizi più attivi e più efficienti.

18 'Les villes ont été rebâties, le niveau de vie a décuplé, la disparition des frontières a assuré la libre circulation des personnes et la multiplication des échanges a favorisé le retour à la prospérité.'
19 PM Cameron also introduced more restrictions for EU migrants who claimed benefits in the UK and argued that the right to free movement was being abused in terms of benefit tourism (e.g. Cameron 2014c, 2014d, 2014e). Apparently, only people who have contributed to the society should be entitled to benefits.
20 'Până la urmă Europa are mai mult de pierdut, decât are de pierdut România, că avem circulație liberă.'
21 The abolition of the Schengen Area would likely be very costly for the Union, as argued in a study made by the German Bertelsmann Foundation (Böhmer et al. 2016).
22 'Locul nostru este in Spațiul Schengen, ca stat membru cu drepturi depline. Aderarea României va consolida securitatea acestuia și va transmite, într-un moment de răscruce, un mesaj politic puternic de sprijin pentru menținerea principiului liberei circulații a persoanelor.'
23 'În plus, avantajele aparenenței României la Uniunea Europeană se resimt pozitiv în viața fiecăruia dintre noi, fie că ne referim la libera circulație a persoanelor, fie la oportunitățile economice sau de educație.'
24 'Noi trebuie să optăm între: "Vrem libera circulație a forței de muncă" sau: "Nu o vrem ca să nu ne mai plece tinerii pregătiți". Eu vă pot spune că România nu pierde prin libera circulație a forței de muncă.'
25
> Diaspora românească a devenit nu doar o forță intelectuală, mai ales în anii de după război și în perioada comunismului, când au plecat mai ales cei care au decis să nu împărtășească anumite valori promovate de conducerea statului la acea vreme, ceea ce a făcut ca în multe țări diaspora românească să fie reprezentată mai ales de aceste valori intelectuale, dar diaspora românească este în momentul de față și o forță economică, așa cum spunea și domnul președinte, după migrația masivă, mai ales în perioada pregătirii aderării României la

Uniunea Europeană și după aderare, când mulți români au beneficiat de acest drept la liberă circulație a persoanelor și a lucrătorilor.

26 'Lo he dicho muchas veces, pero quisiera recalcarlo aquí ante ustedes: una de las ideas-fuerza más importantes en la Unión Europea es la creación de un espacio sin fronteras de prosperidad compartida.'

27 Germany maintained the maximum period of transitional restrictions for both A8 countries (joined in 2004) and A2 countries (joined in 2007), while it provided free access to Croatian workers.

28

Ich komme zum Thema Mindestlohn. Ich stehe dieser Diskussion offen gegenüber. Ich weiß, dass im Zusammenhang mit der Dienstleistungsrichtlinie auf uns Situationen zukommen werden – nicht heute und nicht morgen, aber im Jahr 2011, wenn die komplette Freizügigkeit innerhalb der Europäischen Union erreicht ist -, in denen wir Länder haben, in denen das Lohnniveau deutlich unter dem bei uns liegt, weshalb wir uns überlegen müssen: Wie reagieren wir darauf? Für mich hat die gesamte Diskussion um den Mindestlohn ein Kriterium: Am Ende dieser Diskussion dürfen wir nicht weniger Arbeitsplätze in Deutschland haben, sondern wir müssen mehr Arbeitsplätze in Deutschland haben.

29

Ich glaube, dass wir gerade innerhalb der Europäischen Union auf der einen Seite natürlich die Freizügigkeit haben – das muss man sagen –, aber dass diese Freizügigkeit mit der Erwartung verbunden ist, dass dann hier auch ein Arbeitsplatz wahrgenommen wird und dass das nicht einfach nur ein Kommen nach dem Motto ist, einen Asylantrag zu stellen, wenn die Bedingungen für einen Asylantrag hinterher gar nicht gegeben sind.

30

Das ist nicht die Intention des Freizügigkeitsgesetzes; das heißt, dass man überall in Europa arbeiten darf. Diese Intention schließt nicht ein, dass man überall in Europa vom ersten Tag an auch die gleichen Sozialleistungen bekommt. Deshalb finde ich die Gedanken, die sowohl Frau Nahles als auch Herr Scholz geäußert haben, interessant. Sie verknüpfen sich in gewisser Weise mit dem, was Großbritannien für eine bestimmte Regelung wünscht.

31 'würde der Binnenmarkt massiv darunter leiden.'

32 Transitional arrangements were already imposed when Greece joined the EU in 1981 and when Spain and Portugal joined the Union in 1986. During that time, transitional restrictions were valid in the entire community, while in the twenty-first-century accessions, the old member states could decide whether or not to impose restrictions (see also Currie 2008: 14).

33 In moral terms, however, it would rather appear that it was unfair to judge access to welfare benefits based on one's country of birth, that is, arbitrarily (Huysmans 2000a: 751, Tonkiss 2013a: 90–1). Overall, Home Secretary Reid's utterance approached Eastern European movers fairly positively, while voices that were more critical started to be heard during the subsequent Labour government (see, e.g. the utterance of Smith 2007).

34
> Problema migrației sărăciei este o problemă care, din nefericire, s-a amestecat de prea multe ori cu problema liberei circulații a forței de muncă în Europa. Libera circulație a forței de muncă este un bun câștigat, enorm de valoros, pentru noi toți în Europa. Din păcate, când este vorba despre România, se vede prima dată migrația sărăciei, care nu este semnificativă numeric, și se vede foarte greu și foarte rar se discută un fenomen, care este semnificativ, este problematic pentru România și este un câștig net pentru Germania, este vorba de migrația forței de muncă calificată și foarte calificată care pleacă din România și vine în Germania.

7 Solidarity dimension: Solidarity as the ultimate aim

1 This idea is also closely related to cosmopolitanism (e.g. Delanty and He 2008).
2 In the context of the EU, reflections on solidarity can also be observed in its enlargement policy. For example, the previous enlargements can be seen as widening the solidary community of the EU by introducing new member states, which are intended to become part of 'us' (Jileva 2004, Spohn 2005, Zaborowski 2006).
3 For example, in a Eurobarometer Spring 2019 survey, free movement was polled as the second most positive result after peace (European Commission 2019: T128).
4 In contrast, this could also constitute an example of regional nationalism, as the implication is that the current home countries should be replaced by a European home country instead of another type of unity (Tonkiss 2013a).
5 Commissioner Špidla has also written about immigration in an academic journal, where he explicitly differentiated the 'immigrants' who were defined as people coming from outside the EU, and EU movers. He also lamented the fact that some member states called both groups immigrants and thus categorized them in the same group (Špidla 2009: 17). Although the commissioner's intention was probably to remove the label of immigrant from EU citizens and thus increase the European sense of solidarity, it simultaneously served to classify people as first-class and second-class movers (see also Hansen 2008).
6 The German approach to the EU has generally been positive. However, it has been argued that after the financial crisis, German European identity has changed. Instead of turning to nationalism such as some other countries, German politicians instead emphasized Northern European identity, as opposed to a Southern one (Galpin 2015). This is not, however, visible in the free movement discourses, although a noticeable issue is that no German solidarity-related free movement utterances appeared during the challenging years of the financial crisis.
7
> Die Arbeitnehmerfreizügigkeit ist eine der Grundfreiheiten in der Europäischen Union; auch das fließt in die Statistik ein. Die Wanderung von Arbeitnehmern ist ein notwendiger und – ich sage auch – gewünschter Prozess für das Zusammenwachsen. Wir sollten also nicht allzu sehr Angst davor haben, dass Hochqualifizierte ins Ausland gehen. Wir sollten besser Verbindung mit ihnen halten, damit sie eines Tages zurückkehren. Vielleicht sollten wir uns über eine bessere Betreuung der Deutschen im Ausland Gedanken machen. Je enger unsere Verbindung zu Deutschen im Ausland ist, desto mehr profitieren wir alle

von den Erfahrungen, die sie im Ausland machen, und desto eher können wir ihnen den Weg zurück ebnen.

8

Die Entwicklung der Freizügigkeit aller Unionsbürger ist vielleicht die größte Erfolgsgeschichte des europäischen Einigungsprozesses. Der Zuzug von Unionsbürgern ist eine wirtschaftliche und kulturelle Bereicherung und vielerorts auch eine demografische Notwendigkeit. Deshalb dürfen wir es nicht dem Zufall überlassen, ob und wie gut die Integration von Zuwanderern innerhalb Europas gelingt. Wir müssen die gesellschaftliche Akzeptanz für Zuwanderung auch innerhalb Europas verbessern und eine echte Willkommenskultur schaffen. Denn auch wenn wir unterschiedliche Vergangenheiten haben, geht es darum, dass wir unsere Geschichte gemeinsam erfolgreich weiterschreiben.

9

Es gab in den alten Mitgliedstaaten Ängste und Skepsis zum Beispiel davor, dass sich die Zahl der Mitgliedstaaten der Europäischen Union fast verdoppeln sollte. Viele sahen die Freizügigkeit für Millionen neue EU-Bürgerinnen und EU-Bürger als Bedrohung für den eigenen Arbeitsplatz. Neue Entscheidungsstrukturen mussten entwickelt werden. Europäische Fördermittel mussten zugunsten der neuen Mitgliedstaaten umverteilt werden. Heute erkennen wir, dass sich diese Kraftanstrengung für uns alle gelohnt hat. Sie hat uns nicht zu weniger, sondern sie hat uns zu mehr Wohlstand verholfen. Sie hat uns nicht zu weniger, sondern zu mehr Freiheit verholfen. Sie hat uns nicht zu weniger, sondern zu mehr Vielfalt verholfen. Kurz: Sie hat uns zu mehr Europa verholfen, weil wir Europäer in unserer Geschichte gelernt haben, aus unserer Vielfalt das Meiste zu machen. Die Eigenschaft, die uns dazu befähigt, die uns zur Freiheit in Verantwortung befähigt, ist Toleranz. Sie ist ein wertvolles Gut.

10

Erstens glaube ich, dass das Schengen-Projekt von größter Aktualität ist und dass es allergrößte Gründe gibt, alles zu tun, damit wir die Freizügigkeit innerhalb der Schengen-Grenzen auch weiterhin wirklich leben können. Deshalb haben wir ja auch die Dringlichkeit, die Fragen der Migration zu steuern und auch zu regeln, um aus illegaler Migration legale Migration zu machen. Die temporären Grenzkontrollen, die Sie angesprochen haben, sind zwar Teil des Schengen-Systems, aber sie bergen natürlich auch Gefahren in sich, dass wir, wenn wir die Probleme nicht wirklich lösen, dann auch Schengen nicht so leben können, wie wir das wollen. Ich glaube, Schengen ist sowohl etwas, was die Bürgerinnen und Bürger Europas sehr schätzen, als auch ein Faktor für das Zusammenwachsen Europas und für das Wirtschaftswachstum Europas. Deshalb muss aus meiner Sicht alles darangesetzt werden, Schengen zu erhalten und dann natürlich auch den Ländern, die noch nicht zu Schengen gehören, auch die Möglichkeit zu geben, Teil dieses Schengen-Systems zu werden.

11 'Voi ați avut șansa să creșteți și să vă formați în valorile europene. Oportunitățile de care puteți beneficia sunt uriașe și nu mă refer doar la libertatea de a circula în cadrul

Uniunii sau de a studia oriunde pe teritoriul acesteia. Mă refer la șansa extraordinară de a participa efectiv la construcția viitorului Europei.'

12 'Ne-am dorit libera circulație. O putem avea pe deplin, odată cu intrarea definitivă în spațiul european fără granițe.'

13 On another occasion as well, French President Chirac focused on the practical measures taken by certain states that illustrate how certain member states are *building deeper Europeanness* (Chirac 2007).

14 During President Chirac's term, the Schengen Area only covered fifteen areas; hence, it is no wonder that free movement still appeared a project of only certain states. At its inception, free movement was envisioned for only five member states, but by 2011, twenty-six states were included in the project. Obviously, later French presidents did not consider free movement as a pioneer project of the willing member states.

15

> Dans le même esprit, si la France récuse l'idée d'un directoire – car l'Union a besoin de tous et doit respecter chacun -, je pense qu'il faut absolument permettre aux Etats qui veulent agir ensemble, en complément des politiques communes, de le faire. Ces groupes pionniers, pour lesquels j'ai présenté des propositions dès 2000, doivent pouvoir se constituer autour de tous les pays qui en ont la volonté et les moyens, et rester ouverts à tous ceux qui sont prêts à les rejoindre. C'est ce que nous avons fait avec la monnaie unique, la libre circulation des personnes dans l'espace Schengen ou certaines initiatives de défense. ... C'est-à-dire en rassemblant ses forces, dans le respect de la diversité de ses nations, de ses peuples et de ses cultures. Telle est l'œuvre à laquelle la France, avec ses partenaires, veut apporter toute sa contribution.

16

> Ceux qui ont eu l'idée du tunnel sous la Manche, comme ceux qui ont eu l'idée, il y a plus de vingt ans, du tunnel du Saint-Gothard, avaient à l'esprit une certaine idée de l'Europe. Une Europe qui n'est pas simplement faite de normes, de procédures ou d'institutions. Une Europe qui s'incarne dans des projets, dans des ambitions, dans des volontés de progrès. Une Europe qui investit dans l'innovation, dans la mobilité, dans le développement durable. Une Europe qui assure, et c'est très important, la libre circulation des personnes et des marchandises. C'est cet esprit-là, c'est cette dynamique-là qu'il faut encore insuffler aux pays qui sont membres de l'Union européenne, à ceux qui n'en sont pas membres, mais qui sont dans l'Europe. Nous sommes dans le même ensemble, nous sommes dans le même espace. Nous avons les mêmes volontés, les mêmes espoirs.

17

> Tres grandes naciones, tres de las más antiguas de Europa, España, Francia y Portugal, junto con las instituciones de la Unión representadas por la Comisión y el Banco Europeo de Inversiones, dan un paso muy importante para superar fronteras. Ése es el signo de los tiempos y de nuestro proyecto común: la integración europea: unir, integrar y conectar. Ya acabamos con las fronteras artificiales entre nosotros y ahora queremos acabar con las fronteras naturales. Ta tecnología nos lo permite; pero lo más importante es la voluntad política, la única capaz de superar obstáculos técnicos y burocráticos. Y la voluntad política

queda hoy expresada al máximo nivel para poner en marcha este proyecto, y también los mecanismos y los recursos necesarios para ello.

18

È stato fatto un passo in avanti piccolo ma significativo grazie all'iniziativa dei Paesi del Mediterraneo guidati dall'Italia ovvero Cipro, Grecia e Malta, che un anno e mezzo fa chiesero l'attuazione del principio del burden sharing con la conseguenza che nel programma di Stoccolma per la prima volta si parla di Mediterraneo dal punto di vista della sicurezza, cosa mai avvenuta prima, dell'immigrazione clandestina, del rischio terrorismo, e si attua il principio del burden sharing anche se su base volontaria … Credo che questa sia una richiesta giusta, che interviene nei momenti di difficoltà, di crisi, di emergenza e attua un principio di solidarietà che è uno dei principi fondamentali del sistema sociale europeo. Non vedo francamente obiezioni per cui alla libera circolazione di uomini, di cittadini e di merci si debba derogare in caso di rifugiati, cosicché non possano liberamente circolare neanche nell'area Schengen.

19 Directive on the minimum standards for granting temporary protection in the event of a mass influx of displaced persons and on measures promoting a balance of efforts between member states in receiving such persons and bearing the consequences thereof.

20

Anche su questo l'Europa deve intervenire rapidamente, perché la circolazione nei Paesi dell'Unione di immigrati che hanno titoli per fare richiesta di asilo politico, deve essere resa fluida, possibile. Anche perché sempre più non ci troviamo di fronte a immigrazione 'occupazionale', di chi cerca un lavoro qualunque sia, ma arrivano professionisti, come i siriani, che sfuggono da situazioni di pericolo per la loro vita. E l'Europa li costringe a restare bloccati in Italia perché sbarcano qui. Su questo il nostro pressing sarà sempre più incessante. Anche perché io penso agli immigrati e alla libertà di movimento che va garantita, ripeto, a chi ha i titoli, mentre gli altri vanno rimandati a casa, ma penso anche ai siciliani. Che stanno mostrando come sempre il loro cuore grande, la loro capacità di essere solidali, ma che chiedono, e giustamente, di non essere anche loro messi nella condizione di sentirsi come assediati da immigrati che non stanno bene qui.

21

La gestione dei flussi di migrant verso l'Unione Europea è entrata da tempo in una fase critica, in cui la solidarietà degli Stati membri viene ogni giorno messa a dura prova. Nonostante le recenti iniziative della Commissione e del Consiglio, la chiusura, talvolta non adeguatamente motivate, delle frontiere da parte di alcuni Stati e il diffuso rifiuto di condividere gli oneri di questa sfida epocale mettono a rischio la tenuta dell'Unione. Le proposte della Commissione, che l'Italia appoggia con convinzione, di istituire una Guardia di Frontiera e Costiera europea e le communicazioni 'Back to Schengen' e sulla riforma del Sistem Dublino potranno dare risultati concreti solo se parallelamente la gestione dei flussi migratori passerà dalla fase dell'emergenza a quella di una più ordinata e strategica gestione. Da questa prospettiva appare chiaro come la dimensione esterna della politica migratoria assuma oggi un ruolo fundamentale anche in rapporto alla tenuta di Schengen e al principio di libera circolazione. La gestione dei flussi di migranti non è più sostenibile senza una cooperazione mirata e rafforzata con i Paesi terzi di provenienza e di transito. Molto è stato fatto ma molto di più dobbiamo rapidamente fare se vogliamo scongiurare l'aggravarsi di una crisi sistemica.

22

Segunda, necesitamos una Unión Europea sin fronteras interiores, que gestione las fronteras de la Unión de manera integrada y solidaria. Es decir, una verdadera política de inmigración europea, más eficaz y más solidaria con los países que conformamos su frontera exterior, con más medios europeos y con una dimensión exterior que aúne el diálogo con los países de origen y tránsito, y la cooperación al desarrollo para contribuir a la construcción de un espacio de prosperidad compartido con nuestros vecinos. No se trata de hacer de Europa una fortaleza. Hoy resulta necesario atajar el problema en su raíz: la emigración debe ser una opción y no una obligación para subsistir.

23

Im Moment nehmen nur einige wenige EU-Mitgliedstaaten die große Mehrzahl der Flüchtlinge auf, die nach Europa kommen, allen voran Deutschland. Andere Mitgliedstaaten schauen zu und lassen dabei außer Acht, dass es die EU ist, die sich der weltweiten Migration stellen muss, und dass wir gemeinsam und ihm Geiste der Solidarität reagieren müssen. Was geschieht, wenn wir auf europäischer Ebene nicht gemeinsam handeln, war in den letzten Wochen und Monaten zu beobachten, als an verschiedenen Grenzabschnitten innerhalb des Schengen-Raumes wieder – vorübergehende – Grenzkontrollen eingeführt werden mussten. Auch Deutschland musste angesichts der großen Anzahl von Menschen die Mitte September 2015 eingeführten Grenzkontrollmaßnahmen verlängern. Doch bei diesen Kontrollen werden noch lange keine Menschen abgewiesen. Im Ergebnis wäre das der Gegenentwurf zu einem gemeinsamen europäischen Ansatz. Grenzenlose Einwanderung von Menschen in die Europäische Union und vollständige Bewegungsfreiheit von Flüchtlingen innerhalb Europas sind auf Dauer nicht mit der großen Errungenschaft offener Binnengrenzen zu vereinbaren.

24

Aplicarea libertății de circulație a cetățenilor europeni a pus în evidență și unele dificultăți specifice cu care se confruntă anumite grupuri dezavantajate social. Mă refer cu precădere la etnia Roma, o minoritate transnațională răspândită, în proporții diferite, în toate statele Uniunii. Dimensiunea europeană a problematicii integrării sociale a romilor reclamă, pe lângă politici naționale sistematice de incluziune, și o strategie europeană pentru concertarea politicilor relevante la nivel UE – strategie care se va bucura de tot sprijinul nostru.

25 Indeed, in 2008, President Sarkozy convinced the EU to accept the Pact on Immigration and Asylum where the states committed, inter alia, to end regularization campaigns (see also Vogt 2009).

182 Notes

26
> On fait l'espace Schengen, c'est-à-dire que quelqu'un qui rentre chez nous, rentre chez les autres ou quelqu'un qui rentre chez les autres, rentre chez nous. Dans le même temps, on assiste à des régularisations massives de sans-papiers, sans même que l'on nous demande notre avis. Qui peut croire que cela, c'est l'Europe que veulent les Européens ? Ce n'est pas l'Europe que veulent les Européens.'

8 Setting the scene: Migration policy histories of the analysed countries

1
> (1) Alle Deutschen genießen Freizügigkeit im ganzen Bundesgebiet. (2) Dieses Recht darf nur durch Gesetz oder auf Grund eines Gesetzes und nur für die Fälle eingeschränkt werden, in denen eine ausreichende Lebensgrundlage nicht vorhanden ist und der Allgemeinheit daraus besondere Lasten entstehen würden oder in denen es zur Abwehr einer drohenden Gefahr für den Bestand oder die freiheitliche demokratische Grundordnung des Bundes oder eines Landes, zur Bekämpfung von Seuchengefahr, Naturkatastrophen oder besonders schweren Unglücksfällen, zum Schutze der Jugend vor Verwahrlosung oder um strafbaren Handlungen vorzubeugen, erforderlich ist.

2 In 2004, during Chancellor Schröder's term, Germany also imposed transitional restrictions for the new member states, which were to be lifted at the latest possible date, in 2011. Restrictions were also imposed for Romanian and Bulgarian workers in 2007 as well as for Croatian workers in 2013.
3 With regard to the Maastricht Treaty negotiations, Andrew Moravcsik also observed that the governing CDU party in Germany was in favour of more restrictive common immigration policies as Germany received a disproportionate amount of migrants and refugees compared to other countries in the EC (Moravcsik 1998: 396). Germany was an especially popular target for migrants from Eastern Europe, and the country thus simultaneously supported common immigration policies and EU enlargement, which could be explained both on economic grounds and as a defence against social disruption (Moravcsik 1998: 399–400). Nevertheless, Germany was opposed to enlarging qualified majority voting (QMV) to include immigration matters in the Amsterdam Treaty negotiations, which effectively ended the establishment of a common immigration policy with the signing of the Treaty (Geddes 2000: 117).
4 In the Eurobarometer Spring 2019 survey, as many as 81 per cent of the German respondents reported their support for European immigration policy.
5 France is also infamous for limiting minority and religious rights on the basis of constitutional equality (Balibar 2001, Béland 2003: 66–71, Malik 2015). For example, France is the only EU country that has required a reservation in the minority rights Article 27 of the UN's International Covenant on Civil and Political Rights, based on the claim that there are no national minorities in France, but everyone is equal before the law.
6 Philippe Bourbeau claims that French politicians have increasingly presented migration as a security threat after the 1990s, and especially during Nicolas Sarkozy's

term as the minister of the interior (Bourbeau 2011: 73–7). However, such discussion was mainly concerned with migration from outside the EU, while French politicians approached intra-EU migration more positively.

7 Immigration has also been calculated at the societal level in Italy. For example, a report from 2015 revealed that the contribution of immigration amounts to over ten billion euros per year (Fondazione Leone Moressa 2015).

8 Maroni's Northern League is not predominantly a Eurosceptic party as such, but is characterized by 'diffident acceptance' of the Union, which may also result in calls for more integration (Strumia 2013: 205).

9 In addition, a worker authorization requirement was introduced for Croatian citizens for the initial period of five years, but the transitional restrictions in total were ended on 30 June 2018.

10 It has been argued that the British preferences in immigration matters include (1) strict immigration policies, (2) focus on external instead of internal controls, (3) supranational cooperation in tackling negative externalities caused by other states' policies and in reinforcing the British immigration control (Ette and Gerdes 2007: 107–8).

11 This is related to the observation made by Marcussen et al. in 2001; the mainstream of both main British parties support a 'Europe of nation states' (Marcussen et al. 2001: 112).

12 It can be observed in the British material that, in general, utterances on the EU and on migration become more common before elections. This also tells us something about the EU and migration as contradictory electoral issues as well as about the juxtaposition created by the UK electoral system. The critical approach employed by the politicians in other countries usually concerned migration from third countries; however, in the British case, mainly intra-EU mobility aroused strong feelings.

13 'Europhobia' was also apparent in the rhetoric of the politicians, which supports the argument that the UK citizens see Europe, and especially the new Eastern European migrants, as its 'Other' (Ciupijus 2011, Tonkiss 2013b: 500, Favell 2014: 275–89).

14 Spain is also a desired target or transit route for many African migrants, for example, through the North African cities of Ceuta and Melilla, which are part of the Spanish territory. The border controls in the cities have not always been very well managed, resulting, for example, in fatal shootings of people trying to climb over the walls (Collyer 2012: 505–24). Moreover, other migrants enter Europe through the Canary Islands (Triandafyllidou 2014). These factors may also contribute to the Spanish willingness to support a common European immigration policy.

15 During the financial crisis many Spanish workers, particularly those working in healthcare, moved from Spain to other EU member states (van Riemsdijk 2013: 140). Spain has also been a popular target for retired EU citizens. Eurostat (2019) shows that the total amount of EU citizens in Spain was almost two million in 2018, which is almost half a million more than in the larger neighbouring country, Italy.

16 The restrictions only applied to workers. However, in reality, the restrictions for workers did not allow Spanish authorities to stop Romanian people from coming to Spain; they only restricted the access of Romanian nationals to work or employment benefits. In the beginning of 2011, only 54.3 per cent of Romanians residing in Spain were employed, which makes the Spanish decision less surprising (European Commission 2011).

17 As mentioned before, regularization refers to the legalization of unauthorized migrants, a measure employed by Spain and Italy in particular.

18 An interesting aspect is that there were hardly any discursive differences between different politicians, although Romanian Prime ministers and presidents have often bitterly disagreed over domestic issues. For example, President Iohannis requested the resignation of former prime minister Ponta several times due to allegations of plagiarism and corruption. In autumn 2015, Prime Minister Victor Ponta finally did resign as he was being prosecuted.
19 Already in 1995, a survey about whether Romanians would vote yes or no in a referendum on EU membership resulted in the highest figure in Eastern Europe, with 97 per cent voting in favour (Roper 2000: 117–19).
20 In their study, Sabina Stan and Roland Erne claim that the question of Romanian migration is not only explicable by the sheer difference in the development level of Romania and other European Union countries. Instead, they argue that the growing number of Romanians emigrating from the country relates to the privatization of social and healthcare services, flexibilization of the labour market and the resulting low-cost employment (Stan and Erne 2014: 36).
21 The Commission has also been influential in determining the conditions for the movement of third-country nationals in the EU (Guild 2003: 92–7). The Commissioners did not, however, refer to free movement in the utterances related to organized crime, even though the Commission has been active in establishing internal security cooperation within the Union in order to tackle such crime (Mitsilegas, Monar and Rees 2003: 50).
22 The Italian PD refers to the Democratic Party that was created by a merger of leftist parties during Romano Prodi's term and was also represented by the two later prime ministers, Enrico Letta and Matteo Renzi. The Democratic Party supported Mario Monti's independent government, which is also included in this group. In addition, LN refers to the Northern League that held one post of minister of the interior during the period, employing a fairly different pattern of discourse on common immigration policy than his ally, Silvio Berlusconi's *Forza Italia*. The French UMP is the centre-right party represented by Nicolas Sarkozy, while French PS refers to the Socialist Party, which President François Hollande represented. Finally, the UK Labour has been steered during the period analysed in this book by Tony Blair and Gordon Brown, while the UK Conservative refers to the party that was headed by David Cameron.
23 It is to be noted that the dual-division is ambiguous in the sense that (low-paid) workers can also represent the destitute.

10 Free movement discourses as practical reasoning

1 In his blog, Italian Senator Luigi Manconi proposed in the Italian edition of the *Huffington Post* that it would be necessary to make a recourse to the same directive that Berlusconi's government did in 2011, which would have a strong impact without risking the safety of the refugees (*avrebbe un impatto forte, senza mettere a rischio l'incolumità delle persone in fuga*) (Manconi 2017).

Appendix

1 The utilized keywords included 'Freizügigkeit', 'Verkehr' and 'Mobilität', and all the results were skimmed through to find the relevant utterances.
2 The utilized keywords included 'libre circulation des personnes', 'mobilité' and 'circule*', and the selected documents were skimmed through in order to find the relevant utterances.
3 In the review, I also utilized the search function of the internet browser, with 'circola*' and 'mobilità' as my keywords.
4 In the review process, I also utilized the search function of the internet browser with regard to individual documents, with 'movement' and 'mobility' as my keywords.
5 The internet browser's search function was utilized in the review process of individual documents, with 'circul*', 'movimiento' and 'movilidad' as the keywords.
6 The search function of the internet browser was utilized in the review process of individual documents, with 'mișc*' 'circul*' and 'mobilitate' as the keywords.
7 The keywords included in the search were 'movement' and 'mobility'.

Bibliography

References

Abraham, F. (2015), *Romania since the Second World War: A Political, Social and Economic History*, London: Bloomsbury.
Aggestam, L. (2008), 'Introduction: Ethical Power Europe?', *International Affairs*, 84(1): 1–11.
Alexy, R. (2006), 'Discourse Theory and Fundamental Rights', in A. J. Menéndez and E. O. Eriksen (eds), *Arguing Fundamental Rights*, 15–29, Dordrecht: Springer.
Ambühl, M., and Zurcher, S. (2015), 'Immigration and Swiss-EU Free Movement of Persons: Question of a Safeguard Clause', *Schweizerische Zeitschrift fur Politikwissenschaft*, 21(1): 76–98.
Anderson, B. R. O. (1983), *Imagined Communities: Reflections on the Origin and Spread of Nationalism*, London: Verso.
Aradau, C., Huysmans, J. and Squire, V. (2010), 'Acts of European Citizenship: A Political Sociology of Mobility', *JCMS: Journal of Common Market Studies*, 48(4): 945–65.
Arango, J. (2000a), 'Becoming a Country of Immigration at the End of the Twentieth Century: The Case of Spain', in R. King, G. Lazaridis and C. Tsardanidis (eds), *Eldorado or Fortress? Migration in Southern Europe*, 253–76, Basingstoke: Palgrave Macmillan.
Arango, J. (2000b), 'Explaining Migration: A Critical View', *International Social Science Journal*, 52(165): 283–96.
Arango, J. (2013), 'Exceptional in Europe? Spain's Experience with Immigration and Integration', *Migration Policy Institute*, 1–18
Arango, J., and Martin, P. (2010), 'Best Practices to Manage Migration: Morocco-Spain', *International Migration Review*, 39(1): 258–69.
Arendt, H. (1951), *The Origins of Totalitarianism*, New York: Harcourt, Brace.
Bailes, A. J. K. (2008), 'The EU and a "Better World": What Role for the European Security and Defence Policy?', *International Affairs*, 84(1): 115–30.
Balch, A., Balabanova, E. and Trandafoiu, R. (2014), 'A Europe of Rights and Values? Public Debates on Sarkozy's Roma Affair in France, Bulgaria and Romania', *Journal of Ethnic & Migration Studies*, 40(8): 1154–74.
Balibar, E. (2001), *Nous, citoyens d'Europe? Les frontières, l'État, le peuple*, Paris: La Découverte.
Barbagli, M. (2008), *Immigrazione e sicurezza in Italia*, Bologna: Mulino.
Barbé, E., and Johansson-Nogués, E. (2008), 'The EU as a Modest "Force for Good": The European Neighbourhood Policy', *International Affairs*, 84(1): 81–96.
Bauböck, R. (2009), 'Global Justice, Freedom of Movement and Democratic Citizenship', *Archives Européennes de Sociologie*, 50(1): 1–31.
Bauböck, R. (2013), 'Citizenship and Free Movement', in R. M. Smith (ed.), *Democracy, Citizenship, and Constitutionalism: Citizenship, Borders, and Human Needs*, 343–76, Philadelphia: University of Pennsylvania Press.

Bauböck, R. (2015), 'Morphing the Demos into the Right Shape: Normative Principles for Enfranchising Resident Aliens and Expatriate Citizens', *Democratization*, 22(5): 820–39.

Béland, D. (2003), 'Identity Politics and French Republicanism', *Society*, 40(5): 66–71.

Bellamy, R., Castiglione, D. and Shaw, J. (eds) (2006a), *Making European Citizens; Civic Inclusion in a Transnational Context*, Basingstoke: Palgrave Macmillan.

Bellamy, R., Castiglione, D. and Shaw, J. (2006b), 'Introduction: From National to Transnational Citizenship', in R. Bellamy, D. Castiglione and J. Shaw (eds), *Making European Citizens: Civic Inclusion in a Transnational Context*, 1–30, Basingstoke: Palgrave Macmillan.

Benhabib, S. (2004), *The Rights Of Others: Aliens, Residents, and Citizens*, Cambridge: Cambridge University Press.

Bigo, D. (2000), 'When Two Become One: Internal and External Securitization in Europe', in M. Kelstrup and M. C. Williams (eds), *International Relations Theory and European Integration: Power, Security and Community*, 171–204, London and New York: Routledge.

Bigo, D. (2005), 'Frontier Controls in the European Union: Who Is in control?', in D. Bigo and E. Guild (eds), *Controlling Frontiers: Free Movement into and within Europe*, 49–99, Aldershot: Ashgate.

Bird, M., Odobescu, V., Ferrara, C. and Limontaite, S. (2016), 'Romania and Morocco Have Most Expats in EU Prisons', *EUObserver*, 1 November. Available online https://euobserver.com/investigations/135659 (accessed 27 January 2020).

Blitz, B. K. (2016), *Migration and Freedom: Mobility, Citizenship and Exclusion*, Cheltenham: Edward Elgar.

Bloom, T. and Tonkiss, K. (2013), 'European Union and Commonwealth Free Movement: A Historical-Comparative Perspective', *Journal of Ethnic and Migration Studies*, 39(7): 1067–85.

Böhmer, M., Limbers, J., Pivac, A. and Weinelt, H. (2016), *Abkehr vom Schengen-Abkommen: Gesamtwirtschaftliche Wirkungen auf Deutschland und die Länder der Europäischen Union*, Gütersloh: Bertelsmann Stiftung.

Boia, L. (2001), *Romania: Borderland of Europe*, London: Reaktion.

Bourbeau, P. (2011), *The Securitization of Migration: A Study of Movement and Order*, Abingdon: Routledge.

Brown, C. (2001), 'Ethics, Interests and Foreign Policy', in K. E. Smith and M. Light (eds), *Ethics and Foreign Policy*, 15–32, Cambridge: Cambridge University Press.

Calhoun, C. (2002), 'Imagining Solidarity: Cosmopolitanism, Constitutional Patriotism, and the Public Sphere', *Public Culture*, 14 (July 2000): 147–71.

Carrera, S., Guild, E., Merlino, M. and Parkin, J. (2011), 'A Race against Solidarity: The Schengen Regime and the Franco-Italian Affair', *CESP Liberty and Security in Europe Working Paper*.

Casella Colombeau, S. (2015), 'Policing the Internal Schengen Borders – Managing the Double Bind between Free Movement and Migration Control', *Policing and Society*, 27(5): 480–93.

Castañeda, H. (2010), 'Deportation Deferred: "Illegality", Visibility, and Recognition in Contemporary Germany', in N. De Genova and N. M. Peutz (eds), *The Deportation Regime: Sovereignty, Space, and the Freedom of Movement*, 245–61, Durham, NC: Duke University Press.

Ceccorulli, M., and Fanta, E. (2013), 'The EU and Multilateral Governance of Migration in North and West Africa', in S. Lucarelli, L. van Langenhove and J. Wouters (eds), *The EU and Multilateral Security Governance*, 165–83, London: Routledge.

Cetin, E. (2015), 'The Italian Left and Italy's (Evolving) Foreign Policy of Immigration Controls', *Journal of Modern Italian Studies*, 20(3): 377–97.

Cetti, F. (2012), 'Asylum and the European "Security State": The Construction of the "Global Outsider"', in L. S. Talani (ed.), *Globalisation, Migration, and the Future of Europe: Insiders and Outsiders*, 9–21, London: Routledge.

Chatty, M. (2015), *Migranternas medborgarskap: EU:s medborgarskapande från Romförhandlingarna till idag*, Örebro: Örebro University.

Checkel, J. T. (2007), *International Institutions and Socialization in Europe*, Cambridge: Cambridge University Press.

Chin, R. (2010), 'Guest Worker Migration and the Unexpected Return of Race', in R. Chin, A. Grossmann and G. Eley (eds), *After the Nazi Racial State: Difference and Democracy in Germany and Europe*, 80–101, Ann Arbor: University of Michigan Press.

Ciupijus, Z. (2011), 'Mobile Central Eastern Europeans in Britain: Successful European Union Citizens and Disadvantaged Labour Migrants?', *Work, Employment and Society*, 25(3): 540–50.

Cochran, M. (1999), *Normative Theory in International Relations: A Pragmatic Approach*, Cambridge: Cambridge University Press.

Collyer, M. (2012), 'Migrants as Strategic Actors in the European Union's Global Approach to Migration and Mobility', *Global Networks*, 12(4): 505–24.

Colombo, A., and Sciortino, G. (2004), 'Italian Immigration: The Origins, Nature and Evolution of Italy's Migratory Systems', *Journal of Modern Italian Studies*, 9(1): 49–70.

Commissione Nazionale per il Diritto di Asilo (2019), *Quaderno statistico dal 1990 al 2018*.

Conti, N. (2016), 'The Italian Political Elites and Europe: Big Move, Small Change?', *International Political Science Review*, 38(5): 534–48.

Council of the European Union (2008), European Pact on Immigration and Asylum, 13440/08, 24 September.

Council of the European Union (2016), Council Implementing Decision Setting Out a Recommendation for Temporary Internal Border Control in Exceptional Circumstances Putting the Overall Functioning of the Schengen Area at Risk Delegations, 8835/16, 12 May.

Cross, G. S. (1983), *Immigrant Workers in Industrial France: The Making of a New Laboring Class*, Philadelphia, PA: Temple University Press.

Crowley, J. (2003), 'Locating Europe', in C. A. Groenendijk, E. Guild and P. E. Minderhoud (eds), *In Search of Europe's Borders*, 27–44, The Hague: Kluwer Law International.

Currie, S. (2008), *Migration, Work and Citizenship in the Enlarged European Union*, Abingdon: Ashgate.

Czaika, M., and De Haas, H. (2013), 'The Effectiveness of Immigration Policies', *Population and Development Review*, 39(3): 487–508.

Daily Mail Reporter (2010), 'Romanian President Praises Countrymen for Doing British Jobs in Attack on "lazy Westerners"', *Daily Mail*, 6 August. Available online https://www.dailymail.co.uk/news/article-1300807/Romanian-president-Traian-Basescu-praises-countrymen-claiming-British-benefits.html (accessed 27 January 2020).

de Beus, J. (2006), 'The European Union as Community: An Argument about the Public Sphere in International Society and Politics', in P. van Seters (ed.), *Communitarianism in Law and Society*, 71–107, Lanham, MD: Rowman & Littlefield.

Delanty, G., and He, B. (2008), 'Cosmopolitan Perspectives on European and Asian Transnationalism', *International Sociology*, 23(3): 323–44.

Delanty, G., Jones, P. and Wodak, R. (2008), 'Introduction: Migration, Discrimination and Belonging in Europe', in G. Delanty, R. Wodak and P. Jones (eds), *Identity, Belonging and Migration*, 1–18, Liverpool: Liverpool University Press.

Dennison, J., and Geddes, A. (2018), 'Brexit and the Perils of "Europeanised" Migration', *Journal of European Public Policy*, 25(8): 1137–53.

Deutsch, K. W., Burrel, S. A., Kann, R. A., Lee, M., Lichterman, M., Lindgren, R. E., Loewenheim, F. L. and Van Wagenen, R. W. (1957), *Political Community and the North Atlantic Area : International Organization in the Light of Historical Experience*, Princeton, NJ: Priceton University Press.

Deutsches Reichsgesetzblatt Band (1878), Nr. 20, S. 131, 1878. Verordnung, betreffend die vorübergehende Einführung der Paß- Pflichtigkeit für Berlin.

di Martino, A., Biondi Dal Monte, F., Boiano, I. and Raffaelli, R. (2013), *The Criminalization of Irregular Immigration: Law and Practice in Italy*, Pisa: Pisa University Press.

Díaz, F. A. G. (2014), 'La Reforma Laboral "De Los Jóvenes" En España. Especial Referencia a La Ley 11/2013 Y El Rd-Ley 16/2013', *Revista de Derecho*, 14: 237–76.

Dietz, G. (2003), *The State and the Roma in Spain*, European Roma Rights Center. Available online: http://www.errc.org/roma-rights-journal/the-state-and-the-roma-in-spain (accessed 10 June 2020).

Dimitrova-Grajzl, V., Eastwood, J. and Grajzl, P. (2016), 'The Longevity of National Identity and National Pride: Evidence from Wider Europe', *Research & Politics*, 3(2): 1–9.

Domnar, A. O. (2009), 'When the East Goes West: Romanian Migrants in Italy or How to Deal with Mobility Issues in the EU 27', *Romanian Journal of Political Science*, 9(1): 29–46.

Dower, N. (2007), *World Ethics: The New Agenda*, Edinburgh: Edinburgh University Press.

Drewski, D. (2015), 'Has There Been a European Public Discourse on the Euro Crisis? A Systematic Content Analysis of Newspaper Editorials on the Euro Crisis in Germany and Spain', *Javnost – The Public*, 22(3): 264–82.

Duchêne, F. (1972), 'Europe's Role in World Peace', in R. Mayne (ed.), *Europe Tomorrow: Sixteen Europeans Look Ahead*, 32–47, London: Fontana for Chatham House and P.E.P.

Dudek, C. M., and Pestano, C. (2019), 'Canaries in a Coal Mine: The Cayuco Migrant Crisis and the Europeanization of Migration Policy', *Revista Espanola de Ciencia Politica*, 49: 85–106.

Dunne, T., and Wheeler, N. J. (2001), 'Blair's Britain: A Force for Good in the World?', in K. E. Smith and M. Light (eds), *Ethics and Foreign Policy*, 167–84, Cambridge: Cambridge University Press.

Dustmann, C., and Frattini, T. (2014), 'The Fiscal Effects of Immigration to the UK', *Economic Journal*, 124(580): F593–F643.

Eder, K. (2009), 'A Theory of Collective Identity Making Sense of the Debate on a "European Identity"', *European Journal of Social Theory*, 12(4): 227–47.

Eder, K., and Kantner, C. (2000), 'Transnationale Resonanzstrukturen in Europa', *KZfSS*, Sonderheft (40): 306–31.

Eder, K., and Trenz, H.-J. (2003), 'The Making of a European Public Space: The Case of Justice and Home Affairs', in B. Kohler-Koch (ed.), *Linking EU and National Governance*, 111–32, Oxford: Oxford University Press.

Edmondson, R. (2012), 'Practical Reasoning in Place: Tracing "Wise" Inferences in Everyday Life', in R. Edmondson and K. Hülser (eds), *Politics of Practical*

Reasoning: Integrating Action, Discourse, and Argument, 111–30, Lanham, MD: Lexington Books.

Einaudi, L. (2007), *Le politiche dell'immigrazione in Italia dall'unità a oggi*, Bari: Laterza.

Ellermann, A. (2015), 'Do Policy Legacies Matter? Past and Present Guest Worker Recruitment in Germany', *Journal of Ethnic and Migration Studies*, 41(8): 1235–53.

Elsner, B., and Zimmerman, K. F. (2013), '10 Years after: EU Enlargement, Closed Borders, and Migration to Germany', in M. Kahanec and K. F. Zimmermann (eds), *Labor Migration, EU Enlargement, and the Great Recession*, 85–101, Berlin: Springer.

Encarnación, O. G. (2004), 'The Politics of Immigration: Why Spain Is Different', *Mediterranean Quarterly*, 15(4): 167–85.

Ette, A., and Faist, T. (2007), 'The Europeanization of National Policies and Politics of Immigration: Research, Questions and Concepts', in T. Faist and A. Ette (eds), *The Europeanization of National Policies and Politics of Immigration: between Autonomy and the European Union*, 3–31, Basingstoke: Palgrave Macmillan.

Ette, A., and Gerdes, J. (2007), 'Against Exceptionalism: British Interests for Selectively Europeanizing Its Immigration Policy', in T. Faist and A. Ette (eds), *The Europeanization of National Policies and Politics of Immigration: between Autonomy and the European Union*, 93–115, Basingstoke: Palgrave Macmillan.

European Commission (2011), The Commission Accepts That Spain Can Temporarily Restrict the Free Movement of Romanian Workers, MEMO/11/554, 11 August.

European Commission (2017), Proposal for a Council Implementing Decision Setting Out a Recommendation for Prolonging Temporary Internal Border Control in Exceptional Circumstances Putting the Overall Functioning of the Schengen Area at Risk, COM(2017) 226 final, 2 May.

European Commission (2019), Standard Eurobarometer 91, Annex: Public opinion in the European Union.

Eurostat (2019), Population (demography, migration and projections).

Fahrmeir, A. (2001), 'Governments and Forgers: Passports in Nineteenth-Century Europe', in J. Caplan and J. Torpey (eds), *Documenting Individual Identity: The Development of State Practices in the Modern World*, 218–34, Princeton, NJ: Princeton University Press.

Fairclough, I., and Fairclough, N. (2011), 'Practical Reasoning in Political Discourse: The UK Government's Response to the Economic Crisis in the 2008 Pre-Budget Report', *Discourse & Society*, 22(3): 243–68.

Fairclough, I., and Fairclough, N. (2012), *Political Discourse Analysis*, Abingdon: Routledge.

Fassmann, H., and Münz, R. (1994), 'European East-West Migration, 1945–1992', *International Migration Review*, 28(3): 520–38.

Favell, A. (2008), *Eurostars and Eurocities: Free Movement and Mobility in an Integrating Europe*, Malden: Blackwell.

Favell, A. (2014), *Immigration, Integration and Mobility: New Agendas in Migration Studies, Essays 1998–2014*, Colchester: ECPR Press.

Fierke, K. M., and Wiener, A. (2001), 'Constructing Institutional Interests: EU and NATO Enlargement', in T. Christiansen, K. E. Jørgensen and A. Wiener (eds), *The Social Construction of Europe*, 121–39, London: SAGE.

Finotelli, C., and Arango, J. (2011), 'Regularisation of Unauthorised Immigrants in Italy and Spain: Determinants and Effects', *Documents d'Anàlisi Geogràfica*, 57(13): 495–515.

Fondazione Leone Moressa (2015), *Rapporto annuale sull'economia dell'immigrazione: Stranieri in Italia, attori dello sviluppo*, Bologna: Mulino.

Fossum, J. E. (2003), 'The European Charter between Deep Diversity and Constitutional Patriotism', in A. J. Menéndez, J. E. Fossum and E. O. Eriksen (eds), *The Chartering of Europe: The European Charter of Fundamental Rights and Its Constitutional Implications*, Baden-Baden: Nomos.

Fossum, J. E. (2008), 'Constitutional Patriotism: Canada and the European Union', in P. Mouritsen and K. E. Jørgensen (eds), *Constituting Communities: Political Solutions to Cultural Conflict*, 138–61, London: Palgrave Macmillan.

Fredette, J. (2015), 'Becoming a Threat: The Burqa and the Contestation Over Public Morality Law in France', *Law & Social Inquiry*, 40(3): 585–610.

Frost, M. (1996), *Ethics in International Relations : A Constitutive Theory*, Cambridge: Cambridge University Press.

Frost, M. (2008), *Global Ethics: Anarchy, Freedom & International Relations*, Abingdon: Routledge.

Gabaccia, D. R. (2003), *Emigranti: le diaspore degli italiani dal Medioevo a oggi*, Torino: Einaudi.

Gabaccia, D. R. (2012), *Foreign Relations: American Immigration in Global Perspective*, Princeton, NJ: Princeton University Press.

Galpin, C. (2015), 'Has Germany "Fallen Out of Love" with Europe? The Eurozone Crisis and the "Normalization" of Germany's European Identity', *German Politics & Society*, 33(1): 25–41.

García Juan, L. (2015), 'El discurso de la Unión Europea sobre medidas de integración de inmigrantes y sus derivaciones en España', *Migraciones Internacionales*, 8(1): 127–58.

Garelli, G., and Tazzioli, M. (2013), 'Arab Springs Making Space: Territoriality and Moral Geographies for Asylum Seekers in Italy', *Environment and Planning D: Society and Space*, 31(6): 1004–21.

Gattinara, P. C. (2016), *The Politics of Migration in Italy: Perspectives on Local Debates and Party Competition*, Abingdon: Routledge.

Geddes, A. (2000), *Immigration and European Integration: Towards Fortress Europe?*, Manchester: Manchester University Press.

Geddes, A. (2003), *The Politics of Migration and Immigration in Europe*, London: Sage.

Geddes, A., and Scholten, P. (2016), *The Politics of Migration and Immigration in Europe*, London: Sage.

Gehring, J. S. (2013a), 'Free Movement for Some: The Treatment of the Roma after the European Union's Eastern Expansion', *European Journal of Migration & Law*, 15(1): 7–28.

Gehring, J. S. (2013b), 'Roma and the Limits of Free Movement in the European Union', in W. Maas (ed.), *Democratic Citizenship and the Free Movement of People*, 143–74, Leiden: Martinus Nijhoff.

Geselle, A. (2001), 'Domenica Saba Takes to the Road: Origins and Development of a Modern Passport System in Lombardy-Veneto', in J. Caplan and J. Torpey (eds), *Documenting Individual Identity: The Development of State Practices in the Modern World*, 199–217, Princeton, NJ: Princeton University Press.

Gherghina, S., and Volintiru, C. (2015), 'A New Model of Clientelism: Political Parties, Public Resources, and Private Contributors', *European Political Science Review*, 9(1): 115–37.

Gifford, C. (2016), 'The United Kingdoms Eurosceptic Political Economy', *British Journal of Politics and International Relations*, 18(4): 779–94.

Gil, T. (2012), 'Reasons to Act and Practical Reasoning', in R. Edmondson and K. Hülser (eds), *Politics of Practical Reasoning: Integrating Action, Discourse and Argument*, 95–107, Lanham, MD: Lexington Books.

Giubboni, S. (2007), 'Free Movement of Persons and European Solidarity', *European Law Journal*, 13(3): 360–79.

González-Enríquez, C. (2009), 'Spain, the Cheap Model: Irregularity and Regularisation as Immigration Management Policies', *European Journal of Migration & Law*, 11(2): 139–57.

Government of Romania (2006), Strategie Post-Aderare 2007–2013, 13 December.

Guarnieri, C. (2011), *Il sistema politico italiano*, Bologna: Mulino.

Guild, E. (2000), 'The United Kingdom: Kosovar Albanian Refugees', in J. van Selm (ed.), *Kosovo's Refugees in the European Union*, 67–90, London: Continuum.

Guild, E. (2003), 'The Border Abroad – Visas and Border Controls', in C. A. Groenendijk, E. Guild and P. E. Minderhoud (eds), *In Search of Europe's Borders*, 87–104, The Hague: Kluwer Law International.

Guild, E. (2005), 'The Legal Framework: Who Is Entitled to Move?', in D. Bigo and E. Guild (eds), *Controlling Frontiers: Free Movement into and within Europe*, 14–48, Aldershot: Ashgate.

Guinan, J., and Hanna, T. M. (2017), 'Forbidden Fruit: The Neglected Political Economy of Lexit', *IPPR Progressive Review*, 24(1): 14–24.

Haas, E. B. (1968), *The Uniting Of Europe: Political, Social, and Economic Forces 1950–1957*, Stanford: Stanford University Press.

Habermas, J. (1989), *The Structural Transformation of the Public Sphere: An Inquiry Into Category of Bourgeois Society*, Cambridge: Polity Press.

Habermas, J. (1994a), *Justification and Application: Remarks on Discourse Ethics*, Cambridge: Polity Press.

Habermas, J. (1994b), 'Struggles for Recognition in the Democratic Constitutional State', in A. Gutmann (ed.), *Multiculturalism: Examining the Politics of Recognition*, 107–48, Princeton, NJ: Princeton University Press.

Habermas, J. (1999), *The Inclusion of the Other: Studies in Political Theory*, Cambridge: Polity Press.

Haller, M. (2008), *European Integration as an Elite Process: The Failure of a Dream?*, New York: Routledge.

Hansen, P. (2008), *EU:s migrationspolitik under 50 år: ett integrerat perspektiv på en motsägelsefull utveckling'*, Lund: Studentlitteratur.

Hansen, P., and Jonsson, S. (2017), *Eurafrica: The Untold History of European Integration and Colonialism*, London: Bloomsbury.

Hare, R. M. (1981), *Moral Thinking: Its Levels, Method and Point*, Oxford: Clarendon Press.

Heinikoski, S. (2011), 'Introduction: the European Union as a Security Provider', in P. Hario and S. Heinikoski (eds), *The European Union as a Security Provider*, 1–14, Helsinki: National Defence University.

Heinikoski, S. (2013), 'Laajentumisen moraali: Euroopan unionin laajentumisargumentaatio moraaliteorioiden ja kosmopolitanismin valossa', *Kosmopolis*, 43(2): 3–20.

Heinikoski, S. (2015a), 'Britain and the Other: Moral Perceptions of the Right to Free Movement in the European Commission and in the UK', *Journal on Ethnopolitics and Minority Issues in Europe*, 14(1): 71–92.

Heinikoski, S. (2015b), 'European Identity Challenged. Romanian Politicians Discussing Free Movement from the Perspective of Kinship-based Morality', *Finnish Journal for Romanian Studies*, 1: 57–76.
Heinikoski, S. (2015c), 'Economic Asset or Welfare Tourists? Political Reactions to Eastern European Migrants in the UK', *Siirtolaisuus-Migration*, 42(4): 3–10.
Heinikoski, S. (2016a), 'Vapaan liikkuvuuden rajat Euroopassa 2006–2010: Keskusteluista Italiassa, Ranskassa, Romaniassa ja Euroopan komissiossa', *Kulttuurintutkimus*, 33(1): 3–15.
Heinikoski, S. (2016b), 'Who Should Benefit from Free Movement? A Comparative Study on British and Romanian Political Discourses in the Pre-Brexit Period', *Finnish Journal for Romanian Studies*, 2: 33–52.
Heinikoski, S. (2017a), 'Morals and the Right to Free Movement – Insiders, Outsiders and Europe's Migration Crisis', *Nordic Journal of Migration Research*, 7(1): 47–55.
Heinikoski, S. (2017b), 'Calls of Duty: Romanian Politicians' Deontological Discursive Strategies for Securing Free Movement in the European Union', *New Perspectives*, 25(3): 43–66.
Heller, W. (2013), 'Who Moves within the Country? Who Emigrates? Who Immigrates? Current Migrational Trends in Romania', *Südosteuropa. Zeitschrift für Politik und Gesellschaft*, 2: 244–67.
Holland, D. Fic, T. Rincon-Aznar, A. Stokes, L. and Paluchowski, P. (2011), *Labour Mobility within the EU – The Impact of Enlargement and the Functioning of the Transitional Arrangements*, London: National Institute of Economic and Social Research.
Holmes, C. (1999), 'Hostile Images of Immigrants and Refugees in Nineteeth- and Twentieth-Century Britain', in J. Lucassen and L. Lucassen (eds), *Migration, Migration History, History: Old Paradigms and New Perspectives*, 317–34, Berne: Peter Lang.
Holopainen, M., and Toivonen, M. (2012), 'Weak Signals: Ansoff Today', *Futures*, 44(3): 198–205.
Hooghe, L. (2001), *European Commission and the Integration of Europe*, Port Chester: Cambridge University Press.
Horsti, K., and Pellander, S. (2015), 'Conditions of Cultural Citizenship: Intersections of Gender, Race and Age in Public Debates on Family Migration', *Citizenship Studies*, 19(6–7): 751–67.
Hume, D. (1896), *A Treatise of Human Nature*, Oxford: Clarendon Press.
Huysmans, J. (2000a), 'The European Union and the Securitization of Migration', *Journal of Common Market Studies*, 38(5): 751–77.
Huysmans, J. (2000b), 'Contested Community: Migration and the Question of the Political in the EU', in M. Kelstrup and M. C. Williams (eds), *International Relations Theory and European Integration: Power, Security and Community*, 149–70, Florence: Routledge.
Huysmans, J. (2004), 'A Foucaultian View on Spill-Over: Freedom and Security in the EU', *Journal of International Relations and Development*, 7(3): 294–318.
Huysmans, J. (2006), *The Politics of Insecurity : Fear, Migration and Asylum in the EU*, London: Routledge.
Huysseune, M. (2010), 'A Eurosceptic Vision in a Europhile Country: The Case of the Lega Nord', *Modern Italy*, 15(1): 63–75.
Hyde-Price, A. (2008), 'A "Tragic Actor"? A Realist Perspective on "Ethical Power Europe"', *International Affairs*, 84(1): 29–44.
Janco, A. P. (2014), '"Unwilling": The One-Word Revolution in Refugee Status, 1940–51', *Contemporary European History*, 23(3): 429–46.

Jenkins, B., and Copsey, N. (1996), 'Nation, Nationalism and National Identity in France', in B. Jenkins and S. A. Sofos (eds), *Nation and Identity in Contemporary Europe*, 101–24, London: Routledge.

Jileva, E. (2004), 'Do Norms Matter? The Principle of Solidarity and the EU's Eastern Enlargement', *Journal of International Relations and Development*, 7(1): 3–23.

Johns, M. (2013), 'The Long-Term Future of Polish Migrants in Ireland and Britain', in W. Maas (ed.), *Democratic Citizenship and the Free Movement of People*, 91–113, Leiden: Brill.

Juncker, J.-C. (2017), President Jean-Claude Juncker's State of the Union Address 2017, 12 September.

Kahn, P. W. (2013), 'Imagining Warfare', *European Journal of International Law*, 24(1): 199–226.

Kant, I. (1999), *Metaphysical Elements of Justice: Part I of the Metaphysics of Morals*, Indianapolis: Hackett.

Kelly, L. (2003), 'Bosnian Refugees in Britain', *Sociology*, 37(1): 35–49.

Klekowski von Koppenfels, A., and Höhne, J. (2017), 'Gastarbeiter Migration Revisited: Consolidating Germany's Position as an Immigration Country', in J. Lafleur and M. Stanek (eds), *South-North Migration of EU Citizens in Times of Crisis*, 149–74, Online: Springer.

Kmak, M. (2015), 'Between Citizen and Bogus Asylum Seeker: Management of Migration in the EU through the Technology of Morality', *Social Identities*, 21(4): 395–409.

Knischewski, G. (1996), 'Post-war National Identity in Germany', in B. Jenkins and S. A. Sofos (eds), *Nation and Identity in Contemporary Europe*, 125–51, London: Routledge.

Knox, K. (1997), *Credit to the Nation – A Study of Refugees in the United Kingdom*, London: Refugee Council.

Kochenov, D. (2008), *EU Enlargement and the Failure of Conditionality*, New York: Kluwer Law International.

Koivula, T., and Sipilä, J. (2011), 'Missing in Action? EU Crisis Management and the Link to the Domestic Political Debate', *Cooperation and Conflict*, 46(4): 521–42.

Kratochwil, F. V. (1989), *Rules, Norms, and Decisions: On the Conditions of Practical and Legal Reasoning in International Relations and Domestic Affairs*, Cambridge: Cambridge University Press.

Kriesi, H. (2010), 'Restructuration of Partisan Politics and the Emergence of a New Cleavage Based on Values', *West European Politics*, 33(3): 673–85.

Kriesi, H., Grande, E., Dolezal, M., Helbling, M., Höglinger, D., Hutter, S. and Wüest, B. (2012), *Political Conflict in Western Europe*, Cambridge: Cambridge University Press.

Kuhn, T. (2012), 'Europa ante portas: Border Residence, Transnational Interaction and Euroscepticism in Germany and France', *European Union Politics*, 13(1): 94–117.

Kuhn, T. (2015), *Experiencing European Integration : Transnational Lives and European Identity*, Oxford: Oxford University Press.

Kunelius, R., and Sparks, C. (2001), 'Problems with a European Public Sphere', *Javnost*, 8(1): 5–20.

Lacroix, J. (2009), 'Does Europe Need Common Values? Habermas vs Habermas', *European Journal of Political Theory*, 8(2): 141–56.

Lamers, K., and Schäuble, W. (2014), 'More integration Is Still the Right Goal for Europe', *Financial Times*, 31 August.

Le Monde (2005), 'Le G5 envisage une "force européenne d'intervention" aux frontières de l'UE', *Le Monde*, 13 May. Available online https://www.lemonde.fr/europe/article/2005/05/13/le-g5-envisage-une-force-europeenne-d-intervention-aux-frontieres-de-l-ue_649168_3214.html (accessed 27 January 2020).

Léonard, S. (2010), 'EU Border Security and Migration into the European Union: FRONTEX and Securitisation through Practices', *European Security*, 19(2): 231–54.

Lucassen, L. (2001), 'A Many-Headed Monster: The Evolution of the Passport System in the Netherlands and Germany in the Long Nineteenth Century', in J. Caplan and J. Torpey (eds), *Documenting Individual Identity: The Development of State Practices in the Modern World*, 235–55, Princeton, NJ: Princeton University Press.

Lunn, K. (1996), 'Reconsidering "Britishness": The Construction and Significance of National Identity in Twentieth-century Britain', in B. Jenkins and S. A. Sofos (eds), *Nation and Identity in Contemporary Europe*, 83–100, London: Routledge.

Maas, W. (2007), *Creating European Citizens*, Lanham, MD: Rowman & Littlefield.

Maas, W. (2013), 'Equality and the Free Movement of People: Citizenship and Internal Migration', in W. Maas (ed.), *Democratic Citizenship and the Free Movement of People*, , 9–30, Leiden: Brill.

MacIntyre, A. (1982), *After Virtue: A Study in Moral Theory*, London: Duckworth.

MacIntyre, A. (2006), *Ethics and Politics*, Cambridge: Cambridge University Press.

Mackie, J. L. (1984), 'Rights, Utility and Universalization', in R. G. Frey (ed.), *Utility and Rights*, 86–105, Minneapolis: University of Minnesota Press.

Magnani, N. (2012), 'Immigration Control in Italian Political Elite Debates: Changing Policy Frames in Italy, 1980s-2000s', *Ethnicities*, 12(5): 643–64.

Mäkinen, V. (2013), 'Are There Fundamental Rights for Roma Beggars in Europe?', *Political Theology*, 14(2): 201–18.

Malik, K. (2015), 'The Failure of Multiculturalism', *Foreign Affairs*, 94(2): 21–32.

Manconi, L. (2017), 'Immigrazione, la soluzione (parziale) c'è', *Huffington Post Italia*, 11 July. Available online https://www.huffingtonpost.it/entry/immigrazione-la-soluzione-parziale-ce_it_5cc1a38fe4b0e68bc67b40bb (accessed 27 January 2020).

Manners, I. (2002), 'Normative Power Europe: A Contradiction in Terms?', *JCMS: Journal of Common Market Studies*, 40(2): 235–58.

Manners, I. (2008), 'The Normative Ethics of the European Union', *International Affairs*, 84(1): 45–60.

March, J. G., and Olsen, J. P. (1989), *Rediscovering Institutions: The Organizational Basis Of Politics*, New York: Free Press.

Marcu, S. (2014), 'Mobility and identity in a Wider European Union: Experiences of Romanian Migrants in Spain', *European Societies*, 16(1): 136–56.

Marcussen, M., Risse, T., Engelmann-Martin, D., Knopf, H.-J. and Roscher, K. (2001), 'Constructing Europe? The Evolution of Nation-State Identities', in T. Christiansen, K. E. Jørgensen and A. Wiener (eds), *The Social Construction of Europe*, 101–20, London: Sage.

Marrus, M. R. (1985), *The Unwanted: European Refugees in the Twentieth Century*, New York: Oxford University Press.

Martín-Pérez, A., and Moreno-Fuentes, F. J. (2012), 'Migration and Citizenship Law in Spain: Path-Dependency and Policy Change in a Recent Country of Immigration'. *International Migration Review*, 46(3), 625–55.

Massetti, E. (2015), 'Mainstream Parties and the Politics of Immigration in Italy: A Structural Advantage for the Right or a Missed Opportunity for the Left?', *Acta Politica*, 50(4): 486–505.

Matichescu, M. L., Bica, A., Ogodescu, A. S., Lobont, O.-R., Nicoleta-Claudia, M., Iacob, M. C. and Rosu, S. (2015), 'The Romanian Migration: Development of the

Phenomenon and the Part Played by the Immigration Policies of European Countries',
Revista de Cercetare și Intervenție Socială, 50: 225–39.
Mato Díaz, F. J., and Miyar Busto, M. (2017), 'Immigration Policy and Economic Cycle
Effects on Spousal Reunification in Spain', *Revista Internacional de Sociología*,
75(3): 071.
Mayer, H., and Vogt, H. (eds) (2006), *A Responsible Europe? Ethical Foundations of EU
External Affairs*, Basingstoke: Palgrave Macmillan.
McCarthy, T. (1994), 'Kantian Constructivism and Reconstructivism : Rawls and
Habermas in Dialogue', *Ethics*, 105(1): 44–63.
McMahon, S. (2012), 'North African Migration and Europe's Contextual Mediterranean
Border in Light of the Lampedusa Migrant Crisis of 2011', *European University Institute
Working Paper Series*, 1–11.
McMahon, S. (2015), *Immigration and Citizenship in an Enlarged European Union: the
Political Dynamics of Intra-EU Mobility*, London: Palgrave Macmillan.
Mechi, L. (2013), 'Economic Regionalism and Social Stabilisation: The International
Labour Organization and Western Europe in the Early Post-War Years', *International
History Review*, 35(4): 844–62.
Messina, A. M. (2001), 'The Impacts of Post-WWII Migration to Britain: Policy
Constraints, Political Opportunism and the Alteration of Representational Politics',
Review of Politics, 63(2): 259–85.
Messina, A. M. (2014), 'European Disunion? The Implications of "Super" Diversity for
European Identity and Political Community', in A. Gould and A. M. Messina (eds),
*Europe's Contending Identities: Supranationalism, Ethnoregionalism, Religion, and New
Nationalism*, 54–80, Cambridge: Cambridge University Press.
Mezzadra, S. (2006), 'Citizen and Subject: A Postcolonial Constitution for the European
Union?', *Situations*, 1(2): 31–42.
Mezzadra, S., and Neilson, B. (2013), *Border as Method, or, the Multiplication of Labor*,
Durham, NC: Duke University Press.
Mill, J. S. (2000), *Utilitarianism*, Peterborough: Broadview Press.
Minderhoud, P. (2013), 'Directive 2004/38 and Access to Social Assistance Benefits', in
E. Guild, T. Kostakopoulou and C. Gortázar (eds), *The Reconceptualization of European
Union Citizenship*, 209–26, Leiden: Brill.
Mingione, E., and Quassoli, F. (2000), 'The Participation of Immigrants in the
Underground Economy in Italy BT - Eldorado or Fortress? Migration in Southern
Europe', in R. King, G. Lazaridis and C. Tsardanidis (eds), *Eldorado or Fortress?
Migration in Southern Europe*, 29–56, London: Palgrave Macmillan.
Mitsilegas, V., Monar, J. and Rees, W. (2003), *The European Union and Internal
Security: Guardian of the People?*, Basingstoke: Palgrave Macmillan.
Moch, L. P. (2003), *Moving Europeans: Migration in Western Europe since 1650*,
Bloomington: Indiana University Press.
Molnar, C. A. (2016), 'On the Move and Putting Down Roots: Transnationalism and
Integration among Yugoslav Guest Workers in West Germany', in J. Coy, J. Poley
and A. Schunka (eds), *Migrations in the German Lands, 1500–2000*, 191–208,
New York: Berghahn Books.
Moravcsik, A. (1998), *The Choice for Europe: Social Purpose and State Power from Messina
to Maastricht*, Ithaca, NY: Cornell University Press.
Moravcsik, A. (2002), 'Reassessing Legitimacy in the European Union', *JCMS: Journal of
Common Market Studies*, 40(4): 603–24.

Müller, J.-W. (2006), 'On the Origins of Constitutional Patriotism', *Contemporary Political Theory*, 5(3): 278–96.
Müller, J.-W. (2007), *Constitutional Patriotism*, Princeton, NJ: Princeton University Press.
Münz, R., and Ulrich, R. (1999), 'Immigration and Citizenship in Germany', *German Politics and Society*, 17(4): 1–33.
Nava, M. (2014), 'Sometimes Antagonistic, Sometimes Ardently Sympathetic: Contradictory Responses to Migrants in Postwar Britain', *Ethnicities*, 14(3): 458–80.
Noiriel, G. (1988), *Le creuset francais: histoire de'l immigration XIXe-XXe siècles*, Paris: Seuil.
Noiriel, G. (2018), 'The Role of Immigration in the Making/Unmaking of the French Working Class (Nineteenth and Twentieth Centuries)', in E. Henrich and J. M. Simpson (eds), *History, Historians and the Immigration Debate*, 133–51, Basingstoke: Palgrave Macmillan.
O'Brien, P. (1988), 'Continuity and Change in Germany's Treatment of Non-Germans', *International Migration Review*, 22(3): 109–34.
O'Keeffe, D. (1998), 'Freedom of Movement for Workers in Community Law: Accomplishments and Prospects', in J. Y. Carlier and M. Verwilghen (eds), *Thirty Years of Free Movement of Workers in Europe*, 20–32, Brussels: European Commission.
Odmalm, P. (2005), *Migration Policies and Political Participation: Inclusion or Intrusion in Western Europe?*, Basingstoke: Palgrave Macmillan.
Oliver, T. (2015), 'Europe's British Question: The UK–EU Relationship in a Changing Europe and Multipolar World', *Global Society*, 29(3): 409–26.
Olsen, E. D. H. (2012), *Transnational Citizenship in the European Union: Past, Present, and Future*, London: Continuum.
Olsen, E. D. H. (2014), 'European Citizenship: Toward Renationalization or Cosmopolitan Europe?', in E. Guild, C. J. Gortázar Rotaeche and T. Kostakopoulou (eds), *The Reconceptualization of European Union Citizenship*, 343–60, Leiden: Brill.
Oltmer, J. (2016), 'Foreign Policy and Migration in Central Europe: Functions of the German-Polish Recruitment Treaty of 1927', in J. Coy, J. Poley and A. Schunka (eds), *Migrations in the German Lands, 1500–2000*, 151–72, New York: Berghahn Books.
Onuf, N. G. (1989), *World of Our Making: Rules and Rule in Social Theory and International Relations*, Columbia: University of South Carolina press.
ÓTuathail, G. (2002), 'Theorizing Practical Geopolitical Reasoning: The Case of the United States Response to the War in Bosnia', *Political Geography*, 21(5): 601–28.
Pace, M. (2008), 'The EU as a "Force for Good" in Border Conflict Cases?', in T. Diez, M. Albert and S. Stetter (eds), *The European Union and Border Conflicts: The Power of Integration and Association*, 203–19, Cambridge: Cambridge University Press.
Panagiotidis, J. (2016), 'Sifting Germans from Yugoslavs: Co-ethnic Selection, Danube Swabian Migrants, and the Contestation of Aussiedler Immigration in West Germany in the 1950s and 1960s', in J. Coy, J. Poley and A. Schunka (eds), *Migrations in the German Lands, 1500–2000*, 209–26, New York: Berghahn Books.
Panainte, S., Nedelciuc, V. and Voicu, O. (2013), 'Redobândirea Cetățeniei Române: O Politică Ce Capătă Viziune?', *Fundația Soros România*, 1–19.
Pânzaru, C., and Reisz, R. D. (2013), 'Validity of the Push and Pull Hypothesis for the Explanation of Romanian Migration Flows', *Journal of Social Research and Policy*, 4(1): 93–108.
Papadimitriou, D., and Phinnemore, D. (2008), *Romania and the European Union: From Marginalisation to Inclusion?*, Abingdon: Routledge.

Parker, O. (2013), *Cosmopolitan Government in Europe: Citizens and Entrepreneurs in Postnational Politics*, London: Routledge.
Parker, O., and Catalán, Ó. L. (2014), 'Free Movement for Whom, Where, When? Roma EU Citizens in France and Spain', *International Political Sociology*, 8(4): 379–95.
Parker, O., and Toke, D. (2013), 'The Politics of a Multi-level Citizenship: French Republicanism, Roma Mobility and the EU', *Global Society*, 27(3): 360–78.
Pettit, P. (1997), *Republicanism: A Theory of Freedom and Government*, Oxford: Clarendon Press.
Piedrafita, S., and Torreblanca, J. I. (2005), 'The Three Logics of EU Enlargement: Interests, Identities and Arguments', *Politique Européenne*, 15: 29–59.
Preston, P. W. (2014), *Britain after Empire*, Basingstoke: Palgrave Macmillan.
Prümm, K., and Alscher, S. (2007), 'From Model to Average Student: the Europeanization of Migration Policy and Politics' in Germany', in T. Faist and A. Ette (eds), *The Europeanization of National Policies and Politics of Immigration: Between Autonomy and the European Union*, 73–92, Basingstoke: Palgrave Macmillan.
Quin, J. (1999), 'After Amsterdam – What Next?', Speech by FCO Minister of State at the Clingendael Institute, The Hague, 11 March.
Ram, M. H. (2014), 'Europeanized Hypocrisy: Roma Inclusion and Exclusion in Central and Eastern Europe', *Journal of Ethnopolitics and Minority Issues in Europe*, 13(3): 15–44.
Raz, J. (1978), *Practical Reasoning*, Oxford: Oxford University Press.
Recchi, E. (2008), 'Cross-State Mobility in the EU', *European Societies*, 10(2): 197–224.
Recchi, E. (2013), *Senza Frontiere. La Libera Circolazione delle Persone in Europa*, Bologna: Mulino.
Recchi, E. (2015), *Mobile Europe: The Theory and Practice of Free Movement in the EU*, Basingstoke: Palgrave Macmillan.
Recchi, E., and Salamonska, J. (2014), 'Keeping the European Faith: Collective Identity before and after the Euro-Crisis', *Participazione e Conflitto*, 7(3): 509–31.
Rigo, E. (2007), *Europa di confine: transformazioni della cittadinanza dell'Unione allargata*, Rome: Meltemi.
Rigo, E. (2011), 'Citizens Despite Borders: Challenges to the Territorial Order of Europe', in V. Squire (ed.), *The Contested Politics of Mobility: Borderzones and Irregularity*, 199–215, Abingdon: Routledge.
Risse, T. (2010), *A Community of Europeans? Transnational Identities and Public Spheres*, Ithaca, NY: Cornell University Press.
Risse, T. (2014), 'No Demos? Identities and Public Spheres in the Euro Crisis', *Journal of Common Market Studies*, 52(6): 1207–15.
Roberts, S., and Sakslin, M. (2009), 'Some Are More Equal Than Others: The Impact of Discrimination in Social Security on the Right of Same-Sex Partners to Free Movement in the European Union', *Benefits: The Journal of Poverty & Social Justice*, 17(3): 249–61.
Robertson, G. (1989), *Freedom, the Individual and the Law*, London: Penguin Books.
Roman, M., and Voicu, C. (2010), 'Câteva efecte socioeconomice ale migrației foței de munc ă asupra țărilor de emigra ție', *Cazul României*, 7(7): 50–65.
Roos, C. (2019), 'The (De-)Politicization of EU Freedom of Movement: Political Parties, Opportunities, and Policy Framing in Germany and the UK', *Comparative European Politics*, 17(5): 631–50.

Roos, C., and Westerveen, L. (2020), 'The Conditionality of EU Freedom of Movement: Normative Change in the Discourse of EU Institutions', *Journal of European Social Policy*, 30(1): 63–78.

Roper, S. D. (2000), *Romania: The Unfinished Revolution*, Florence: Gordon & Breach.

Roper, S. D. (2005), 'The Politicization of Education: Identity Formation in Moldova and Transnistria', *Communist and Post-Communist Studies*, 38(4): 501–14.

Rorty, R. (1989), *Contingency, Irony, and Solidarity*, Cambridge: Cambridge University Press.

Rorty, R. (1999), 'Human Rights, Rationality and Sentimentality', in O. Savić (ed.), *The Politics of Human Rights*, 67–83, London: Verso.

Rorty, R. (2000a), *Philosophy and Social Hope*, London: Penguin Books.

Rorty, R. (2000b), 'Response to Jurgen Habermas', in R. B. Brandom (ed.), *Rorty and His Critics*, 56–64, London: Blackwell.

Rosenberg, C. D. (2018), *Policing Paris: The Origins of Modern Immigration Control between the Wars*, Ithaca, NY: Cornell University Press.

Rumford, C. (2007), 'Does Europe Have Cosmopolitan Borders?' *Globalizations*, 4(3): 327–39.

Ruzza, C., and Fella, S. (2009), *Reinventing the Italian Right: Territorial Politics, Populism and 'Post-Fascism'*, London: Routledge.

Sallinen, H. (2013), *Intergovernmental Advocates of Refugees: The Refugee Policy of the League of Nations and the International Labour Organization in the 1920s and 1930s*, Helsinki: University of Helsinki.

Sánchez Alonso, B. (2011), 'La política migratoria en España Un análisis de largo plazo', *Revista Internacional de Sociología*, 69(M1): 243–68.

Sangiovanni, A. (2017), 'Non-Discrimination, in-Work Benefits, and Free Movement in the EU', *European Journal of Political Theory*, 16(2): 143–63.

Sasse, G. (2005), 'Securitization or Securing Rights? Exploring the Conceptual Foundations of Policies Towards Minorities and Migrants in Europe', *Journal of Common Market Studies*, 43(4): 673–93.

Schain, M. (2008), *The Politics of Immigration in France, Britain, and the United States: A Comparative Study*, Basingstoke: Palgrave Macmillan.

Schmidtke, O. (2015), 'Between Populist Rhetoric and Pragmatic Policymaking: The Normalization of Migration as an Electoral Issue in German Politics', *Acta Politica*, 50(4): 379–98.

Schuster, A., and Toniollo, M. G. (2015), *La famiglia omonogenitoriale in Europa. Diritti di cittadinanza e libera circolazione*, Roma: Ediesse.

Searle, J. R. (2001), *Rationality in Action*, Cambridge: MIT Press.

Searle, J. R. (2010), *Making the Social World: The Structure of Human Civilization*, Oxford: Oxford University Press.

Shaw, J. (2007), *The Transformation of Citizenship in the European Union: Electoral Rights and the Restructuring of Political Space*, Cambridge: Cambridge University Press.

Shutes, I., and Walker, S. (2018), 'Gender and free movement: EU migrant women's access to residence and social rights in the UK', *Journal of Ethnic and Migration Studies*, 44 (1): 137–53.

Siebold, A. (2013), 'Between Borders: France, Germany, and Poland in the Debate on Demarcation and Frontier Crossing in the Context of the Schengen Agreement', in A. Lechevalier and J. Wielgohs (eds), *Borders and Border Regions in Europe – Changes, Challenges and Chances*, 129–44, Bielefield: transcript Verlag.

Simpson, J. H. (1938), 'The Refugee Problem', *International Affairs*, 17(5): 607–28.

Sjursen, H. (2002), 'Why Expand? The Question of Legitimacy and Justification in the EU's Enlargement Policy', *Journal of Common Market Studies*, 40(3): 491–513.
Sjursen, H. (ed.) (2006a), *Questioning EU Enlargement: Europe in Search of Identity*, London: Routledge.
Sjursen, H. (2006b), 'The European Union between Values and Rights', in H. Sjursen (ed.), *Questioning EU Enlargement: Europe in Search of Identity*, 203–15, London: Routledge.
Sjursen, H. (2012), 'A Certain Sense of Europe? Defining the EU through Enlargement', *European Societies*, 14 (November): 37–41.
Sjursen, H., and Smith, K. E. (2004), 'Justifying EU Foreign Policy: The Logics Underpinning EU Enlargement', in B. Tonra and T. Christiansen (eds), *Europe in Change: Rethinking European Union Foreign Policy*, 126–41, Manchester: Manchester University Press.
Skran, C. M. (1995), *Refugees in Inter-War Europe: The Emergence of a Regime*, Oxford: Clarendon Press.
Smith, K. E., and Light, M. (2001), *Ethics and Foreign Policy*, Cambridge: Cambridge University Press.
Špidla, V. (2009), 'Immigration Policies in the European Union', *New Presence: The Prague Journal of Central European Affairs*, 11(1): 17–18.
Spohn, W. (2005), 'National Identities and Collective Memory in an Enlarged Europe', in K. Eder and W. Spohn (eds), *Collective Memory and European Identity: The Effects of Integration and Enlargement*, 1–16, Aldershot: Ashgate.
Springford, J. (2013), 'Is Immigration a Reason for Britain to Leave the EU?', Centre for European *Reform*.
Squire, V. (2009), *The Exclusionary Politics of Asylum*, New York: Palgrave Macmillan.
Stan, S., and Erne, R. (2014), 'Explaining Romanian Labor Migration: From Development Gaps to Development Trajectories', *Labor History*, 55(1): 21–46.
Stanek, J. L. M. (2017), *South-North Migration of EU Citizens in Times of Crisis*, London: Springer.
Stângaciu, A. (2016), 'Transnational Perspective of the Romanian Migration in Spain and Italy after 1990', *Studia Europaea*, 61(3): 67–91.
Startin, N. (2015), 'Have We Reached a Tipping Point? The Mainstreaming of Euroscepticism in the UK', *International Political Science Review*, 36(3): 311–23.
Staver, A. (2013), 'Free Movement for Workers or Citizens? Reverse Discrimination in European Family Reunification Policies', in W. Maas (ed.), *Democratic Citizenship and the Free Movement of People*, 57–90, Leiden: Brill.
Steinmeier, F.-W., and Ayrault, J.-M. (2016), 'A Strong Europe in a World of Uncertainties', Joint declaration by the Foreign Ministers of Germany and France.
Steinmetz, G. (1993), *Regulating the Social: The Welfare State and Local Politics in Imperial Germany*, Princeton, NJ: Princeton University Press.
Sternberger, D. (1963), *Staatsfreundschaft*, Berlin: Suhrkamp.
Strumia, F. (2013), *Supranational Citizenship and the Challenge of Diversity: Immigrants, Citizens, and Member States in the EU*, Leiden: Brill.
Talani, L. S. (2012), 'The internal and external dimension of the "Fortress Europe"', in L. S.Talani (ed.), *Globalisation, Migration, and the Future of Europe: Insiders and Outsiders*, 61–80, London: Routledge.
Tallis, B. (2015), *A Moveable East: Identities, Borders & Orders in the Enlarged EU and Its Eastern Neighbourhood*, Manchester: University of Manchester.
Tammikko, T. (2017), 'The New Frontex and the Future of Schengen – A Brick Fortress, or a Castle Made of Sand?', *FIIA Briefing Paper*.

Taylor, C. (1985), *Philosophical Papers. 2, Philosophy and the Human Sciences*, Cambridge: Cambridge University Press.
Taylor, C. (1993), *Reconciling the Solitudes: Essays on Canadian Federalism and Nationalism*, Montreal: McGill-Queen's University Press.
Taylor, C. (1994), *Multiculturalism: Examining the Politics of Recognition*, Princeton, NJ: Princeton University Press.
Taylor, C. (1999), 'Conditions of an Unforced Consensus on Human Rights', in J. R. Bauer and D. Bell (eds), *The East Asian Challenge for Human Rights*, 124–44, Cambridge: Cambridge University Press.
Thieleman, E. R., and Dewan, T. (2007), 'The Myth of Free-Riding: Refugee Protection and Implicit Burden-Sharing', in V. Guiraudon and G. Lahav (eds), *Immigration Policy in Europe: The Politics of Control*, 151–69, New York: Routledge.
Thielemann, E., and Schade, D. (2016), 'Buying into Myths: Free Movement of People and Immigration', 87(2): 139–47.
Tonkiss, K. (2013a), *Migration and Identity in a Post-National World*, London: Palgrave Macmillan.
Tonkiss, K. (2013b), 'Constitutional Patriotism, Migration and the Post-National Dilemma', *Citizenship Studies*, 17(3): 491–504.
Tonkiss, K. (2013c), 'Post-National Citizenship without Post-National Identity? A Case study of UK Immigration Policy and Intra-EU Migration', *Journal of Global Ethics*, 9(1): 35–48.
Torpey, J. (1998a), 'Le contrôle des passeports et la liberté de circulation. Le cas de l'Allemagne au XIXe siècle', *Genèses*, 30: 53–76.
Torpey, J. (1998b), 'Coming and Going: On the State Monopolization of the Legitimate "Means of Movement"', *Sociological Theory*, 16(3): 239–59.
Torpey, J. (2000), *The Invention of the Passport: Surveillance, Citizenship and the State*, Cambridge: Cambridge University Press.
Torpey, J. (2001), 'The Great War and the Birth of the Modern Passport System', in J. Caplan and J. Torpey (eds), *Documenting Individual Identity: The Development of State Practices in the Modern World*, 256–70, Princeton, NJ: Princeton University Press.
Traynor, I. (2015), 'Italy threatens to Give Schengen Visas to Migrants as EU Ministers Meet', *The Guardian*, 16 June.
Triandafyllidou, A. (2014), 'Multi-Levelling and Externalizing Migration and Asylum: Lessons from the Southern European Islands', *Island Studies Journal*, 9(1): 7–22.
Tsoukala, A. (2005), 'Looking at Migrants as Enemies', in D. Bigo and E. Guild (eds), *Controlling Frontiers: Free Movement into and within Europe*, 161–92, Aldershot: Ashgate.
Ugur, M. (1995), 'Freedom of Movement vs. Exclusion: A Reinterpretation of the "Insider" – "Outsider" Divide in the European Union', *International Migration Review*, 29(4): 964–99.
Vaciago, G. (2015), *Un'anima per l'Europa*, Bologna: Mulino.
van de Steeg, M. (2004), 'Does a Public Sphere Exist in the EU? An Analysis of the Content of the Debate on the Haider Case', *EUI Working Paper SPS*, 45 (2004/5): 609–34.
van Munster, R. (2009), *Securitizing Immigration: The Politics of Risk in the EU*, Basingstoke: Palgrave Macmillan.
van Riemsdijk, M. (2013), 'Politics of Free Movement in the European Union: Recognition and Transfer of Professional Qualifications', in W. Maas (ed.), *Democratic Citizenship and the Free Movement of People*, 115–42, Leiden: Brill.

Viñas, A. (2000), 'The Enlargement of the European Union: Opportunities and Concerns for Spain', *Mediterranean Politics*, 5(2): 76–92.
Vogt, H. (2009), 'The Borders of European Tolerance', in I. Pernice, B. von Egelhardt, S. H. Krieg, I. Ley and O. Salidas (eds), *Europa jenseits seiner Grenzen: historische, politologische und rechtliche Zugriffe*, 211–25, Baden-Baden: Nomos.
Wagner, R. (2015), '"Transnational Civil Dis/Obedience" in the Danish Family Unification Dispute', *European Political Science Review*, 7(1): 43–62.
Wallace, H., Pollack, M. A. and Young, A. R. (2010), *Policy-Making in the European Union*, Oxford: Oxford University Press.
Walton, D. (2007), *Media Argumentation: Dialectic, Persuasion and Rhetoric*, New York: Cambridge University Press.
Walzer, M. (1983), *Spheres of Justice: A Defense of Pluralism and Equality*, Oxford: Martin Robertson.
Walzer, M. (1994), *Thick and Thin: Moral Argument at Home and Abroad*, Notre Dame: University of Notre Dame Press.
Walzer, M. (1997), *On Toleration*, New Haven: Yale University Press.
Weber, M. (1978), *Economy and Society: An Outline of Interpretive Sociology*, Berkeley: University of California Press.
Weil, P. (1995), 'Racisme et discrimination dans la politique francaise de l'immigration', *Vingtième Siècle. Revue d'histoire*, 47: 77–102.
Weil, P. (2017), 'Denaturalization and Denationalization in Comparison (France, the United Kingdom, the United States)', *Philosophy and Social Criticism*, 43(4–5): 417–29.
Weiler, J. (1998), *The Constitution Of Europe: 'Do The New Clothes Have An Emperor?' And Other Essays on European Integration*, Cambridge: Cambridge University Press.
Weiler, J. (2002), 'A Constitution for Europe? Some Hard Choices', *Journal of Common Market Studies*, 40(4): 563–80.
Wessler, H., Peters, B., Brüggemann, M., Kleinen-von Königslöw, K. and Sifft, S. (eds) (2008), *Transnationalization of Public Spheres*, Basingstoke: Palgrave Macmillan.
Wodak, R. (2001), 'The Discourse-Historical Approach', in R. Wodak and M. Meyer (eds), *Methods of Critical Discourse Analysis*, 63–94, London: Sage.
Wodak, R. (2009), *The Discourse of Politics in Action: Politics as Usual*, New York: Palgrave Macmillan.
Wodak, R., and Boukala, S. (2015), '(Supra) National Identity and Language: Rethinking National and European Migration Policies and the Linguistic Integration of Migrants', *Annual Review of Applied Linguistics*, 35: 253–73.
Wodak, R., and Riesigl, M. (2001), *Discourse and Discrimination: Rhetorics of Racism and Antisemitism*, New York: Routledge.
Wodak, R., De Cillia, R. and Reisigl, M. (2009), *The Discursive Construction of National Identity*, Edinburgh: Edinburgh University Press.
World Bank Group (2019), 'Migration and Remittances: Recent Developments and Outlook', *Migration and Development Brief* 31.
Young, I. M. (2000), *Inclusion and Democracy*, Oxford: Oxford University Press.
Zaborowski, M. (2006), 'More Than Simply Expanding Markets: Germany and EU Enlargement', in H. Sjursen (ed.), *Questioning EU Enlargement: Europe in Search of Identity*, 104–20, London: Routledge.
Žagar, I. (2010), 'Topoi in Critical Discourse Analysis', *Lodz Papers in Pragmatics*, 6(1): 3–27.
Zapata-Barrero, R., and De Witte, N. (2007), 'The Spanish Governance of EU borders: Normative Questions', *Mediterranean Politics*, 12(1): 85–90.
Zimmerman, A. (2006), 'Decolonizing Weber', *Postcolonial Studies*, 9(1): 53–79.

Analysed documents

Alfano, A. (2013), 'Ue, Alfano incontra Rajoy su crescita, occupazione e immigrazione', 25 November.
Alfano, A. (2014a), 'Immigrazione, monito del governo all'Ue', Intervista del ministro dell'Interno Angelino Alfano al giornale *La Sicilia*, 21 May.
Alfano, A. (2014b), 'Alfano: 'L'Europa risponda, l'Italia non aspetta", Intervista del ministro dell'Interno al quotidiano *Corriere della Sera*, 24 August 24.
Alfano, A. (2015a), 'Alfano: rivedere le procedure di Schengen', Intervista al ministro Alfano, di Marco Ballico sul quotidiano Il Piccolo, 11 December.
Alfano, A. (2015b), '«Schengen non si tocca»', Intervista del ministro Alfano al quotidiano Corriere della Sera, 31 August.
Alfano, A. (2015c), 'Alfano: islamici, denunciate', Intervista al ministro dell'Interno Angelino Alfano al quotidiano La Nazione, 13 January.
Alfano, A. (2016), '«Rimpatri o sarà caos, le quote una delusione»', Intervista del ministro dell'Interno Angelino Alfano al quotidiano Il Messaggero, 27 January.
Alliot-Marie, M. (2007), 'Déclaration de Mme Michèle Alliot-Marie, ministre de l'intérieur, de l'outre-mer et des collectivités territoriales, sur la création et la mission de l'Agence nationale des titres sécurisés en vue de la sécurisation des titres d'identité et sur l'obligation de l'Etat de se moderniser et de se réformer', Charleville-Mézières, 17 December.
Amato, G. (2006), 'Amato: 'Cosí vedo l'Italia multietnica', Intervista al Ministro dell'Interno sui temi dell'immigrazione nell'inserto Metropoli del quotidiano La Repubblica – 'Scelte urbanistiche dei Comuni e scuola decisive per l'integrazione', 19 November.
Amato, G. (2007a), 'Amato: "Quel diritto dei cittadini alla sicurezza che dobbiamo saper garantire"', Lettera del ministro dell'Interno Giuliano Amato al direttore del quotidiano *Il Messaggero*, 1 October.
Amato, G. (2007b), 'La UE debe perfeccionar las normas sobre movimientos de personas', Intervista a Giuliano Amato di *El Pais*, 13 November.
Amato, G. (2007c), 'Rome demande una modification des règle de libre circulation dans l'Union europèenne', Intervista a Giuliano Amato di *Le Monde*, 14 November.
Andor, L. (2010), 'Moving Forward on the Posting of Workers Directive', SPEECH-10-100, Oviedo, 17 March.
Andor, L. (2011), 'The Commission Accepts That Spain Can Temporarily Restrict the Free Movement of Romanian Workers', IP/11/960, Brussels, 11 August.
Andor, L. (2012), 'A Strong Employment Agenda – The Pathway to Economic Recovery', SPEECH/12/588, 6 September.
Andor, L. (2013a), 'Youth guarantee, Social Investment Package and Free movement of workers from Bulgaria and Romania', SPEECH/13/173, Brussels, 28 February.
Andor, L. (2013b), 'Building a Single European Labour Market Must Be Part of the EU's Recovery Strategy', SPEECH/13/472, Brussels, 28 May.
Andor, L. (2013c), 'Free Movement of People: Five Actions to Benefit Citizens, Growth and Employment in the EU', IP/13/1151, Brussels, 25 November 25.
Andor, L. (2014a), 'Labour Mobility in the European Union – The Inconvenient Truth', SPEECH/14/114, Bristol, 10 February.
Andor, L. (2014b), 'Moving towards the Facts: Mobility in the Nordic-Baltic Region', SPEECH/14/193, Tallinn, 3 March.

Bibliography

Andor, L. (2014c), 'Free Movement of Workers: Commissioner Andor Welcomes Parliament's Approval of Directive', STATEMENT/14/67, Brussels, 12 March.

Avramopoulos, D. (2014), 'Remarks of Dimitris Avramopoulos, Commissioner for Migration, Home Affairs and Citizenship, at the End of the Home Affairs Council', Brussels, 5 December.

Avramopoulos, D. (2015), 'Remarks of Commissioner Dimitris Avramopoulos at the Press Conference on the Preparation of the 20 November Justice and Home Affairs Council and the Firearms Package', Brussels, 18 November.

Avramopoulos, D. (2016a), 'Remarks by First Vice-President Timmermans and Commissioner Avramopoulos to the European Parliament Plenary Session', Brussels, 12 May.

Avramopoulos, D. (2016b), 'Statement by Commissioner Avramopoulos on the Occasion of the 31st Anniversary of the Schengen Agreement', Brussels, 14 June.

Avramopoulos, D. (2016c), 'Remarks by Commissioner Avramopoulos to the Committee on Federal and European Affairs of the Bavarian Parliament on 26 April', Munich, 26 April.

Avramopoulos, D. (2016d), 'Remarks by Commissioner Avramopoulos at the Readout of the College Meeting of 23 March 2016', Brussels, 23 March.

Avramopoulos, D. (2016e), 'Remarks of Commissioner Avramopoulos at the Press Conference on 4 March 2016 Ahead of the Meeting of EU Heads of State or Government on 7 March 2016', Brussels, 4 March.

Avramopoulos, D. (2016f), 'Keynote Speech by Commissioner Avramopoulos at the 2016 Harvard European Conference: Europe at the Crossroads of the Migration and Security Crises', Cambridge, MA, 20 February.

Avramopoulos, D. (2016g), 'Remarks by Commissioner Avramopoulos at the Press Conference after the Informal Meeting of Ministers of Home Affairs', Amsterdam, 25 January.

Barroso, J. M. (2005), 'Choosing to Grow – a New Agenda for Growth and Jobs', SPEECH/05/188, Warsaw, 18 March.

Barroso, J. M. (2006a), '2006 European Year of Workers' Mobility', SPEECH/06/109, Brussels, 20 February.

Barroso, J. M. (2006b), 'More Europe Where It Matters!', SPEECH/06/168, Strasbourg, 15 March.

Barroso, J. M. (2006c), 'Remarks by the President', SPEECH/06/525, Berlin, 22 September.

Barroso, J. M. (2007), 'Enlargement of the Schengen Area: Achieving the European Goal of Free Movement of Persons', IP/07/1968, Brussels, 20 December.

Barroso, J. M. (2008), 'Building the Europe of the Future: A Europe of Citizens, Opportunities and Culture', SPEECH/08/267, The Hague, 24 May.

Barroso, J. M. (2009), 'EU Enlargement – 5 Years after', SPEECH/09/83, Prague, 2 March.

Barroso, J. M. (2010), 'Working Together to Improve the Danube Region', SPEECH/10/623, Bucharest, 8 November.

Barroso, J. M. (2011a), 'Migration Flows and Asylum and Their Impact on Schengen', SPEECH/11/322, Strasbourg, 10 May.

Barroso, J. M. (2011b), 'Statement by President Barroso at the "Youth on the Move – Make it Happen" Event', SPEECH/11/343, Antwerp, 17 May.

Barroso, J. M. (2011c), 'Statement by President Barroso Following the European Council', SPEECH/11/475, Brussels, 24 June.

Barroso, J. M. (2011d), 'Debate on the Closing of the Hungarian Presidency', SPEECH/11/496, Strasbourg, 5 July.

Barroso, J. M. (2012a), 'Speech by President Barroso: "Europe's future budget – Investing for Growth"', SPEECH/12/213, Brussels, 22 March.
Barroso, J. M. (2012b), 'Speech by President Barroso at the Employment Policy Conference "Jobs for Europe"', SPEECH/12/587, Brussels, 6 September.
Barroso, J. M. (2013), 'Speech by President Barroso at the 17th Tourism Summit', SPEECH/13/1002, Berlin, 2 December.
Barroso, J. M. (2014a), 'Speech by President Barroso on the Review of the Lithuanian Presidency', SPEECH/14/15, Strasbourg, 14 January.
Barroso, J. M. (2014b), 'Speech by President Barroso on the Greek Presidency', SPEECH/14/17, Strasbourg, 15 January.
Barroso, J. M. (2014c), 'Discours du Président Barroso: S'engager pour l'Europe', SPEECH/14/78, Brussels, 30 January.
Barroso, J. M. (2014d), 'Remarks by President Barroso Following His Meeting with the President of Romania, Traian Băsescu', SPEECH/14/132, Brussels, 14 February.
Barroso, J. M. (2014e), 'Reforming Europe in a Changing World', SPEECH/14/131, London, 14 February.
Barrot, J. (2008), '"Freedom, Security and Justice: What Will Be the Future?": Commission Launches Wide-Ranging Public Consultation to Define Future Priorities Relating to Freedom, Security and Justice', IP/08/1405, Brussels, 25 September.
Barrot, J. (2009), 'Free Movement and Residence Rights of EU Citizens and Their Families: The Commission Gives Guidance for Better Transposition and Application of Directive 2004/38/EC for the Benefit of Member States and EU Citizens', IP/09/1077, Brussels, 2 July.
Băsescu, T. (2006), 'Presedintele Romaniei, Traian Basescu, a oferit astazi, 01 iulie a.c., la Palatul Cotroceni, un dejun oficial elevilor olimpici la istorie si profesorilor indrumatori din Republica Moldova', Bucharest, 1 July.
Băsescu, T. (2007a), 'Discursul la întâlnirea ministerială Dunăre-Marea Neagră cu tema "Către un parteneriat durabil pentru gospodărirea integrată a apelor" (București, 23 februarie 2007)', Bucharest, 23 February.
Băsescu, T. (2007b), 'Discursul la Congresul Mondial al Asociației Internaționale a Chirurgilor, Medicilor Gastroenterologi și Oncologi', Bucharest, 5 September.
Băsescu, T. (2008a), 'Discursul la întâlnirea de început de an cu Șefii Misiunilor Diplomatice acreditați la București', Bucharest, 23 January.
Băsescu, T. (2008b), 'Alocuținea președintelui Românei, Traian Băsescu, la recepția oferită cu ocazia Zilei Europei', Bucharest, 8 May.
Băsescu, T. (2008c), 'Alocuțiunea la deschiderea reuniunii Consiliului General al Uniunii Internaționale a Notariatului', Bucharest, 13 June.
Băsescu, T. (2009a), 'Mesajul în fața Camerelor reunite ale Parlamentului (București, 14 aprilie 2009)', Bucharest, 14 April.
Băsescu, T. (2009b), 'Discursul la conferința "High Level Conference on the Security Situation of Roma in Europe"', Bucharest, 12 October.
Băsescu, T. (2009c), 'Discursul la întâlnirea cu autoritățile publice locale și cu reprezentanți din învățământul preuniversitar și universitar. (Satu Mare, 25 octombrie 2009)', Satu Mare, 25 October.
Băsescu, T. (2009d), 'Discursul la întâlnirea cu reprezentanți ai administrației publice locale, ai cadrelor didactice și ai mediului de afaceri din județul Iași (Iași, 31 octombrie 2009)', Iași, 31 October.
Băsescu, T. (2009e), 'Discursul la întâlnirea cu reprezentanți ai administrației publice din județul Teleorman', Roșiorii de Vede, 4 November.

Băsescu, T. (2010a), 'Discursul la întâlnirea cu cadrele didactice şi cu studenţii de la Universitatea Alexandru Ioan Cuza din Iaşi (Iaşi, 28 aprilie 2010)', Iaşi, 18 April.
Băsescu, T. (2010b), 'Discursul la seminarul cu tematica Europa Centrală – Centrul Europei? (Băile Tuşnad, 24 iulie 2010)', Băile Tuşnad, 24 July.
Băsescu, T. (2010c), 'Discursul la Reuniunea Anuală a Diplomaţiei Române (Palatul Cotroceni, 1 septembrie 2010) preşedintelui României, Traian Băsescu', Bucharest, 1 September.
Băsescu, T. (2010d), 'Mesajul în faţa Camerelor reunite ale Parlamentului (21 septembrie 2010)', Bucharest, 21 September.
Băsescu, T. (2011), 'Discursul la întâlnirea de început de an cu Şefii Misiunilor Diplomatice acreditaţi la Bucureşti', Bucharest, 20 January.
Băsescu, T. (2012), 'Discursul la întâlnirea anuală cu Şefii Misiunilor Diplomatice acreditaţi în România', Bucharest, 19 January.
Băsescu, T. (2013a), 'Speech of the President of Romania, Mr. Traian Băsescu, at the Annual Meeting of the Heads of the Diplomatic Missions in Romania', Bucharest, 13 January.
Băsescu, T. (2013b), 'Alocuţiunea preşedintelui României, domnul Traian Băsescu, în cadrul Celei de-a cincea ediţii a Forumului Global al Alianţei Civilizaţiilor', 27 February.
Băsescu, T. (2013c), 'Declaraţia de presă comună a preşedintelui României, domnul Traian Băsescu, şi a preşedintelui Consiliului European, domnul Herman van Rompuy', 25 April.
Băsescu, T. (2013d), 'Traian Băsescu la TVR: Următorul proiect pentru România trebuie să fie "Vrem să ne întregim ţara!"', 27 November.
Băsescu, T. (2014a), 'Discursul preşedintelui României, domnul Traian Băsescu, la Întâlnirea Anuală cu Şefii Misiunilor Diplomatice acreditaţi în România', Bucharest, 15 January.
Băsescu, T. (2014b), 'Eliminarea de către Parlamentul European a regimului de vize în spaţiul UE aplicabil cetăţenilor Republicii Moldova', 27 February.
Băsescu, T. (2014c), 'Declaraţia de presă a preşedintelui României, domnul Traian Băsescu', Bucharest, 11 March.
Băsescu, T. (2014d), 'Discursul preşedintelui României, domnul Traian Băsescu, la Reuniunea Anuală a Diplomaţiei Române', 29 August.
Băsescu, T. (2014e), 'Mesajul preşedintelui României, domnul Traian Băsescu, cu ocazia intrării în vigoare a deciziei privind introducerea Republicii Moldova printre statele ai căror cetăţeni vor putea circula fără viză în spaţiul Schengen', 28 April.
Berlusconi, S. (2008), 'Intervista del Presidente del Consiglio, Silvio Berlusconi, al quotidiano *Unione Sarda*', Rome, 7 September.
Berlusconi, S. (2010a), 'Intervista del Presidente Berlusconi a "Le Figaro"', 15 September.
Berlusconi, S. (2010b), 'Intervista del Presidente Berlusconi a "La Stampa"', 28 January.
Berlusconi, S., and Sarkozy, N. (2011), 'Lettera congiunta a Herman van Rompuy e José Manuel Barroso', Rome, 26 April.
Blair, T. (2005), 'The Labour Party, Britain Forward, Not Back', Dover, 22 April.
Blair, T. (2006), 'Joint Press conference with the Prime Minister of Slovakia', Bratislava, 9 March.
Boc, E. (2009a), 'Primul-ministru Emil Boc a avut o intrevedere cu Jovan Krkobabic, vice prim-ministru al Republicii Serbia pe probleme sociale', 24 February.
Boc, E. (2009b), 'Primul-ministru Emil Boc s-a intalnit cu reprezentanti ai comunitatii romane din Italia', 26 September.

Boc, E. (2010), 'Declarații susținute de primul-ministru Emil Boc și Boyko Borissov, prim-ministru al Republicii Bulgaria, la inaugurarea liniei de feribot Turnu Măgurele-Nicopole', 19 March.
Brown, G. (2010), 'Speech on Controlling Immigration for a Fairer Britain', London, 31 March.
Brown, G. (2008), 'Speech on Managed Migration and Earned Citizenship', London, 20 February.
Brown, G. (2009), 'Speech on Immigration', Ealing, West London, 12 November.
Cameron, D. (2010), 'A transcript of Prime Minister David Cameron's Press Conference at the Close of the European Council in Brussels on 16 September', 16 September.
Cameron, D. (2011), 'Prime Minister's Speech on Immigration', London, 10 October.
Cameron, D. (2012), 'David Cameron "Prepared to Halt Immigration of Greeks into UK"', *The Guardian*, 3 July.
Cameron, D. (2013), 'Free Movement within Europe Needs to Be Less Free', *Financial Times*, 26 November.
Cameron, D. (2014a), 'David Cameron's Speech to the Conservative Conference', London, 1 October.
Cameron, D. (2014b), 'David Cameron: Speech on Immigration', London, 28 November.
Cameron, D. (2014c), 'David Cameron and Angela Merkel Press Conference', London, 27 February.
Cameron, D. (2014d), 'David Cameron's Statement on G7 Summit: June 2014', London, 11 June.
Cameron, D. (2014e), 'European Council June 2014: David Cameron's Speech', London, 27 June.
Cameron, D. (2015a), 'PM Statement in Poland: 10 December 2015', Warsaw, 10 December.
Cameron, D. (2015b), 'PM Statement on Talks in Romania, 9 December 2015', Bucharest, 9 December.
Cameron, D. (2015c), 'Prime Minister's Speech on Europe', London, 10 November.
Cameron, D. (2015d), 'David Cameron and Angela Merkel in Berlin: Press Conference', Berlin, 29 May.
Cameron, D. (2015e), 'PM Speech on Immigration', London, 21 May.
Cameron, D. (2015f), 'Eastern Partnership Summit in Riga: PM Press Conference', Riga, 20 May.
Cameron, D. (2015g), 'European Council March 2015: Pre-Council Press Conference', Brussels, 20 March.
Cameron, D. (2015h), 'David Cameron and Angela Merkel press conference', London, 7 January 2015.
Cameron, D. (2015i), 'A New Settlement for the United Kingdom in a Reformed European Union', Letter to the President of the European Council Donald Tusk London, 10 November.
Cameron, D. (2016a), 'PM Statement in Hungary, 7 January 2016', Budapest, 7 January.
Cameron, D. (2016b), 'PM Speech at Caterpillar on the EU Referendum: 28 April 2016', Peterborough, 28 April.
Cameron, D. (2016c), 'PM Speech at PwC on Economic Security in the EU: 5 April 2016', Birmingham, 5 April.
Cameron, D. (2016d), 'PM Statement in Bavaria on EU Reform, 7 January 2016', Bavaria, 7 January.

Cameron, D. (2016e), 'PM speech at O2 on the EU referendum: 23 February 2016', Slough, 23 February.
Cameron, D. (2016f), 'PM Statement Following European Council Meeting: 19 February 2016', Brussels, 19 February.
Cameron, D. (2016g), 'PM's Statement at Press Conference in Copenhagen: 5 February 2016', Copenhagen, 5 February.
Cameron, D. (2016h), 'PM Speech in the Czech Republic, 22 January 2016', Prague, 22 January.
Cameron, D. (2016i), 'European Council Meeting 28 June 2016: PM Press Conference', Brussels, 28 June.
Cancellieri, A. (2012), 'Emergenza umanitaria decretata dal Governo in relazione al flusso migratorio proveniente dal Nord Africa', Audizione del ministro dell'Interno Annamaria Cancellieri alla Commissione straordinaria per la tutela e la promozione dei diritti umani del Senato della Repubblica, 27 November.
Cazeneuve, B. (2015a), 'Déclaration de M. Bernard Cazeneuve, ministre de l'intérieur, sur la position de la France concernant les mesures de lutte contre le terrorisme adoptées au niveau européen à la suite des attentats perpétrés à Paris et à Saint-Denis, à Bruxelles le 20 novembre 2015, Brussels, 20 November.
Cazeneuve, B. (2015b), 'Déclaration de M. Bernard Cazeneuve, ministre de l'intérieur, sur le renforcement de la sécurité ferroviaire après l'attentat déjoué du Thalys Amsterdam – Paris, notamment sur les lignes internationales à grande vitesse, à Paris le 29 août 2015, Paris, 29 August.
Cazeneuve, B. (2015c), 'Interview de M. Bernard Cazeneuve, ministre de l'intérieur, à BFM TV le 6 novembre 2015, sur l'éventualité de confier à des prestataires privés l'utilisation des radars embarqués dans des véhicules banalisés, le rétablissement de l'ordre à Moirans (Isère), l'organisation de la conférence Climat, la crise migratoire et la lutte contre le trafic de drogue', Paris, 6 November.
Cazeneuve, B. (2015d), 'Interview de M. Bernard Cazeneuve, ministre de l'intérieur, à France 3 le 25 mars 2015, sur la situation des migrants à Calais, l'accueil des demandeurs d'asile syriens et irakiens et l'organisation d'un "partage de l'asile" au niveau des pays de l'Union européenne', Paris, 25 March.
Cazeneuve, B. (2016a), 'Déclaration de M. Bernard Cazeneuve, ministre de l'intérieur, sur la nécessité du renforcement de la coopération européenne en matière de lutte contre le terrorisme, Amsterdam le 25 janvier 2016', Amsterdam, 25 January.
Cazeneuve, B. (2016b), 'Interview de M. Bernard Cazeneuve, ministre de l'intérieur, au journal "Le Parisien" du 6 février 2016, sur la gestion par la Grèce des flux migratoires, Paris, 6 February.
Cazeneuve, B., Avramopoulos, D., de Kerchove, G. and Holder, E. (2015), 'Réunion européenne et internationale sur la lutte contre le terrorisme: Déclaration conjointe', Paris, 11 January.
Chirac, J. (2005a), 'Débat de M. Jacques Chirac, Président de la République, avec des jeunes à TF1', 14 April.
Chirac, J. (2005b), 'Conférence de presse conjointe de MM. Jacques Chirac, Président de la République, Gerhard Schroeder, Chancelier de la République fédérale d'Allemagne et Aleksander Kwasniewski, Président de la République de Pologne', Nancy, 19 May.
Chirac, J. (2005c), 'Déclaration de M. Jacques Chirac, Président de la République, notamment sur le maintien de la paix dans le monde, l'aide au développement, la construction européenne et sur les relations économiques internationales', Paris, 29 August.

Chirac, J. (2005d), 'Tribune de M. Jacques Chirac, Président de la République, dans *Le Figaro* et dans plusieurs journaux européens', 26 October.
Chirac, J. (2007), 'Conférence de presse de M. Jacques Chirac, Président de la République, notamment sur la construction européenne, les relations franco-allemandes et sur la situation au Proche et Moyen Orient', Berlin, 25 March.
Cioloş, D. (2015), 'Premierul Cioloş a prezentat principalele concluzii ale reuniunii Consiliului European de la Bruxelles şi poziţia României pe temele discutate', Bruissels, 18 December.
Cioloş, D. (2016a), 'Premierul Dacian Cioloş a participat la evenimentul "Diaspora românească, vector de dezvoltare"', Bucharest, 23 February.
Cioloş, D. (2016b), 'Declaraţii comune susţinute de premierul Dacian Cioloş şi de preşedintele Parlamentului European, Martin Schulz', Brussels, 16 February.
Cioloş D. (2016c), 'Premierul a participat la cea de-a IV-a ediţie a Eurosfat, cu tema "Este România pregătită pentru examenul de maturitate în UE? Ameliorarea profilului european al României în perspectiva Preşedinţiei Consiliului 2019"', Brussels, 6 May.
Cioloş D. (2016d), 'Interviul premierului Dacian Cioloş acordat postului francez LCI – MYTF1', Paris, 9 June.
Clarke, C. (2005), 'Liberty and Security: Striking the Right Balance', Speech by Charles Clarke, Then Home Secretary, to the European Parliament in October 2005.
de Maizière, T. (2010), 'Das Bürgertum muss stolz sein', Interview mit Bundesinnenminister Dr. Thomas de Mazière in *der Zeit*, 16 September.
de Maizière, T. (2014), 'Schutz im Internet verbessern', 14 April.
de Maizière, T. (2015a), 'Rede des Bundesinnenministers anlässlich der Migrationskonferenz 2015', Berlin, 14 April.
de Maizière, T. (2015b), '"Es bedarf eines gemeinsamen Bandes"', Interview mit dem Bundesinnenminister Dr. Thomas de Maizière, *Märkische Oderzeitung*, 19 January.
de Maizière, T. (2015c), 'Die Muslime müssen sich distanzieren', Interview mit dem Bundesinnenminister Dr. Thomas de Maizière über islamischen Terror in Europa, echte und unechte Flüchtlinge und die Umsetzung der Masseneinwanderungsinitiative der SVP, *Schweiz am Sonntag*, 2 February.
de Maizière, T. (2016). '"Eine enge Zusammenarbeit ist in der Flüchtlingskrise und in der Flüchtlingsbewegung notwendig"', Genf, 18 January.
de Villepin, D. (2005), 'Article de M. Dominique Galouzeau de Villepin, ministre de l'intérieur, de la sécurité intérieure et des libertés locales, sur le site de l'UMP', 10 April.
de Villepin, D. et al. (2005), 'Déclaration commune de M. Dominique Galouzeau de Villepin, ministre de l'intérieur, de la sécurité intérieure et des libertés locales, M. Otto Schily, ministre de l'intérieur allemand, M. José Alonso, ministre de l'intérieur espagnol, M. Giuseppe Pisanu, ministre de l'intérieur italien et M. Charles Clarke, ministre de l'intérieur anglais', Déclaration commune du G5, Paris, 12 May.
Díaz, J. F. (2014), 'Comparecencia del Ministro del Interior, a petición propia, para informar sobre los hechos acaecidos en la frontera de la Ciudad Autónoma de Ceuta el pasado 6 de febrero', Comisión de Interior del Congreso de los Diputados, 13 February.
Díaz, J. F. (2015a), 'El ministro del Interior anuncia que el Puerto de Palamós será declarado frontera exterior de Schengen', Palamós, 9 March.
Díaz, J. F. (2015b), 'Jorge Fernández Díaz propone la aprobación de un Programa Europeo de Retorno como medida eficaz para hacer frente a las redes de tráfico de seres humanos y al drama humanitario del Mediterráneo', 16 June.
Frattini, F. (2005), 'SIS II: Commission Presents a Set of Proposals for Enlarging the Schengen Area to the New Member States', IP/05/651, Brussels, 1 June.

Frattini, F. (2006), 'Enhancement of Free Movement and Residence Rights for EU Citizens: A New Milestone in EU Integration Process', IP/06/554, Brussels, 2 May.

Frattini, F. (2007a), 'Application of Directive 2004/38/EC on the Right of Citizens of the Union and Their Families to Move and Reside Freely within the Territory of the Member States (Debate)', Strasbourg, 12 November.

Frattini, F. (2007b), 'Declaration by Vice-President Frattini on the Occasion of the Grand Opening of the New Premises of Frontex in Warsaw', IP/07/419, Brussels, 27 March.

Frattini, F. (2008), 'Providing Europe with the Tools to Bring Its Border Management into the 21st Century', SPEECH/08/142, Brdo (Slovenia), Mar 12, 2008.

Friedrich, H.-P. (2011), 'Europa ist ein großer Arbeitsmarkt für uns alle', Interview mit Bundesinnenminister Dr. Hans-Peter Friedrich und Claude Guéant in *L'Express*, 7 December.

Friedrich, H.-P. (2012a), 'Erfolgsmodell "Blaue Karte EU"', 1 August.

Friedrich, H.-P. (2012b), 'Deutsch-Niederländische Integrationskonferenz', 4 September.

Friedrich, H.-P. (2013), 'Rat der Justiz- und Innenminister in Luxemburg', 6 June.

Guéant, C. (2011), 'Déclaration de M. Claude Guéant, ministre de l'intérieur, de l'outre-mer, des collectivités territoriales et de l'immigration, sur la politique de l'immigration dans le cadre de l'Union européenne', Paris, 31 August.

Hollande, F. (2013), 'Intervention du Président de la République devant le Parlement européen', 5 February.

Hollande, F. (2014), 'L'Europe que je veux (tribune dans Le Monde)', Paris, 8 May.

Hollande, F. (2015a), 'Déclaration de M. François Hollande, Président de la République, sur la question des réfugiés et sur l'appartenance de la Grande-Bretagne à l'Union européenne, à Bruxelles le 17 décembre 2015', Brussels, 17 December.

Hollande, F. (2015b), 'Interview de M. François Hollande, Président de la République, sur son déplacement aux Caraïbes, la collectivité d'Outre-mer de Saint-Martin et sur la Grande-Bretagne et l'Union européenne, à Saint-Martin le 8 mai 2015', Saint-Martin, 8 May.

Hollande, F. (2015c), 'Déclaration de M. François Hollande, Président de la République, sur les défis et priorités de l'Union européenne, à Strasbourg le 7 octobre 2015', Strasbourg, 7 October.

Hollande, F. (2015d), 'Déclaration de M. François Hollande, Président de la République, sur les efforts en faveur des conditions de vie des étudiants, à Paris le 1er octobre 2015', Paris, 1 October.

Hollande, F. (2015e), 'Déclaration de M. François Hollande, Président de la République, sur la politique sociale au sein de l'Union européenne, à Paris le 29 septembre 2015', Paris, 29 September.

Hollande, F. (2015f), 'Point de presse de M. François Hollande, Président de la République, sur la crise des réfugiés, les logiciels truqués des moteurs diesel de onze millions de véhicules Volkswagen et sur la Grande-Bretagne et l'Union européenne, à Londres le 22 septembre', London, 22 September.

Hollande, F. (2015g), 'Conférence de presse de M. François Hollande, Président de la République, sur les défis et priorités de la politique gouvernementale, à Paris le 7 septembre 2015', Paris, 7 September.

Hollande, F. (2015h), 'Déclaration conjointe de M. François Hollande, Président de la République, et Mme Angela Merkel, Chancelière fédérale allemande, sur la crise des migrants, à Berlin le 24 août 2015', Berlin, 24 August.

Hollande, F. (2015i), 'Déclaration de M. François Hollande, Président de la République, sur les efforts en faveur des entreprises, à Paris le 17 juin 2015', Paris, 17 June.

Holande, F. (2016a), 'Déclaration de M. François Hollande, Président de la République, sur les défis et priorités de la politique étrangère de la France, à Paris le 21 janvier 2016', Paris, 21 January.

Hollande, F. (2016b), 'Déclaration de M. François Hollande, Président de la République, sur la Grande-Bretagne et l'Union européenne, la crise des réfugiés, l'Accord de Paris sur le climat et sur les questions économiques, à Paris le 22 juin 2016', Paris, 22 June.

Hollande, F. (2016c), 'Interview de M. François Hollande, Président de la République, dans "Les Echos" du 30 juin 2016, sur la décision des Britanniques de quitter l'Union européenne, la loi travail, la politique économique du gouvernement, la présidentielle aux Etats-Unis et sur le référendum concernant l'aéroport de Notre-Dame-des-Landes', Paris, 30 June.

Hollande, F. (2016d), 'Conférence de presse de M. François Hollande, Président de la République, sur la décision des Britanniques de quitter l'Union européenne, les priorités de la construction européenne, un attentat terroriste en Turquie, la réduction des déficits et sur l'accord franco-britannique concernant les migrants, à Bruxelles le 29 juin 2016', Brussels, 29 June.

Hollande, F. (2016e), 'Déclaration de M. François Hollande, Président de la République, sur le tunnel de Saint-Gothard en Suisse et sur la construction européenne, à Saint-Gothard le 1er juin 2016', Saint-Gothard, 1 June.

Hollande, F. (2016f), 'Déclaration de M. François Hollande, Président de la République, sur les relations entre la France et les Pays-Bas, à Paris le 10 mars 2016', Paris, 10 March.

Hollande, F. (2016g), 'Conférence de presse de M. François Hollande, Président de la République, sur la politique européenne en matière de réfugiés, la situation en Syrie et sur la place du Royaume-Uni dans l'Union européenne, à Bruxelles le 20 février 2016', Brussels, 20 February.

Hollande, F. (2016h), 'Interview de M. François Hollande, Président de la République, avec France Inter le 19 février 2016, sur les relations entre le Royaume-Uni et l'Union européenne, le crise migratoire, la construction européenne, la lutte contre le terrorisme, la réforme du code du travail, la politique économique et sur l'élection présidentielle de 2017', Paris, 19 February.

Hollande, F. (2016i), 'Déclaration de M. François Hollande, Président de la République, sur le centenaire de la bataille de Verdun, la réconciliation franco-allemande et sur la construction européenne, à Verdun le 29 mai 2016', Verdun, 29 May.

Hollande, F. (2016j), Conférence de presse de M. François Hollande, Président de la République, sur le choix des Britanniques de quitter l'Union européenne et sur la construction européenne, à Bruxelles le 28 juin 2016', Brussels, 28 June.

Hollande, F., and A. Merkel (2013), 'Déclaration du Conseil des ministres franco-allemand à l'occasion du cinquantième anniversaire du Traité de l'Élysée', Berlin, 22 January.

Hollande, F., and M. Rutte (2014), 'Déclaration commune sur le Partenariat entre la République française et le Royaume des Pays-Bas', The Hague, 20 January.

Hortefeux, B. (2009), 'Déclaration de M. Brice Hortefeux, ministre de l'intérieur, de l'outre-mer et des collectivités territoriales, sur la coopération policière internationale, notamment en matière de lutte contre les réseaux d'immigration irrégulière, le terrorisme et le crime organisé', Paris, 1 September.

Hortefeux, B. (2010), 'Déclaration de M. Brice Hortefeux, ministre de l'intérieur, de l'outre-mer et des collectivités territoriales, sur la mise en oeuvre des mesures d'évacuation des campements illicites des Roms en situation irrégulière', Paris, 30 August.

Iohannis, K. (2015a), 'Primirea de către Președintele României, domnul Klaus Iohannis, a domnului Philip Hammond, ministrul de Externe al Regatului Unit al Marii Britanii și Irlandei de Nord', Bucharest, 14 January.
Iohannis, K. (2015b), 'Declarația de presă a Președintelui României, domnul Klaus Iohannis, după Reuniunea Consiliului European Informal', Brussels, 12 February.
Iohannis, K. (2015c), 'Declarația de presă comună a Președintelui României, domnul Klaus Iohannis, și a Cancelarului Republicii Federale Germania, doamna Angela Merkel', Berlin, 26 February.
Iohannis, K. (2015d), 'Alocuțiunea Președintelui României, domnul Klaus Iohannis, la întâlnirea cu reprezentanți ai minorității românești din Serbia', Serbia, 16 July.
Iohannis, K. (2016a), 'Discursul Președintelui României, domnul Klaus Iohannis, susținut la recepția oferită cu prilejul Zilei Europei', Bucharest, 9 May.
Iohannis, K. (2016b), 'Alocuțiunea Președintelui României, domnul Klaus Iohannis, susținută la întâlnirea cu reprezentanți ai unor companii române și germane', Bucharest, 22 June.
Jourová, V. (2015), 'Speech by Věra Jourová at Conference on European Citizenship and Justice – European citizenship: our common rights and values', Luxembourg, 14 September.
Juncker, J. C. (2015a), 'Speech by President Juncker at the BusinessEurope Day Event', Brussels, 26 March.
Juncker, J. C. (2015b), 'Speech by President Juncker at the EP Plenary – Preparation of the European Council Meeting of 17–18 December 2015', Strasbourg, 16 December.
Juncker, J. C. (2016), 'Speech by Jean-Claude Juncker, President of the European Commission – Preparation of the European Council Meeting of 18 and 19 February 2016', Brussels, 3 February.
Letta, E. (2013), 'Keynote Address from Enrico Letta, Prime Minister of Italy'. Annual dinner Bruegel "Sketching the Contours of the New World Economy", Brussels, 9 September.
Letta, E., and Hollande, F. (2013), 'Dichiarazione congiunta (Italy-France Joint Declaration)'. XXXI Vertice Italo-Francese, Rome, 20 November.
Letta, E., and R. Niblett (2013), 'Italy and the UK in an Evolving EU', London: Chatham House, 16 July.
Letta, E., and Rajoy, M. (2014), 'Dichiarazione congiunta (Italy-Spain Joint Declaration)', Vertice Italia-Spagna, Rome, 27 January.
Malmström, C. (2010), 'Schengen Borders Code Evaluated: Commission Concerned about Reported Difficulties for Travellers', IP/10/1329, Brussels, 13 October.
Malmström, C. (2011), 'Commission Proposes Better Management of Migration to the EU', IP/11/532, Brussels, 4 May.
Malmström, C. (2012a), 'The Importance of Safeguarding Schengen', SPEECH/12/78, Brussels, 8 February.
Malmström, C. (2012b), 'New Report and Survey Give a Snapshot of Migration, Asylum and Free Movement in the EU', IP/12/552, Brussels, 1 June.
Malmström, C. (2013), 'Commission Reports on EU Free Movement', IP/13/496, Brussels, 3 June.
Malmström, C. (2014), 'Cecilia Malmström's Acceptance Speech When Receiving the "Estrella de Europa" Award in Zaragoza', SPEECH/14/429, Zaragoza, 4 June.
Maroni, R. (2008a), 'Romania e Libia, chiuse le falle'. Intervista del ministro Maroni al quotidiano La Padania', 23 September.

Maroni, R. (2008b), 'Maroni: 'Chiederò di aumentare i militari nelle città. Sui campi nomadi Bruxelles ha dovuto farmi ragione', Intervista del ministro Roberto Maroni al quotidiano *Il Messaggero*, 5 September.

Maroni, R. (2008c), 'Audizione del Ministro dell'interno, Roberto Maroni, in merito alle misure avviate per migliorare l'efficacia della normativa in materia di immigrazione', Camera dei deputati, 15 October.

Maroni, R. (2010a), 'Audizione sulla proposta di regolamento del Parlamento europeo e del Consiglio recante modifica del regolamento (CE) n. 2007/2004 del Consiglio che istituisce un'Agenzia europea per la gestione della cooperazione operativa alle frontiere esterne degli Stati membri dell'Unione europea (Frontex) (COM(2010)61 def.)', Camera dei Deputati, 18 May.

Maroni, R. (2010b), 'Maroni: giusto espellere i rom. Saremo più duri di Sarkozy', Intervista del ministro dell'Interno al quotidiano *il Corriere della Sera*, 21 August.

Maroni, R. (2010c), 'Interrogazione a risposta immediata n. 3-01239 dell'On. Marco Giovanni Reguzzoni ed altri sui risultati conseguiti dal Governo in ordine alla questione dei campi nomadi abusivi ed iniziative in ambito comunitario per la revisione della disciplina della libera circolazione', Camera dei Deputati, 22 September.

Maroni, R. (2010d), 'Audizione del Ministro dell'interno, On. Roberto Maroni nell'ambito dell'indagine conoscitiva sulle nuove politiche europee in materia di immigrazione', Comitato parlamentare di controllo sull'attuazione dell'accordo di Schengen, di vigilanza sull'attività di Europol, di controllo e vigilanza in materia di immigrazione, 12 October.

Maroni, R. (2011a), 'Audizione del Ministro dell'interno Roberto Maroni sui recenti sviluppi della situazione nel Mediterraneo', Commissioni congiunte, 2 March.

Maroni, R. (2011b), 'Informativa sulla questione dei flussi migratori provenienti dal Nord Africa', Senato della Repubblica, 7 April.

Maroni, R. (2011c), 'Audizione del Ministro dell'interno, Roberto Maroni, sui recenti sviluppi degli eccezionali flussi migratori dalla Tunisia e dalla Libia e sulle iniziative che il Governo intende assumere in materia di immigrazione', Camera dei Deputati, 12 April.

May, T. (2010), 'Immigration: Home Secretary's Speech', 5 November.

May, T. (2011), 'Justice and Home Affairs (JHA) Brussels 12 May 2011: Post-Council Statement – Written Statements To Parliament', House of Commons, 9.

May, T. (2012), 'G6 Meeting: London 20 to 21 November 2012 – Written Statements to Parliament', House of Commons, 29 November.

May, T. (2013a), 'Written Statement to Parliament Justice and Home Affairs: Pre-Council Statement – June 2013', House of Commons, 5 June.

May, T. (2013b), 'Written Statement to Parliament Justice and Home Affairs: Pre-Council Statement – December 2013', House of Commons, 4 December.

May, T. (2013c), 'Written Statement to Parliament Justice and Home Affairs: Post-Council Statement', House of Commons, 12 December.

May, T. (2014a), 'Written Statement to Parliament Justice and Home Affairs: Post-Council Statement, January 2014', House of Commons, 30 January.

May, T. (2014b), 'Written Statement to Parliament G6: Krakow', House of Commons, 24 February.

May, T. (2014c), 'Written Statement to Parliament Justice and Home Affairs: Post-Council Statement, March 2014', House of Commons, 12 March.

May, T. (2014d), 'Written Statement to Parliament Justice and Home Affairs: Post-Council Statement', House of Commons, 16 October.

May, T. (2014e), 'Written Statement to Parliament Justice and Home Affairs: Pre-Council Statement', House of Commons, 27 November.
May, T. (2015a), 'Justice and Home Affairs Post-Council Statement: Written Statement – HCWS425', 19 March.
May, T. (2015b), 'Justice and Home Affairs Pre-Council Statement: Written Statement – HCWS351', 5 March.
May, T. (2015c), 'Justice and Home Affairs Post-Council Statement: Written Statement – HCWS311', London, 17 November.
May, T. (2016), 'Justice and Home Affairs Post-Council Statement: Written Statement – HCWS31', London, 26 May.
Merkel, A. (2006a), 'Rede von Bundeskanzlerin Dr. Angela Merkel auf dem 18. DGB-Bundeskongress', Berlin, 24 May.
Merkel, A. (2006b), 'Rede von Bundeskanzlerin Dr. Angela Merkel auf der Konferenz "Globalisierung fair gestalten"', Berlin, 22 November.
Merkel, A. (2007a), 'Rede von Bundeskanzlerin Dr. Angela Merkel zur Jahreseröffnung der Deutschen Börse', Franfurt/Main, 22 January.
Merkel, A. (2007b), 'Rede von Bundeskanzlerin Dr. Angela Merkel auf dem Europäischen Sozialstaatskongress des DGB', Berlin, 13 March.
Merkel, A. (2008), 'Rede von Bundeskanzlerin Dr. Angela Merkel auf dem "National Forum on Europe"', Dublin, 14 April.
Merkel, A. (2009), 'Regierungserklärung von Bundeskanzlerin Dr. Angela Merkel zum Europäischen Rat am 10./11. Dezember 2009 in Brüssel und zur UN-Klimakonferenz vom 7. Bis 18. Dezember 2009 in Kopenhagen vor dem Deutschen Bundestag', Berlin, 17 December.
Merkel, A. (2010a), 'Rede von Bundeskanzlerin Merkel bei der Festveranstaltung der acatech – Deutsche Akademie der Technikwissenschaften e. V', Berlin, 19 October.
Merkel, A. (2010b), 'Frachtgutkontrollen weltweit besser abstimmen', 3 November.
Merkel, A. (2010c), 'Pressekonferenz von Bundeskanzlerin Merkel nach dem Europäischen Rat in Brüssel', 16, September.
Merkel, A. (2011), 'Stabilität und Wettbewerbsfähigkeit für die Eurozone', 10 March.
Merkel, A. (2012a), 'Fachkräftegipfel auf Schloss Meseberg', 5 June.
Merkel, A. (2012b), 'Pressestatements von Bundeskanzlerin Angela Merkel, Bundesminister Philipp Rösler, DIHK-Präsident Prof. Hans Heinrich Driftmann und dem DGB- Bundesvorsitzenden Michael Sommer nach dem Gespräch mit Sozialpartnern', 5 June.
Merkel, A. (2013a), 'Rede der Bundeskanzlerin zum 50. Jahrestag der Unterzeichnung des Élysée-Vertrages', Berlin, 22 January.
Merkel, A. (2013b), 'Rede von Bundeskanzlerin Merkel beim Jahresempfang der Wirtschaft 2013', Mainz, 18 February.
Merkel, A. (2013c), 'Die Kanzlerin im Gespräch', 20 April.
Merkel, A. (2013d), 'Pressekonferenz zum 6. Integrationsgipfel der Bundesregierung', 28 May.
Merkel, A. (2014a), 'Regierungserklärung von Bundeskanzlerin Merkel', Deutscher Bundestag, 29 January.
Merkel, A. (2014b), 'Rede von Bundeskanzlerin Merkel vor den beiden Häusern des britischen Parlaments', London, 27 February.
Merkel, A. (2014c), 'Europa gemeinsam besser machen', 27 February.
Merkel, A. (2014d), 'Pressekonferenz von Bundeskanzlerin Merkel und dem britischen Premierminister Cameron', 27 February.

Merkel, A. (2014e), 'Pressekonferenz von Bundeskanzlerin Merkel nach dem Europäischen Rat am 23. und 24. Oktober 2014', 24 October.

Merkel, A. (2014f), 'Rede von Bundeskanzlerin Merkel an der Universität Auckland', 14 November.

Merkel, A. (2014g), 'Pressekonferenz zum 7. Integrationsgipfel am 1. Dezember 2014', 1 December.

Merkel, A. (2015a), 'Pressekonferenz von Bundeskanzlerin Merkel und dem britischen Premierminister Cameron', 7 January 2015.

Merkel, A. (2015b), 'Wir wissen zu wenig über den Islam', *Frankfurter Allgemeine Zeitung*, 16 January.

Merkel, A. (2015c), 'Regierungserklärung von Bundeskanzlerin Merkel', Berlin, 16 December.

Merkel, A. (2015d), 'Regierungserklärung von Bundeskanzlerin Merkel', Berlin, 15 October.

Merkel, A. (2015e), 'Rede von Bundeskanzlerin Merkel am 7. Oktober 2015 vor dem Europäischen Parlament', Strasbourg, 7 October.

Merkel, A. (2015f), 'Rede von Bundeskanzlerin Merkel bei der Tageszeitung "Asahi Shimbun" am 9. März 2015', Tokio, 9 March.

Merkel, A. (2015g), 'Pressekonferenz von Bundeskanzlerin Merkel und dem Premierminister von Singapur, Lee Hsien Loong', Berlin, 3 February.

Merkel, A. (2015h), 'Pressekonferenz von Bundeskanzlerin Merkel und dem rumänischen Präsidenten, Johannis', Berlin, 26 February.

Merkel, A. (2015i), 'Pressekonferenz von Bundeskanzlerin Merkel und dem Premierminister des Vereinigten Königreiches Großbritannien und Nordirland, Cameron', Berlin, 29 May.

Merkel, A. (2015j), 'Sommerpressekonferenz von Bundeskanzlerin Merkel', Berlin, 31 August.

Merkel, A. (2015k), 'Pressekonferenz von Bundeskanzlerin Merkel am 18. Dezember 2015 zum Abschluss des Europäischen Rats', Brussels, 18 December.

Merkel, A. (2016a), 'Regierungserklärung von Bundeskanzlerin Merkel', Berlin, 28 June.

Merkel, A. (2016b), 'Rede von Bundeskanzlerin Merkel zum "Tag des deutschen Familienunternehmens" der Stiftung Familienunternehmen am 10. Juni 2016', Berlin, 10 June.

Merkel, A. (2016c), 'Regierungserklärung von Bundeskanzlerin Merkel', Berlin, 17 February.

Merkel, A. (2016d), 'Rede von Bundeskanzlerin Merkel beim Festakt zum 125. Geburtstag von Walter Eucken am 13. Januar 2016', Freiburg, 13 January.

Merkel, A. (2016e), 'Rede von Bundeskanzlerin Merkel beim Jahresempfang der Wirtschaft 2016 am 11. Januar 2016', Mainz, 11 January.

Merkel, A. (2016f), 'Pressekonferenz von Bundeskanzlerin Merkel und dem rumänischen Ministerpräsidenten Cioloş, Berlin, 7 January.

Mikl-Leitner, J., Friedrich, H. P., Teeven, F. and May T. (2013), Letter to the President of the European Council.

Monti, M. (2012a), 'Bruxelles: Conferenza stampa del Presidente Mario Monti al termine del Consiglio Europeo', 2 March.

Monti, M. (2012b), 'Dall'UE con ottimismo. Intervista alla "Rossiyskaya Gazeta"', 23 July.

Pisanu, G. (2005), 'Anche l'Italia chiuderà le porte per bloccare il terrore islamico', *Il Giornale*, 13 July.

Ponta, V. (2012a), 'Primul-ministru Victor Ponta a reconfirmat, cu ocazia vizitei efectuate astăzi în Republica Moldova, determinarea României de a-și respecta toate angajamentele asumate în relația bilaterală', 17 July.

Ponta, V. (2012b), 'Primul-ministru Victor Ponta a participat la emisiunea "Vocile Străzii", de la Realitatea TV', 2 September.

Ponta, V. (2012c), 'Victor Ponta: Este prima vizită oficială de când premierul sârb, Ivica Dačić, a fost investit. Din 2008, niciun premier român nu a efectuat vreo vizita oficială la Belgrad, în Republica Serbia', Belgrad, 18 October.

Ponta, V. (2013a), 'Interviu acordat de premierul Victor Ponta pentru Adevărul TV', 19 March.

Ponta, V. (2013b), 'Germania profită de românii care au emigrat', Interviul acordat de premierul Victor Ponta cotidianului *Frankfurter Allgemeine Zeitung*, 10 June.

Ponta, V. (2013c), 'Declarații de presă susținute de premierul Victor Ponta, la finalul vizitei efectuate la Bruxelles', 15 November.

Ponta, V. (2014a), 'Mesajul Prim-ministrului Victor Ponta, cu ocazia liberalizării vizelor pentru cetățenii Republicii Moldova', 28 April.

Ponta, V. (2014b), 'Primul-ministru Victor Ponta a fost invitatul emisiunii "Bună seara, România!", la postul de televiziune B1 TV', 7 July.

Popescu-Tăriceanu, C. (2005), 'Tăriceanu: Franța ne susține în demersul nostru pentru Uniunea', *Amos News*, 10 August.

Popescu-Tăriceanu, C. (2006), 'Tariceanu si Emma Nicholson prin Giulesti', 9AM News, 4 November.

Popescu-Tăriceanu, C. (2007), 'Today, PM Calin Popescu – Tariceanu has met with Mr. Norbert Lammert, President of Bundestag. The two officials have reviewed a series of topics of common interest on the bilateral and European agenda', 30 October.

Popescu-Tăriceanu, C. (2008), 'Premierul Călin Popescu-Tăriceanu și premierul Silvio Berlusconi au ținut o conferință de presă comună după Summit-ul interguvernamental româno-italian', Rome, 9 October.

Prodi, R. (2006), 'Sintesi dell'intervento del Presidente del Consiglio, Romano Prodi, alla presentazione del XVI Dossier Statistico sull'immigrazione', Rome, 25 October.

Prodi, R. (2007a), 'Address by the Prime Minister to the Conference of Slovak Ambassadors', Bratislava, 18 July.

Prodi, R. (2007b), 'Discorso del Presidente del Consiglio Romano Prodi in Campidoglio', Campidoglio, 23 March.

Rajoy, M. (2012a), 'Conferencia de prensa del primer ministro del Reino Unido y del Presidente del Gobierno', London, 21 February.

Rajoy, M. (2012b), 'Discurso del Presidente del Gobierno en el Pleno del Congreso de Diputados para informar de las Conclusiones del Consejo Europeo', Madrid, 14 March.

Rajoy, M. (2013a), 'Discurso del Presidente del Gobierno en la clausura del foro "Europa: próximas etapas", del Instituto de Gobernanza', Paris, 28 May.

Rajoy, M. (2013b), 'Conferencia de prensa del Presidente del Gobierno y del Presidente de la República Francesa después de la XXIII Cumbre Hispano-Francesa', Madrid, 27 November.

Rajoy, M. (2014a), 'Discurso del Presidente del Gobierno en la clausura de la Conferencia Internacional Proyecto de Europa, organizada por el Consejo por el Futuro de Europa del Instituto Berggruen para la Gobernanza', Madrid, 28 February.

Rajoy, M. (2014b), 'Conferencia de prensa del Presidente del Gobierno después de la reunión del Consejo Europeo', Brussels, 21 March.

Rajoy, M. (2014c), 'Declaraciones del Presidente del Gobierno a su llegada a Bruselas', Brussels, 27 May.

Rajoy, M. (2014d), 'Declaraciones del Presidente del Gobierno después de la cena de trabajo de los jefes de Estado y de Gobierno de la Unión Europea', Brussels, 27 May.

Rajoy, M. (2014e), 'Conferencia de prensa del Presidente del Gobierno antes de la Cumbre polaco-española', Gdansk, 23 June.

Rajoy, M. (2014f), 'Conferencia de prensa del Presidente del Gobierno después de la reunión del Consejo Europeo', Brussels, 27 June.

Rajoy, M. (2014g), 'Intervención del Presidente del Gobierno en el Pleno del Congreso de los Diputados para informar sobre el Consejo Europeo de los días 26 y 27 de junio de 2014', Madrid, 9 July.

Rajoy, M. (2014h), 'Declaraciones del Presidente del Gobierno antes de la reunión del Consejo Europeo', Brussels, 30 August.

Rajoy, M. (2014i), 'Discurso del Presidente del Gobierno en la apertura del curso académico en el Colegio de Europa', Brujas, 23 October.

Rajoy, M. (2014j), 'Rajoy reclama a la UE solidaridad y medios frente a la inmigración', *El Mundo*, 28 February.

Rajoy, M. (2015a), 'Conferencia de prensa del presidente del Gobierno y del presidente de la República de Rumanía', Madrid, 13 July.

Rajoy, M. (2015b), 'Declaraciones del presidente del Gobierno después de la primera sesión de trabajo del Consejo Europeo', Brussels, 17 December.

Rajoy, M. (2015c), 'Declaraciones del presidente del Gobierno después del Consejo Europeo extraordinario', Brussels, 23 April.

Rajoy, M. (2015d), 'Intervención del presidente del Gobierno después de la reunión del Consejo Europeo', 18 December.

Rajoy, M. (2015e), 'Conferencia de prensa del presidente del Gobierno, del presidente de la República Francesa, del primer ministro de Portugal y del presidente de la Comisión Europea después de la cumbre sobre interconexiones europeas', 4 March.

Rajoy, M. (2015f), 'Conferencia de prensa del jefe de Gobierno del principado de Andorra y del presidente del Gobierno', 8 January.

Rajoy, M. (2016a), 'Conferencia de prensa del presidente del Gobierno después de la reunión del Consejo Europeo', Brussels, 19 February.

Rajoy, M. (2016b), 'Declaraciones del presidente del Gobierno a la Agencia EFE sobre propuestas de los partidarios del "Brexit"', Madrid, 1 June.

Rajoy, M. (2016c), 'Declaración institucional del presidente del Gobierno después del referéndum en el Reino Unido', Madrid, 24 June.

Rajoy, M. (2016d), 'Intervención del presidente del Gobierno en el Pleno del Congreso de los Diputados, de forma extraordinaria por la urgencia de la materia y por encontrarse en funciones, sobre los Consejos Europeos de los días 18 y 19 de febrero, y de los días 17 y 18 de marzo', Diputados', Madrid, 6 April.

Rajoy, M. (2016e), 'Declaraciones del presidente del Gobierno a su llegada a Bruselas', Brussels, 18 February.

Reding, V. (2010), 'Statement on the Latest Developments on the Roma Situation', SPEECH/10/428, Brussels, 14 September.

Reding, V. (2011), 'Europe at the Crossroads: An Opportunity for Optimism', SPEECH/11/446, Brussels, 16 June.

Reding, V. (2012), 'The EU and the UK: Continuing to Fulfil Winston Churchill's Vision?', SPEECH/12/155, London, 1 March.

Reding, V. (2013a), 'Main Messages: Citizens' Dialogue in Sofia', Sofia, 23 July.

Reding, V. (2013b), 'Main Messages: Trieste Citizen's Dialogue', SPEECH/13/706, Trieste, 16 September.

Reding, V. (2013c), 'Free Movement of People: Five Actions To Benefit Citizens, Growth And Employment In The EU', Press Release, Brussels, 25 November.

Reding, V. (2014), 'Free Movement: European Commission Publishes Study on Integration of Mobile EU Citizens in Six Cities', Press Release, Brussels, 11 February.

Reichters, M. (2014), 'Fighting Abuse of EU Citizens' Right to free Movement: Commission Helps Member States Tackle Marriages of Convenience', IP/14/1049, Brussels, 26 September.

Reid, J. (2006), 'Security, Freedom and the Protection of Our Values', A Speech by Then Home Secretary, John Reid, to DEMOS, 9 August.

Renzi, M. (2014), 'Camera dei Deputati – Replica del Presidente del Consiglio Matteo Renzi', 25 February.

Renzi, M. (2015), 'Statement at the European Parliament Debate on the Review of the Italian Presidency', Strasbourg, 13 January.

Renzi, M. (2016), 'La lettera del premier Matteo Renzi inviata il 15 aprile ai presidenti di Commissione e Consiglio Ue, Jean-Claude Juncker e Donald Tusk', Rome, 15 April.

Rubalcaba, A. P. (2010a), 'Sesión plenaria núm. 166', 17 June.

Rubalcaba, A. P. (2010b), 'Sesión núm. 46 (extraordinaria)', Palacio del Congreso de los Diputados, 6 July.

Rubalcaba, A. P. (2011), 'Rubalcaba afirma que reformar Schengen no es urgente – Internacional', 10 May.

Sarkozy, N. (2006a), 'Déclaration de M. Nicolas Sarkozy, ministre de l'intérieur et de l'aménagement du territoire et président de l'UMP, sur la République, la nation et la réforme de l'Etat, la "rupture" avec des droits sociaux "opposables", dont le droit au logement', Périgueux (Dordogne), 12 October.

Sarkozy, N. (2006b), 'Déclaration de M. Nicolas Sarkozy, ministre de l'intérieur et de l'aménagement du territoire et président de l'UMP, sur ses propositions pour sortir de la crise institutionnelle européenne après les rejets du référendum sur le traité constitutionnel en France et aux Pays-Bas, et la modernisation du financement de l'UE et de la vie politique en Europe, les frontières de l'Europe', Brussels, 8 September.

Sarkozy, N. (2006c), 'Déclaration de M. Nicolas Sarkozy, ministre de l'intérieur et de l'aménagement du territoire et président de l'UMP, sur l'immigration', Paris, 11 December.

Sarkozy, N. (2007), 'Déclaration de M. Nicolas Sarkozy, Président de la République, sur la construction européenne, notamment l'apport du Traité européen simplifié', Strasbourg, 13 November.

Sarkozy, N. (2008a), 'Déclaration de M. Nicolas Sarkozy, Président de la République, sur les priorités de la présidence française de l'Union européenne', Paris, 30 January.

Sarkozy, N. (2008b), 'Déclaration de M. Nicolas Sarkozy, Président de la République, devant le Parlement européen, sur le bilan de la Présidence française du Conseil de l'Union européenne', Strasbourg, 16 December.

Sarkozy, N. (2009), 'Déclaration de M. Nicolas Sarkozy, Président de la République, sur l'action de la France en faveur de la construction européenne', Nîmes, 5 May.

Sarkozy, N. (2010a), 'Déclaration en Conseil des ministres de M. Nicolas Sarkozy, Président de la République, sur les questions de sécurité, notamment l'annonce de la nomination d'un nouveau préfet de l'Isère et de la tenue d'une réunion sur les gens du voyage et les Roms', Paris, 21 July.

Sarkozy, N. (2010b), 'Discours de Nicolas Sarkozy à Grenoble', Grenoble, 30 July.

Sarkozy, N. (2011), 'Conférence de presse de M. Nicolas Sarkozy, Président de la République, notamment sur la crise de la zone euro, la situation en Libye et le retrait d'Afghanistan des renforts militaires français et américains', Brussels, 24 June.
Sarkozy, N. (2012), 'Déclaration de M. Nicolas Sarkozy, candidat à l'élection présidentielle, sur la lutte contre le terrorisme, l'énergie nucléaire, l'immigration, l'Union européenne, l'emploi et sur les relations franco-allemandes, à Ormes (Loiret) le 26 mars 2012', Ormes, 26 March.
Schäuble, W. (2007), 'Rede des Bundesministers des Innern, Dr. Wolfgang Schäuble, zu den Konsequenzen der Auswanderung Hochqualifizierter aus Deutschland vor dem Deutschen Bundestag', Berlin, 12 October.
Schäuble, W. (2008), 'Schengen nach der Erweiterung – eine erste Bilanz', Berlin, 15 October.
Schäuble, W. (2009), 'Europa – Komfortzone, Schicksalsgemeinschaft, Zukunftsaufgabe', 16 June.
Schäuble, W., Pereira, R. and Mate, D. (2008), 'Schengen in Freiheit', Gemeinsamer Namensbeitrag der Innenminister von Deutschland, Dr. Wolfgang Schäuble, Portugal, Dr. Rui Pereira und Slowenien, Dragutin Mate, zu Beginn der letzten Etappe der EU-Trio-Ratspräsidentschaft in Die Welt', 8 January.
Schily, O. (2005), 'Rede von Bundesminister Otto Schily zur Eröffnung der Generalversammlung der IKPO Interpol', Berlin, 19 September.
Schröder, G. (2005), 'Regierungserklärung von Bundeskanzler Gerhard Schröder vor dem Deutschen Bundestag', Berlin, 17 March.
Smith, J. (2007), 'Shared Protections, Shared Values: Next Steps on Migration', 5 December.
Smith, J. (2008), 'House of Commons Hansard Ministerial Statements', 28 October.
Špidla, V. (2006), 'Free Movement of Workers since the 2004 Enlargement Had a Positive Impact – Commission Report Finds', IP/06/130, Brussels, 8 February.
Špidla, V. (2008a), 'Situation of the Roma in Italy (debate)', Strasbourg, 20 May.
Špidla, V. (2008b), 'Free Movement of Workers Is Goof for Europe's Economy', IP/08/1729, Brussels, 28 November.
Špidla, V. (2009), 'Statement in Response to the Strikes in the UK', SPEECH/09/36, Brussels, 4 February.
Thyssen, M. (2015a), 'Speech by Commissioner Marianne Thyssen on Europe's Vision for Fair Labour Mobility', Dublin, 13 November.
Thyssen, M. (2015b), 'Free Movement: End of the First Phase of Transitional Period for Croatian Workers', Brussels, 1 July.
Thyssen, M (2015c), 'Free Movement: New Commission Report on Mobility of Croatian Workers', Brussels, 29 May.
Thyssen, M. (2015d), 'Intervention of Commissioner Marianne Thyssen at 3rd Labour Mobility Congress', 23 April.
Valls, M. (2013a), 'Déclaration de M. Manuel Valls, ministre de l'intérieur, en réponse à une question sur l'immigration des Roms en provenance de Roumanie et de Bulgarie', Assemblée nationale, 15 May.
Valls, M. (2013b), 'Déclarations de M. Manuel Valls, ministre de l'intérieur, en réponse à une question sur l'adoption par le Sénat d'un amendement ouvrant la voie à la dépénalisation du stationnement et à une question sur les occupations illicites de terrains par les gens du voyage', Assemblée nationale, 9 July.
Valls, M. (2013c), 'Interview de M. Manuel Valls, ministre de l'intérieur, à RMC', 5 September.

Valls, M. (2013d), 'Interview de M. Manuel Valls, ministre de l'intérieur, à France Inter le 24 septembre 2013, sur l'évacuation du campement de Roms de la rue de Carvin (Lille-Sud), l'intégration des Roms dans la société française et l'entrée éventuelle de la Roumanie dans l'espace Schengen', 24 September.

Valls, M. (2014), 'Déclaration de M. Manuel Valls, ministre de l'intérieur, sur le bilan des réformes en matière de lutte contre la délinquance en 2013, la mise en place du logiciel de rédaction des procédures de la police nationale et les priorités opérationnelles de la politique de sécurité en 2014', Paris, 23 January.

Zapatero, J. L. R. (2005), 'Conferencia de prensa del Presidente del Gobierno después de la reunión del Consejo Europeo', Brussels, 23 March.

Zapatero, J. L. R. (2006), 'España permitirá la libre entrada de trabajadores de los nuevos miembros de la UE', 9 March.

Zapatero, J. L. R. (2007), 'Conferencia de prensa del Presidente del Gobierno y del Presidente del Consejo de Ministros de Italia después de la Cumbre hispano-italiana', 20 February.

Zapatero, J. L. R. (2008), 'Transcripción de las intervenciones de Zapatero y Rajoy', 4 March.

Zapatero, J. L. R. (2009), 'Discurso y posterior coloquio del Presidente del Gobierno para presentar los objetivos de la Presidencia española de la Unión Europea en un acto organizado por la Asociación de Periodistas Europeos', Madrid, 12 February.

Zapatero, J. L. R. (2010a), 'Conferencia de prensa del Presidente del Gobierno después del Consejo Europeo extraordinario', Brussels, 16 September.

Zapatero, J. L. R. (2010b), 'Entrevista al Presidente del Gobierno en el programa 'En días como hoy', de Radio Nacional de España', 1 October.

Zapatero, J. L. R. (2011), 'Conferencia de prensa del Presidente del Gobierno después de la reunión del Consejo Europeo', Brussels, 24 June.

Index

agreement dimension 25–7, 35–60
Alfano, Angelino 48–50, 67, 106, 155–6
asylum 2, 16, 21–3, 80, 82–3, 90, 106, 120, 129, 134, 144, 181 n.25
   seeker(s) 47, 49, 65, 81, 90, 101, 106, 108, 118, 129, 144

Barroso, José Manuel 27, 53, 64, 74, 82–3, 85, 100, 138, 159–60
Băsescu, Traian 43, 72, 88, 102–3, 108–9, 158–9
Bauböck, Rainer 5, 63, 94, 169 n.38
Berlusconi, Silvio 11, 28, 41, 45, 52, 69, 86, 130–1, 140, 155–6, 165 n.14, 168 n.30, 184 n.22, 184 n.1
border control 2, 14, 17, 20–1, 40, 45–50, 54, 64–6, 69, 91–2, 100, 102, 107, 120–1, 129, 146, 166 n.17, 183 n 14
Brexit 27, 29, 51, 53, 55, 57, 65–6, 73, 102, 127, 131–3, 135, 138, 146
Bulgaria 50, 132, 134, 162 nn.8, 9, 167 n.25, 174 n.11, 182 n.2

Cameron, David 42, 51, 55–6, 65, 71, 74, 87, 92–3, 109–10, 132–3, 156–7, 175 n.19, 184 n.22
Cold War 119, 122
community dimension 25–7, 61–75
conservative 131–5, 140, 156–7, 184 n.22
constitution, constitutional 18, 36, 44, 73, 120, 128, 158, 182 n.5
   patriotism 31, 36–8, 45, 51, 59–60, 63, 127, 164 n.2
Council of the European Union 2, 22, 28, 54
Croatia 13, 162 nn.8, 9
Cyprus 13, 105, 162 n.9

deep diversity 11, 26, 31, 62–3, 68–73
de Maizière, Thomas 56, 66–7, 107–8, 144, 153–4

Denmark 16, 20, 54, 65, 93, 162 n.6, 163 n.14
Deutsch, Karl W. 99–100, 108, 111
discourse-historical approach 25, 30
discourse analysis 10, 27, 30, 125
   critical 30, 163 n.1
Dublin (system) 22, 107, 162–3 n.14, 180 n.21

ethical power 8, 161 n.5
ethics 9, 62, 97, 135
   virtue ethics 9, 61
European Council 47–8, 53, 55, 110, 158
European Parliament 45–7, 53, 102
Europeanness 1, 9–10, 12, 31, 67, 97, 100–1, 103–4, 108, 111–12, 129, 137, 152

fascism 16, 116

Greece 19, 49, 70, 105, 176 n.32

Habermas, Jürgen 8–9, 26, 35–7, 164 n.1
Hare, R. M. 26, 77–8, 95
Hollande, François 49, 57, 65–6, 68, 74, 80, 86, 103–4, 128–9, 154–5, 184 n.22

identification 14–15, 26, 30–1, 61–3, 73, 75

Juncker, Jean-Claude 47, 57, 106, 136, 159–60

Kant, Immanuel 26, 36, 77, 110

League of Nations 15–16
liberal 73, 121, 132–3, 137, 156, 158–9
   intergovernmentalism 78–9, 173 n.3

May, Theresa 50–1, 55–6, 92, 132–3, 156–7, 163 n.9

Merkel, Angela 43, 49–50, 56–7, 66, 69, 74, 84–5, 89–91, 93, 101–2, 125, 146, 153–4, 163 n.9, 171 nn.26–7
migration crisis (so-called) 2, 49–50, 73, 75, 80, 83, 118, 125, 127, 129, 138, 148, 152
mobility studies 3, 5
Moldova 72, 74–5, 122–3, 136–7, 143, 172 n.32, nn.33, 34

Nansen passport 15–16
nationalism, nationalist(ic) 5, 148, 171 n.25, 172 n.30, 177 n.6
  regional nationalism 69, 71, 73, 177 n.4
normative social science 3, 7

Olsen, Espen D. H. 5, 79, 99

Ponta, Victor 44, 87–8, 158–9, 184 n.18
post-national dilemma 5, 36–7
practical reasoning 1, 3, 10–12, 25–7, 30–3, 44, 125, 143, 149, 151, 163 n.1
public sphere 8–9, 36, 152

Rajoy, Mariano 54–5, 64–5, 67, 81–2, 89, 104, 107, 135, 157–8, 180 n.16
regularization 2, 22, 109, 117, 120–1, 134, 163 n.15, 181 n.25, 183 n.17
rights-based 26–7, 37, 58, 136
Roma 5–6, 37–44, 48, 57–9, 105, 108–9, 115, 128, 130, 135–8, 140, 143, 148, 164 n.7, 165 n.10, 175 n.17, 181 n.24
Rorty, Richard 97–100, 105
refugee(s) 16, 65, 108, 116, 119–20

Sarkozy, Nicolas 39–40, 59, 70, 80, 82, 109, 128–9, 154–5, 164 n.3, 181 n.25, 184 n.22
Schengen Area 6, 11, 13, 17, 19–21, 43, 46–51, 56–7, 59, 63–4, 68, 70, 80, 82, 84, 87–8, 92, 103, 105, 107, 109, 128, 131, 136–7, 162 n.9, 175 n.21, 179 n.14
securitization 6, 117, 164 n.3
socialism, socialist(s) 40, 59, 115, 128–9, 133, 154, 157, 184
solidarity dimension 25–7, 97–112
spill-over theory 78–9
Switzerland 16–17, 66

Taylor, Charles 26–7, 61–3, 73, 75
terrorism, terrorist(s) 47–51, 65–6, 69, 105, 115, 128–9, 132, 146, 166 n.21, 180 n.18
transactionalism 99–100
  negative transactionalism 12, 26, 31, 100, 108, 110–11, 129, 133
transitional restrictions 13, 19, 44, 72, 84, 86, 91, 123, 132–5, 138, 162 nn.7–8, 164 n.8, 167 n.25, 176 nn.27, 32, 182 n.2, 183 n.9
transnational 4, 9, 73, 108, 181
Turkey 23, 49, 70, 122, 123

utilitarian, utilitarianism 95, 126, 128, 133, 138, 143, 145, 149, 152, 169 n.37, 173 n.1
utility dimension 25–7, 77–95

welfare 15, 27, 51, 71, 87, 93–5, 99, 136
  benefits 58, 91, 93, 140, 176 n.33
  chauvinism 50, 146, 149
  state 6, 14, 132
  tourism, tourist(s) 2, 51, 94, 144, 146–7
World War 10, 13–16, 39, 42, 113, 117, 119, 138, 171 n.25
  First World War 13–16, 113
  Second World War 10, 16, 39, 42, 117, 119, 138, 171 n.25

youth 68, 144–5, 170 n.17

Zapatero, José Luis Rodríguez 42, 47–8, 81–2, 135, 157–8

www.ingramcontent.com/pod-product-compliance
Lightning Source LLC
Chambersburg PA
CBHW072230290426
44111CB00012B/2038